VIEW
FROM THE CRADLE

O. Weininger

VIEW
FROM THE CRADLE

Children's Emotions
in Everyday Life

Otto Weininger

Foreword by
Clifford Scott

London
KARNAC BOOKS

First published in 1993 by
H. Karnac (Books) Ltd.
58 Gloucester Road
London SW7 4QY

British Library Cataloguing in Publication Data.
A catalogue record for this book is available from the British Library.

Weininger, Otto
  View from the Cradle: Children's Emotions
  in Everyday Life
  I. Title
  155.4
  ISBN 1-85575-037-6

Printed in Great Britain by BPCC Wheatons Ltd, Exeter

ACKNOWLEDGEMENTS

I am grateful to all the young children, and their parents, who granted me the opportunity to be an observer in their homes and to become, in a sense, a family friend, so that their "natural setting of familyness" could be maintained. I also thank those children who gave me the privilege of listening to their private ideas, concerns, worries, and their sense of comfort and discomfort.

Mary Morris's helpfulness and diligence never fail to amaze me. She patiently read the manuscript and helped me to reorganize it and make "sense" of those passages that needed clarification. Mary is continually encouraging and supportive, and I am very thankful.

I very much appreciate the help that Joyce Townsend gave me. To her fell the lot of trying to decipher all the changes in the manuscript and to reorganize the paragraphs. She did this magnificently and in addition managed to find the proper place for all the bits and pieces, drawings and figures.

Sylvia Singer and Johanna Cutcher were always there—ready to help and give their support. Even when I thought things had bogged down, they spurred me on to continue.

I am very appreciative of all these people and of the many students, especially Romi Malik, who helped by listening to me with critical ears and by adding their own examples to clarify theory.

CONTENTS

FOREWORD

Clifford Scott

The history of "education" is long, that of "psychoanalysis" is short. Freud came from biology, physiology, embryology, and neurology to psychoanalysis. His daughter, Anna, came to analysis through education, as did several of those closely associated with Melanie Klein's analytic discoveries. Melanie Klein herself came to child analysis through being asked to try to analyse children during her early years, as her two papers, "The Development of the Child" (1923a) and "The Role of School in the Libidinal Development of the Child" (1924), show so well. She was also stimulated, of course, by her attempts to analyse her own children, as Freud himself was by his attempts to analyse his daughter. Klein's chief associate who came to analysis was Susan Isaacs, whose writing on her work in nursery schools on the intellectual and emotional growth of children—*Intellectual Growth in Young Children* (1930) and *Social Development in Young Children* (1933)—have become classics.

The writings of Melanie Klein stimulated the author of this book, who is a professor in The Department of Applied Psychology at the Ontario Institute for Studies in Education, a centre of innovative work on the development of children since 1965 and affiliated with the University of Toronto, which grants degrees to those trained at this Institute to the Ph.D. level.

The author wrote a text in 1984, *The Clinical Psychology of Melanie Klein*, and, with his associates, founded a journal in 1983, first called *The Journal of the Melanie Klein Society*, and later, in 1990, called *Melanie Klein and Object Relations*. Dr Weininger's interest, knowledge, and experience have bridged educational and clinical domains. With dedicated efforts to contribute to the appreciation and development of the applications of Melanie Klein's work to understanding and helping children with difficulties, in 1989 he published *Children's Phantasies: The Shaping of Relationships* and, in 1992, *Melanie Klein: From Theory to Reality*.

Out of the welter of "phantasies" during development, discriminations lead to the recognition of fantasy, sensation, perception, conceptions related to concurrent development of feelings of love, hate, grief, fear, guilt, mourning, along with maturation related to actions with the world of living and non-living objects. Gradually, over the last century or so, the importance of vicissitudes of instincts and, more recently, of the history of waking and sleeping life, and that of early prenatal and postnatal development, dreams, daydreams, plans, and actions, and the awesome role of these interrelated complexities, have become increasingly recognized. In this book Dr Weininger describes the uses made of a model of short-term therapy that takes this richness and complexity of the development of psychic life into account. These treatments are profusely illustrated, and there are as well vignettes that point to episodes in longer-term treatment. The creative work with a small group of children, day students in a treatment centre for difficult young children, shows a new respect for the way a gradual introduction to short periods of a new type of atmosphere of treatment can over time have a positive and profound effect on the group. Anyone beginning child analysis, astounded by the way a child can begin and continue to make use of what happens in the confidentiality and containing security of such new situations, will be grateful indeed for Dr Weininger's courage in attempting to work with small groups and for telling us, in this book, about the results of this work.

Knowledge of such work should be a source of stimulus and support to that increasing number of people who work with children and who achieve success of a kind and degree that seems to be almost miraculous to those of us who become acquainted with it. On second thought, we realize that their success is not miraculous but is the result of the work of those people who hope that with time, sympathy, and understanding they can learn to pass on what they have learned from others.

PREFACE

I n this book, I write about the experiences that I was able to
have with many young children in several settings, a Child
Study Center, day treatment centres for seriously emotionally disturbed children, and with many children in individual
play psychotherapy and in their homes. I have concentrated on
the details that I have been able to watch and to listen to as
young children played and talked about their play and their
concerns. I have tried to understand these children from the
theoretical framework that has been provided for us by Melanie
Klein, who also watched and listened to many young children
and provided us with understanding about their loves, hates,
fears, and anxieties. She wrote inspiringly about children's
loves and the ways in which their feelings frustrated them,
created discomfort, as well as helped them to mature. Her
accounts of the many children she observed helped me to look
at children's play, language, and emotions and to continue to
discover how children make sense out of their world.

* * *

I have generally followed Melanie Klein's lead in terms of her use of the generic "he", "his", and "him" to refer to children of both sexes. The text will be unimpeded this way and will enable the reader to concentrate on what really counts: the remarkable ideas of Melanie Klein.

VIEW
FROM THE CRADLE

CHAPTER ONE

Mental representation:
the internal container

A group of two-and-a-half-year-olds were engaged in a variety of activities—painting, colouring, ripping paper, piling blocks, and pushing cars on the floor. They played separately for a time and then got together periodically to look at what another child was doing. Following this, they would just continue on with their own activity again. After one girl had finished her painting, she looked at it with a wide joyous smile and seemed so pleased with her work that she hugged herself as she jumped up and down in front of her painting. At another point in the morning, a boy who had managed to pile several blocks one on top of the other looked at his structure and then, grabbing his crotch with both hands and bending over, began to jump up and down. Like the girl, he also had a very pleased smile on his face, and both children shouted out their happiness at their creations by saying such words as "terrific", "lovely", "wow", "great", and "look, look". While the jumping about, the pleasure and even the words were similar for both, their way of expressing their pleasure was different in the way that they held themselves: the boy held his crotch, and the girl hugged herself, wrapping her arms about her chest.

I think that the ways these children were expressing them-selves were not just an outcome of their parents' sensitivity and capacity to respond to their pleasures, but represented the children's responses to their own bodily sensations. Young children experience their emotions as a physical sense of them-selves. This comes about as a result of having been physically held and hugged and psychologically watched, listened to, and contained by their mothers/caretakers who watched and listened enough.

Mothers contain their babies during pregnancy and after birth. They physically hold them in ways that make them feel comfortable and safe. Mothers who seem to be able to adjust themselves to their babies' needs, who seem to recognize that they have to make the "fit" with their babies (not the other way around), are more capable of maintaining themselves as their babies' containers—the holders and guardians of their babies' emotions and physical sensations. By this I mean that mothers are able to realize how much feeling and sensation their babies can endure at any one time, and, when these stimuli are too much, they reduce them—for example, by leaving a situation with their babies, or by lowering the sound level of the radio. Some days the babies are just unable to withstand very much, and most mothers, then, do not feel overwhelmed, but, rather, they realize that their babies need a little more of their time and energy than usual, and they give it easily and freely. Such mothers are able to "hold on to" their babies' distress without having to turn away or become angry with them or feel that they caused this distress. These mothers have a good sense of themselves and of their capacity to be an adequate container for their babies. They seem to know how important it is to help their babies deal with excessive amounts of anxiety, distress, and confusion.

When mothers are able to hold their babies like this, babies are able to maintain their interest in and concern about their world, which is generally continuously changing. It is their mothers' capacity to change their attention to their babies that enables babies to maintain themselves and to continue to main-tain a sense of themselves, in spite of their constantly shifting states. I think that when the two children I described above held themselves, they did so as a reconstruction of their phantasy, which held them together as babies. When feelings are too strong, children may become confused, even when these are happy, joyful feelings. Even the early giggles or sneezes may at first be something to wonder at, until the confusion is accepted admiringly and happily. A beautiful example is in watching how the mother will place a finger just where her baby is ready to grasp it. In these examples, the pleasure derived from their productions was such as to create in these children sufficiently intense physical sensations and feelings that they had to hold themselves concretely, as their mothers must have done when they were young babies experiencing strong feelings.

The fact that the boy held his crotch and the girl hugged her chest suggests that boys and girls have different phantasies of the ways they need to be contained. For the girl, it is as if the good experiences could turn frightening if she could not make sure that her internal self, made up of both physical and emotional aspects, was not falling apart, and so she held herself together by hugging herself. The boy held himself together by making sure that his penis would not fall off, as if this external organ had become the concrete symbol of his internal integrity and holding it allowed him to maintain his pleasure while integrating physical and emotional aspects of the experience. Rather than become overwhelmed by their obvious joy, the children held what they phantasized as their "important parts" and thus maintained their integrity and coherence.

Phantasy, which Klein indicates is the child's earliest mental activity, refers to the primitive representations that develop in the baby's mind as the baby responds to its own needs, distress, tension, and contact with the outer world (Isaacs, 1948; Weininger, 1989). It seems to be the best name for the infant's activity before sensation and imagination or fact and fancy or phantasy are separated. As a result of this interaction between the internal and external worlds of the baby, internal representations arise that are not necessarily the true or even correct sensory image of what is "really out there" in the outer world but, rather, the representation that becomes the mental processes or the mental activity of the baby's mind.

The baby experiences these mental processes as a result of the interaction between the phantasy and the container. That is, the baby's representation of reality will carry just as much correspondence to the "real world" as the interactive relationship of phantasy and container will allow. Of course, as we grow older, our representations of the world grow closer and closer to what reality is actually like, although even as adults we sometimes cannot take in reality, either because it is too painful or because our distress is too great. Mental activity gradually changes as phantasy becomes less omnipotent and the container becomes more capable. The container gradually becomes an integrated internal aspect of the child's mental life. That is, the child becomes his own container as the child is able to deal with the distortion created by phantasy and to recognize his capacity to cope with both distress and pleasure on his own. To be able to do this, the external maternal container must gradually be able to relinquish the function of siphoning off, or taking charge of, the child's feelings. The adequate container has allowed the child to take over more and more control of his feelings and needs.

When this occurs, the child is able to acquire a mental representation of the satisfying interactive relationship. This representation is capable, not only of maintaining the goodness of the container, but also of allowing the child to anticipate consequences and to risk experiences. The child now has a "good internal object" (Klein, 1948; Weininger, 1984) and can hold and keep this object in both pleasurable and discomforting experiences. Consequently, when the child is experiencing joy and happiness, he is able to hold on to the phantasy of satisfaction and is able to try to integrate the physical aspects of the pleasure (hugging oneself) with the emotional, if not cognitive elements of the feeling.

The internal objects are formed from primitive phantasies of the people in the baby's world. As these phantasies become more accurate, they then become internal representations of reality. This mental representation now helps the child to be separated from his primary relationship with mother. The baby has begun to realize that mother returns after she leaves and can now trust this cognitive element. The anxiety, rage, and discomfort that the child had previously felt upon maternal separation can now be internally evaluated, judged, and transformed into the concept of "safe to be without her" for perhaps a short time at 8 months, a longer time at 15 months, and an even longer time at three years of age. Whatever may be the length of time for safe and comfortable separation, it is necessary that the child has acquired the mental representation of the good internal objects. Now the child is able to hold his feelings, sensations, and needs for longer and longer lengths of time. That is, the child is able to hold himself "together" when he recognizes that mother is not there. At first this separation is a painful experience, but when the original maternal container has been adequate, the child gradually learns to trust his mental representation without feeling that "mother has gone because I've been bad and destroyed her" or that "mother is bad" and "I never want to see her again".

However, some maternal separations may be very disturbing to children, particularly when the child has to try to cope with other difficult experiences at the same time. For example, the child who feels uncomfortable or distressed needs the comfort of a good external maternal container. The child needs this person to help to cope with the pain of difficult experiences. No matter how strong the internal representation is, a separation is felt as a loss, as very different from a "real mother here and now". For example, it is not unusual for a five-year-old child who has been able to develop a good internal representation of the mother as a container to have difficulty separating from mother on the first day of school. This child may have attended birthday parties without mother, gone to sports events with other children, or attended concerts with other adults, yet on the first morning of school this child does not want the mother to leave the classroom. The anxiety of being in a new classroom with a new adult, new peers, and new toys is just too much for many children to cope with alone. They need their container back again for a little while, just long enough for them to realize that they can trust their internal representation of "safety"— that is, trust themselves to cope in this new reality situation.

When the external container is available at such times, most children are then able to recognize their own sense of independence and are able to see that they can do something in the outer world to make the situation more comfortable for themselves. Some children may want to bring their "teddy bear" from home for a few days, others play with familiar toys at the new school, still others look for a friend among the strangers at school. In addition, when they realize that they can make an impact upon this new world of the classroom, they become more comfortable and are ready to look around at the new things this new classroom provides for them. That is, when children can see that they can feel safe in the new environment by reactivating the internal "safe" representation of the container, then they are prepared to seek out new ways of working with the outer world. They are now prepared to find meaning in this mostly unknown world by beginning to play with new materials and new children and to explore the characteristics of these new situations.

However, when the block structure collapses or the doctor play does not attract any patients, the child may need the confirmation that the teacher can provide by becoming, for a very short while, the child's container. This allows the child to create an extension and an elaboration of the original mental representation that at one time did contain most anxieties and distresses. If the original container, the mother, is adequate, then others can help the child by becoming temporary or transient containers. These are new substitute containers, which may represent substitutes for the "good mother" and be accepted for a time but nevertheless are used as a new substitute container. Relationships with other adults are created, and these help the child to maintain interest and curiosity in the outer world.

I was watching a four-year-old girl trying to staple a long, thin piece of paper so that it would become a head-band. She managed to staple one end of the paper but could not manage to hold the two ends together and staple them at the same time. After several attempts she looked as if she were about to cry. However, the teacher, who had seen what was happening, came over to her and said, "I think it's hard to hold the paper together and staple it all at the same time. I'd like to help if you tell me what you'd like me to do." The child did not say anything but handed her the strip of paper, and the teacher held the ends together, making enough room for her to staple the ends together. The girl was visibly relieved, put the band on her head, smiled, and went over to a mirror to look at herself. She then announced: "You know, I look older with my band on." I think she was saying, "You know, I've just seen that another person can relieve my distress. I can trust other relationships, so that

I can now extend my original internal representation of trust. I've grown up a bit."

Most children extend their original internal representation before they go to nursery school. However, when they do go to these schools, they are confronted with new tasks, new information, and new people, and they must extend their representations further in order to learn. If they are unable to do so, then the new information must be rejected and is not understood, for it becomes too threatening. Some children find new ideas and information a danger to their narrow and fragile sense of self, because a poor original container did not provide a continuous sense of being cared for, whatever the experienced feelings, needs, and sensations, and allowed limited explorations. In order to maintain a sense of self-integrity—albeit limited—such a child has to curtail feelings, needs, and sensations. Thus, when this child is in a classroom, he has to limit new information, because there are few ways in which the original container can be extended and elaborated. New relationships may be avoided, and aloneness, aloofness, or aggressiveness may be substituted.

The child with a capacity to accept others' assistance and to risk anxiety is very different (Miller, Rustin, Rustin, & Shuttleworth, 1989).

> His mother's attention to him will have enabled him to develop a capacity to attend to what is going on and to be increasingly curious about it. From his experience of being thought about by his mother he will have become able to begin to reflect on his own experience. The legacy of his pleasure in being cared for seems to be found in his expectations of, and capacity for, enjoyment in an increasing range of relationships and activities which he is able to invest with meaning. [p. 51]

CHAPTER TWO

Early eating problems associated with paranoid and depressive anxieties

Eating disorders and problems such as anorexia nervosa and bulimia have received much attention in adolescence but very little attention in the earlier years, except in the failure-to-thrive syndrome that some unfortunate infants experience, where food refusal may be a symptom. In this chapter I would like to examine eating problems in infants and small children and their origins and dynamics.

Feeding difficulties are closely associated with children's earliest anxieties within the paranoid or the depressive position (Klein, 1935; Segal, 1973; Weininger, 1989). Within the paranoid position the feeding problems are connected to getting "bad" food, while in the depressive position feeding problems are related to endangering the good object by eating it. I will describe how I think these problems develop.

Most of us have been able to observe a baby being fed and have recognized the pleasure that the baby gains from being nursed. Perhaps this is one of the first experiences of satisfaction that the baby is able to gain from the external world. The baby has to deal with the external world from the moment of birth. If the experience is pleasant, then the baby's response will generally be satisfaction. If the experience is unpleasant, then the response will generally be anger, frustration, and aggression. The baby's eventual response is determined not only by the way we interpret these experiences for the baby as pleasant or unpleasant, but also by the way in which the baby is able to experience them. This is often determined by the way the baby is prepared for the eating experience and what has happened prior to the feeding.

If the baby is well and happy, the response to being offered the breast is usually to suck and to have a good feed. However, if the baby is upset, perhaps because it has had to wait too long for food, then the response to being offered the breast may be to refuse it or to turn away and cry even more. These reactions are seen as a result of the baby's unconscious phantasies. The satisfactions and frustration that the baby thereby experiences will affect and be affected by these phantasies. In the first instance, the baby phantasizes the breast as a giving and nurturing object and is able to accept it, but in the second instance the unconscious phantasy is that of a breast that has become bad and is now attacking and revengeful. Essentially, the discomfort and pain that the baby experiences in being hungry is translated into being deprived and frustrated. These feelings result in reactions of anger and hatred, which are directed towards the object that is now phantasized as the depriving object—the depriving breast. Because the feeling of being uncomfortable persists, the baby maintains the phantasized attack upon the depriving breast, but now when being offered the breast, the baby does not perceive a nurturing breast, but, rather, one that will, in turn, attack (because of the baby's phantasized attacks upon it). The baby, anticipating a revengeful breast, turns away from it—crying and usually with considerable anger.

I have often listened to young mothers talk about the feeding of their babies. In one instance, the young mother went to feed her baby within the prescribed time as laid down by her paediatrician. This mother was following instructions in trying to raise her two-month-old son. The baby had been crying for about 20 minutes, and, while the mother was quite prepared to feed her baby, she felt she would have been wrong in doing so because she had been told that she then would "raise a

monster who would never let go". So she waited for the prescribed hour, and when it arrived she went to feed the baby. By
this time her milk was flowing and dribbling, so that the baby
would have no difficulty in getting the milk. She picked up her
baby and put him to her full breast. However, the baby, upon
getting its lips moist from the milk, turned away with a very
loud shriek, which the mother interpreted as "extreme fear".
She tried to comfort him by placing the nipple in his mouth, but
his reactions to this were always fright and even "terror", and
so she stopped and put the baby back into his cot. She had also
been told to let the baby "cry it out" (whatever "it" was). The
baby howled for a short time and then fell asleep. When the
baby awakened, she was at his side and immediately began to
feed him. This time he took the nipple and sucked easily.

In this example, the baby's state of discomfort (and maybe
pain) was too much for him to endure, and thus comfort by way
of feeding could not be accepted. This is the sort of explanatory
statement I often hear, but I think it is only part of the baby's
state of feeling. It is true that the baby is very uncomfortable,
but it is not just that condition that does not allow the baby
to feed. It is the unconscious phantasy that the breast has
become an attacking, revengeful object that forces the baby to
turn away from the breast and remain hungry, uncomfortable,
and distressed. At that moment, nothing can satisfy the baby,
who is in a state of terror. To try to feed him at that time is only
to create more and more discomfort for him. In a way, then,
what this mother did was correct. Since she did not know what
to do, she followed the "advice given" and put him back in his
cot. I think that the baby's state of distress was even too much
for the baby to endure, and sleep was the only alternative
answer for him. We know that when babies are overstimulated
or very upset, they often fall asleep. This provides them with
the opportunity, not only of removing themselves from the discomfort, but also of recovering from the painful experience. I
suggested to the mother that she need not wait for "prescribed
feeding hours" but that she feed her baby when he seemed
hungry and, if he was crying, that she not try to feed him but
hold him and talk to him about how he might be feeling and
how she could help him feel better. Then, when he was not
crying and had become calm, she should be able to feed him.

It is also important to recognize that, if the baby is afraid that the breast will be attacking and if this feeling is not adequately relieved, then the baby always approaches the feed with a certain anxiety, and the expected pleasure and satisfaction is never really achieved. When the baby experiences a feeling of dissatisfaction related to the breast, feelings of anger and aggression are felt, and the breast is phantasized to have turned bad and to have become revengeful. No adequate feed can take place under these conditions.

Some children who have had a poor nursing experience have shown particular "grab-and-run" food behaviour. By this I mean that these children do not seem to be able to sit with their families at a meal and often "eat on the run". They take some food from the table and eat it in another room, or they go under the table to eat it.

In one example, a young girl of three years seemed to be unable to eat with her mother and father and insisted that she eat her food under the table. The parents at first thought that this was "cute", but then, when this behaviour continued for a few weeks, they become angry with her and insisted that she eat at the table, sitting on the chair. The child refused, and mealtimes became battles of who was going to get their way. Usually the mealtime became so chaotic that the child was told to go to her bedroom until she could sit at the table. Since she did not return to the table, the mother was usually forced to bring a plate of food for her to eat in her room. Then the child was able to eat.

I think that eating in the presence of her parents had become terrifying for this child, whose history indicated that she had not had a good nursing experience. Her mother had tried to breast-feed her, but this had been unsatisfactory both to the mother and to the baby and was quickly given up as "a bad job". The bottle was offered, but in such a way as to suggest (to me, at least) that the mother did not want to have anything to do with feeding her baby now that she thought herself to be an inadequate mother. She usually propped the bottle so that the baby could suck but neither baby nor mother had to hold the bottle. Feeds became perfunctory and, while relieving of hunger, could not have carried the satisfaction of comfort involved in the pleasurable feeling of being held and talked to by the mother. This method of feeding continued, and the girl was weaned to a feeding cup by about ten months. The mother was proud of her daughter, and her daughter seemed to do well. The food problem did not start again until the daughter had a "very bad cold" and had to be fed in her bedroom. When she was well again, she did not want to eat at the table but insisted on eating under the table.

I connect the early uncomfortable nursing experiences to the later eating problem. I think that the baby must have experienced the breast as attacking and revengeful as a result of the unconscious phantasies experienced in relation to this unsatisfying breast. The breast-feed was changed to a bottle-feed and then to the cup-feed. At no time did the mother describe the transition as anything other than, "It became more comfortable for her and for me". Breast-feeding was a very difficult job for the mother, and then, when the bottle was given, it was "propped" and not generally hand-held by the mother. When feeding is not good, it is altered to phantasies of an attacking object. The only way that the baby fed "easily" was alone and without help. It was as if the baby could diminish her unconscious phantasy of an attacking breast when the mother was not present or at least was not feeding her. Thus the "not feeding her directly" situation was helpful to both mother and daughter. I think a recurrence of the original feeding situation occurred when the child became quite ill and was given her food in her room. By having her food in her room and feeding herself (her mother sat at her bed but did not feed her), the daughter phantasized that her illness was a revengeful attack. She was sick because she had been angry and aggressive to someone, something, or some phantasy, and eating alone became her experience of being safe from other attacks upon her. As Segal (1973) points out so clearly,

> the actual breast, therefore, when it does return to feed the baby is not felt as a good feeding breast, but is distorted by these phantasies into a terrifying persecutor. [p. 14]

We think that in dealing with excessive frustration the baby uses projection as an early ego defence mechanism. The baby projects its anger towards the breast. Rather than recognizing that it is angry at the breast for not taking away the uncomfort-

able and even painful hunger, the baby views the breast as
hating and being angry with the baby. The baby projects the
feelings that it cannot contain within itself. These feelings are
too powerful to be held by the baby as they make it feel much
too uncomfortable. It is as if the baby's only way of getting rid of
these strong feelings is to "put them into something else"—to
project them into another object—and in that way relieve some
of the feelings of pain although these are now replaced by a
wariness and suspiciousness of something else. However, perhaps this state feels safer for the baby, as it may be easier to
become wary and suspicious than to recognize one's own internal state. Projection, then, is the mechanism that very early in
life helps to preserve some degree of coherency in the ego and
may even help to preserve the ego from annihilation as a result
of excessively strong hostile and destructive feelings. The baby
also projects goodness (derived from comfortable satisfying feelings) onto the breast. In this way, through projection of good
and bad feelings, the baby builds a view of its object world.

However, while projection occurs as an early ego defence
mechanism, introjection is also occurring. In introjection the
baby is taking into himself aspects that are occurring within
the external world. These bits of experiences are being absorbed, but always under the surveillance of the unconscious
phantasy life of the baby. If the phantasy is of a good and
nurturing external world, then a good and nurturing object is
being taken in, and this introjection becomes relieving of internal discomfort. If the phantasy is of an attacking external world
(because of the baby's uncomfortable experiences), then what
is introjected also becomes attacking and persecuting.

The baby takes things in by mouth—it "mouths" everything
that it can get hold of. But the first experiences of mouthing
that bring some "lasting" satisfaction come from feeding. Along
with the food, the baby is also taking in other aspects of the
outside world, such as the way it is held, the way it is spoken
to, the way it is diapered, the way it is stroked, the way its hair
is brushed, the way it is bathed, and countless other ways
that help the baby to gain information about the world. However, I think that most of the tactile and kinaesthetic ways that
the baby takes in information are influenced by the ways in
which it feeds. If the feedings are comfortable, pleasurable, and

pain-relieving, then the baby is able to accept other "kinds" of information and not phantasize them as persecutory. In other words, learning about one's world and even one's self appears predicated upon effective and nurturing feedings.

Projection forces the child to experience his world in a particular way—good or bad—and introjection confirms this world for him. What the baby "takes in" is under the influence of the way in which the baby has "given out". If the baby has given out goodness because of feelings of comfort, then the world is taken in as a kindly and beneficial world, and the baby is all the more willing to go on and explore that world. If this is not so, then the baby is quite unwilling to explore and learn about its world because it is sure that the world is an angry place. The baby has projected its anger (due to its frustrations) onto the outside objects. Whatever it takes in is either bad and persecutory or has to be carefully screened so that the baby does not take in the bad bits, which, in turn, will only make whatever good exists in the baby turn bad. The baby will take in too much bad "information", and this will be damaging to the goodness that exists, usually with the eventual phantasy that the bad will take over the good and destroy it altogether.

In one very interesting example that I was able to observe, a group of 10 three-year-olds were having a Valentine's Day party, with lots of red foods available for all the children—red candy hearts, red cakes and cookies, and red jelly cut into the shape of hearts. The children seemed particularly pleased with the red jelly hearts, and several of them were eating them with considerable gusto. There was enough of everything, so the children did not have to store their food by taking big piles onto their plates. They usually took another piece after they finished the one they were eating. Three children stood out for me.

One girl placed a couple of read jelly hearts on her plate and began "very gingerly" to poke at the hearts with her finger. She had a strange expression on her face—somewhat questioning, but with a tinge of fear. After a few pokes she stuck her finger into the heart so that it went through the heart. She did this until the hearts on her plate were in bits and could not be recognized as "hearts". At this point she smiled and gobbled the bits. Then she put two more on her plate and proceeded to do the whole thing over again. In fact, she did this five times.

I think that the hearts represented phantasized "bad" objects, and the only way she was able to take them in was by making them into "not hearts" and small bits, so that whatever her phantasy of these objects, they were no longer the dangerous or perhaps persecuting objects they once were as whole hearts. I sat beside her and asked her if she was afraid of the hearts. She looked at me sharply as if she were angry and said, "You're silly". I persisted, this time saying that I thought that maybe the sharp points on the hearts might stick into her. She agreed with this and said, "I have to make them small so they'll be okay". I said I thought that "jelly" doesn't hurt when you put it in your mouth. She answered, "Well, it does, especially when it's so thick and hard". She continued to stick her finger into the jelly hearts and eat the bits. This child is a very loud child in the group play-room. She runs around screaming at other children and does not seem able to settle into any activity. The teachers have talked about her and are concerned about her behaviour.

Another child, a three-and-one-half-year-old boy, was giving cookies to another child, piling them upon his neighbour's plate even though the other boy did not want them to be there and kept pushing them off. The boy continued to take cookies and put them on the other's plate, and the other child kept pushing them off his plate. I sat down with them and said, "It looks like you want to give Corey all the cookies". He answered, "I can't eat them 'cause they make me sick". I asked if he had been told not to eat anything at the party. He replied that he could eat anything he wanted to, but he added, "I just know that these cookies will make me sick, and my Mummy will be mad at me".

I interpreted this as his wanting all the cookies and said so to him, adding, "I can get you a bag, and you can take cookies home with you if you want". He said that he couldn't because he'd have to give some away, or else his Mummy would be mad at him. I said, "You think your Mummy gets mad at you a lot". He did not answer but went on to put more cookies on his neighbour's plate. I then suggested that maybe Corey could make the cookies okay—that if the cookies were on Corey's plate, that maybe he could then eat them. At this point Corey said, "eat these", and the child ate the cookies with what appeared to me as some relief.

I think that the child did want to eat the cookies but that his greed for them was so great that he phantasized that eating too much would make him sick—no doubt a statement that his parents had made, and not an uncommon statement at that. It is not so much that parents may say these things as that children have a phantasy of what is going to happen to them as a result of the feelings they have. If the child is greedy, then he perceives himself to be "bad", and if he eats "too much", he believes he will get sick and his mother will be angry. The child is greedy because he feels he has not received enough to fill himself or has not had the opportunity to get enough to fill himself because "greedy children are punished". I found it very interesting that the "power of making him sick" was removed by placing the cookies on his neighbour's plate. When his neighbour then told him to eat these cookies, it seemed all right for him to do so—and he did. The introjection of these cookies no longer contained bad characteristics, and they were sufficiently free of badness to allow him to eat them.

I later discovered that this boy has an infant sister, and that he has been having trouble eating. He was never a good eater, but now he is having problems and does not want to eat very much. I suggested to the parents that they might feed him from his sister's dish and that they ought to make sure that they always said that there was enough food for him and his sister. The parents were able to carry out this suggestion, and about a week later they told me that they had fewer meal-time problems with him. He really enjoyed eating from his sister's plate as she ate her food. Klein (1936) states:

> The child's earliest experiences of painful external and internal stimuli provide a basis for phantasies about hostile external and internal objects, and they contribute largely to the building up of such phantasies. [p. 292]

These painful external and internal stimuli are changed as a result of changes in unconscious phantasies. This occurs as a result of the reality making an impact on the phantasy. If a child's phantasy is of an attacking and revengeful external object, then the child will have to do everything possible to try to avoid or minimize these attacks. However, if the child is able to "feel" that the external object is neither angry nor attacking, then gradually the image of this object changes to one that is nurturing or at least neutral at first.

If the baby is fed when it is hungry and is able to feel the pleasures of the feed, not only from the disappearance of the hunger pains but also from the satisfaction felt and expressed by a loving mother, then the child, through projective and introjective processes, builds a phantasy of the external object as a kind, giving, nurturing, and safe object. However, our society seems to insist on "regularity of feedings", on a "schedule" such that the baby is quickly placed on a feeding routine. The baby is then not able to experience the pleasure and relief of discomfort easily, has to wait too long for this relief, and the phantasy of the good object as satisfying and comforting becomes one of the bad object and discomforting. However, the breast, given when needed by the baby, reinforces the phantasy of a good internal object.

This internal good object eventually becomes stronger and more powerful and is able to overcome those periods of discomfort when the food does not come on time. At such times the baby's unconscious phantasy is not of attack because of discomfort with the result of fear or revenge, but, rather, the ego is sufficiently capable, because of the continued goodness of the internal object, to wait without becoming disorganized and/or fearful of annihilation. If satisfaction does not come quickly enough, then the very feelings of discomfort are enough to make the baby feel that it will not survive. However, when food has come when needed by the baby, then the baby does not have the feeling of disorganization and is able to feel sufficiently strong to wait. In a sense, the baby can feed upon its own goodness, imagining that it has the good breast inside itself. The object that has been introjected is a good object, capable of sustaining the baby due to this omnipotent hallucinatory phantasy. Of course, the baby will not be able to wait forever, and if the needed feed is not forthcoming, then the parent will gradually see the baby become fussier and more and more difficult to calm. The good hallucination begins to change and becomes less capable of staving off the pain and discomfort and becomes "bad" as the child becomes angrier.

Feeding babies when they "demand feedings" allows the phantasy of an introjected object to be good and to make the baby feel that its own goodness is powerful and lasting. It is these good experiences that the baby has with its mother that alter the angry unconscious phantasy and, thereby, alter the persecuting and frightening feelings related to the external object. The baby begins to trust the good object. In this way the baby is moving in the direction of being able to adapt more effectively to reality. If the baby feels continually frustrated and uncomfortable, then reality is something to be avoided. If the baby feels comfortable and has a trust in its own internal objects, then the baby is better able to cope with reality and not be as frightened of possible frustration and will even be able to deal with some degree of frustration from reality. The trust in the goodness of the object reduces the persecutory phantasies and allows the baby to tolerate reality. Mother is felt as a nurturing comfort-providing person, and the baby is able to tolerate periods of time when mother is not there without the feelings of excessive discomfort. The mother as an introjected object is satisfying, caring, and protective, and this allows the baby not only to withstand some frustration but also to explore a world that is seen as exciting and non-threatening.

I think we see a growth in the baby's behaviour from patterns that are demanding and aggressive to ones that are quiet, exploratory, and happy. Most babies at first demand feeds frequently, and these demands are made noisily, even aggressively. One mother said that her baby of two-and-one-half months just pounced on her nipple every time it was offered. She continued feeding the baby whenever he seemed hungry, and gradually, within another month, his behaviour changed. He seemed to become "thoughtful". He patted her breasts, smiled at her, gurgled to her in-between food-gulps, and generally seemed very happy and contented. He trusted his internal picture of a good breast always available and did not have to attack it aggressively. He also was able to look around and gurgle afterwards, as if he were "taking in the room after his feed". If the mother had reacted with aggression by stopping him from grabbing the nipple, I think this would have been experienced as a revengeful breast, and the ease with which he was later feeding would have been disturbed. I do not think he would have been the "easy feeder" he became, nor would he have "taken in the room" as he did. This very early feeding experience also influences the way in which information about the rest of the world is taken in.

As the baby acquires teeth, its phantasies alter to biting and tearing at the nipple. Again there is a surge of aggressiveness, which is expressed as biting the object—the nipple and breast. I think that this surge of aggression, which is usually short-lived, is a result of the baby recognizing that the object is outside of himself and that the phantasy of it being inside and always available for his comfort is just not so. The baby is maturing, and most mothers begin a process of weaning and introducing other foods to the baby at about this time. This change in feeding disturbs the trust the baby has in its internal objects—the mother is not responding and reacting in the same old trustworthy ways, the mother is unpredictable and not as satisfying, and so the baby reacts with aggression. He has to regain a feeling of trust in his internal objects and a trust in the goodness of reality and mother. He has to learn that biting may hurt his gums and/or the nipple but not, for example, his toy or his spoon.

This sadism is often seen in young children of three and four years of age. I recall a four-year-old boy who took all the big dinosaurs and opened their rubber mouths as wide as he could and squashed all the baby dinosaurs into the big dinosaurs' mouths. After he did this, he shook the large dinosaur and said, "See, the babies are all inside, and you can even hear them". I asked if they were angry at being inside. He answered, "I don't care. They need to be inside because they want to get all the food." I recognized that he felt that the only way they would be fed was by being inside the large animal and asked him if the babies were not being fed enough. He said, "You're stupid. I said that the big dinosaurs get all the food. The babies can't get any. They're not big enough yet." I asked if they would get out after they had enough food. He answered, "No, they need to stay there because they'll never be big enough."

I recommended that the mother recognize the feeding situation as a difficult one for her son at that time and that she ask him if she could feed him at meal-times, allowing him to feed himself if he wanted to. I explained some aspects of his phantasy, and she was able to feed him, with the effect that his play changed to not having the baby dinosaurs in the larger

ones, but having them feed side-by-side. He did not say anything about this at all. He just had them stand at the trough
and feed. They fed for the whole session while he played with
paper, glue, and coloured bits of wool and string, making a
collage, which, he announced, he was making for his mother. I
suggested that he needed to make her feel good and to show her
he loved her. He agreed. The phantasy of having taken food
from her insides and perhaps destroying her insides and her
internal babies was too much for him to bear without trying to
make some reparation. He was able to do this after he found
that reality was not as terrible and "unfeeding" as he imagined.

In another situation, which is related to feeding but is displaced, a two-year-old boy suddenly began to gag every time
his mother changed his "poopy nappy". When she had removed
the soiled nappy and was folding it to put it in the waste bin, he
began to gag and sounded as if he were about to vomit. In fact,
on a very few occasions he did vomit a bit. His mother, quite
distressed by this, also noted that when his father changed his
nappy, he generally did not gag. Neither father nor mother
gagged when changing the nappy, although his father had had
some difficulty originally in changing his soiled nappies. His
mother began to give him a "farm book" when she was about to
change his nappy. As she removed the nappy, she talked about
the baby ducks, horses, and other animals he was looking
at, asking ,"How many do you see. Tell me how many babies
you see. Tell me about the babies. They're all small babies, and
they eat a lot, and that makes their Mummies very happy."
When she did this, he did not gag. Perhaps he was distracted,
although if there were any other odour he would certainly smell
it. I think that the boy's faeces represented angry bits of himself, which in phantasy could destroy his mother. His mother
chose a baby farm book and chose to let him tell her about
numbers, and so I think that the faeces, which had become
phantasized hostile bits because of angry feelings towards his
mother, changed. Numbers acted as reparation, and faeces
were no longer hostile bits.

In talking with his mother, I discovered that she had begun
a part-time job a short while before this. I think that his angry
feelings towards her were occasioned by her not being at home
for him when he felt he needed or wanted her. The fear was that

he was losing his mother and that if she left him, he might lose his good internal mother. The child's phantasy of having harmed her is reinforced by her not being there, perhaps experienced as punishment for his harm. Her acceptance of his hostility and offering numbers as a way of making reparation allowed him to alter his phantasy of a frustrating and depriving environment. Sublimation of hostility by the use of numbers helped him with the fear that his excrement might damage her. Numbers seem "to have a genital symbolic cathexis" (Klein, 1923, p. 71).

The fear of one's own faeces as a persecutor (as a result of aggressive phantasy) may give rise to the very frightening idea that one's body is full of persecutors, and that one is being poisoned or at least harmed on the inside. I think that this phantasy gives rise to hypochondriacal fears.

During one play psychotherapy session, a young girl told me that she needed "to go to the bathroom and do number 2". I asked if she would let me take her to the toilet and that I would wait just outside the toilet stall. She reluctantly agreed. She seemed to both want me to come with her and yet not want me to be there. I interpreted this as related to her hostile faeces in the following way: she told me that she does not like to go to the toilet because it makes her all dirty and she won't let her mother "clean her up". I offered the interpretation that she was afraid that her "poop" might hurt her mother and so she kept it in and did not go to the toilet very often. She agreed and said, "It's because it's so messy". When I suggested that she often felt a sort of sick feeling in her stomach, she also agreed, and we continued:

ME: "I think that maybe you think your poop is bad."

SHE: "I don't think of poo."

ME: "Maybe it's like being afraid to poo and hurt Mummy yet being afraid to hold it in because it could make you sick."

SHE: "My Mummy already told me that."

ME: "Sometimes we feel sick because we're afraid someone will hurt us if we poop."

What I tried to do was put into words her phantasy, indicating the relation between dangerous persecutory faeces and hypochondriacal fears. We went to the toilet. She defecated and proudly told me how she wiped herself. I told her that she was safe, that her faeces wouldn't harm her or Mummy, and that she was doing such a good job taking care of herself. She said that she wouldn't tell her mother about this "just yet". She wanted to wait to be sure that she wouldn't get sick any more!

Sometimes babies and children try to avoid feeding altogether. This difficult feeding situation may last only for a few days, or may, at other times, go on in a chronic way for several months.

In one case, a child of three years refused to eat anything but continued to drink from his bottle. Whenever food was presented to him, he got up from the table and went into his bedroom. If his mother or father followed him, he looked very sad and refused to talk with either parent. He remained in his room for a short while and then reappeared at the table, but would neither sit at the table nor accept any food.

When we spoke about this, his parents said that they had tried everything. They had tried to give him his favourite foods; they tried bribing him with gifts and visits to special places; they tried forcing him by sitting him at the table and trying to force-feed him; they spanked him; and they told him how angry and upset they were. However, nothing worked, and Jonathan had not eaten for over two weeks. He continued to drink from his bottle but refused any foods.

I asked if a similar situation had ever happened. His parents recounted an event when Jonathan was four months old and he was being breast-fed. His mother became sufficiently ill to be hospitalized for ten days, and Jonathan was fed from a bottle with a prepared milk. He took the milk at first with no problems, but within two days he began to gag and vomit whenever he had finished or had drunk several millilitres of milk. He continued to gag and vomit until his mother returned, tried unsuccessfully to breast-feed him, and eventually gave him a bottle. He took the bottle, at first with the same effect of gagging and vomiting, but soon accepted the bottle without any further problems. His later feeding history was uneventful, except that he did not want to eat solids, and most of his food was mashed into a paste-like consistency. The present situation had not occurred before, and the parents were very worried because Jonathan was losing weight.

I questioned the parents about his sadness. They said that he seems like a good little boy but is not as energetic as other children his age. He often plays alone building houses and then tries to look into the house by lying on the floor and peering at the blocks. He is in his room more than the parents like, and while they often invite him to be with them, he "wants to be alone". As we talked about his aloneness, his sadness, and his food refusal, his parents expressed their own sadness as well as their anger that they were unable to help him. I suggested that perhaps Jonathan may have felt very greedy for everything that the parents have, and "in his mind he wanted to eat everything up, including his parents". They noted that before this feeding problem he seemed to be very loving and wanted to sit with them, hugging them, but mostly hugging mother, with what he called "big squeezes".

I think that Jonathan gradually felt very loving towards his mother and that his own needs to want and to take more and more from her became very frightening to him. In his phantasy he would introject the desired object—that is, he would "eat her all up". These feelings became very frightening to him and, I think, aroused his earlier fears related to having lost his mother. The phantasy was that he took too much from her, and as a result she went away. She went to the hospital, but, as far as a baby of four months would be concerned, she was gone, she was destroyed, and he would feel that he had been responsible for this. I think his earlier feeding problem was related to the loss of his mother phantasized as a result of his greedy devouring impulses. Now his impulses had become very strong again—he wanted to give her "big squeezes"—which, I think, is an indication of increased greed, with the fear that he could devour her, and she would be lost again. Food refusal was his way of stopping his own greedy impulses, and, by being willing to feed by the bottle, he imagined that she would not go away. In his mind she had come back after he began feeding by bottle, even though he did have some difficulty at first—again a difficulty occasioned by his early sadistic impulses.

Jonathan's parents had told me about his sadness and his aloneness, which I think was expressive of aspects of the depressive position. He needed to make sure that he would not damage the goodness of the nurturing object by eating it. He had experienced sadness, which, he imagined, was due to his devouring impulses, and she was lost to him for a time. Now his feelings had become strong again, and he wanted to preserve the good object by not eating it.

I suggested that the parents talk about how much food they had, that they take Jonathan shopping with them, that they ask him to cook and help them prepare meals, and that they suggest that Jonathan could eat with them or close by if he wished and that he did not have to go into his room because they "would be safe with him in the room". This latter suggestion would indicate that they knew about certain aspects of his anger towards them. I also suggested they tell him that they knew he was very hungry, and that there was so much food "that they'd be able to fill the whole refrigerator" and that it would "still be full even after they finished eating". This interpretation was an attempt to let him know that his mother's body would not be depleted by the meal—taking, as my cue, his building houses and peering into them to see if they remained all right after an imagined feed. Jonathan's eating improved, but his sadness was still evident, and at this point I recommended that he should become involved in play psychotherapy.

These examples illustrate feeding difficulties associated with children's phantasies within both the paranoid and the depressive positions. Within the paranoid position, persecutory anxieties turn feeding into an experience in which the child fears being poisoned and destroyed. The child fears that if food is taken in, his insides will be endangered. Food is equated with external objects that are desired but, if devoured, then the child will not only poison himself, but will also encounter retaliation from the parent from whom the child imagines he has greedily taken. This "doubled-barrelled" paranoid reaction is related to the greed and envy children have for the satisfactions and pleasures they phantasize parents are experiencing.

Within the depressive position, the child wants to make sure that the good object is preserved and may do this by not eating. The child phantasizes, for example, that a good object exists within him and that the child needs to protect it from any outside dangers by not taking "any more in"—that is, by not eating any more. This is imagined as an attempt to maintain love from mother, by saying, "See, I'm not taking any more from you. I'm not eating you up. You don't have to worry. I'm protecting you from any of my attacks by not robbing you and leaving you full." It is primarily the child's phantasized attacks upon the mother that he is preventing. This non-eating then reduces the child's anxiety and is at the service of maintaining a coherence in the ego. The anxiety results from the hostile impulses. The fear of retaliation is not only from the object but also from the child's superego, which forces the child to feel guilt for potential eating and injury to the object that is both loved and envied.

At first, in the early phases of the depressive position the superego exerts very strong demands for "good behaviour"— that is, not to take too much from the mother. The baby or child may then stop eating so much, phantasizing that he is demanding too much; or the child may stop eating certain foods, phantasizing that certain foods represent certain of his parent's bodily organs; or the child may vomit while or after being fed, phantasizing this as an attempt to give the devoured object back to the parent; or the child may just stop eating, phantasizing that he is now successful in not devouring the object. In this latter way the superego will no longer be persecutory, because it has been placated, since the child is not taking any foods from the parent (Tustin, 1958). Now, strangely, the child may even seem calm, if not contented. The loved object will remain, both externally and internally, and the child is "perfect" (Klein, 1935):

> The stronger the anxiety is of losing the loved object, the more the ego strives to save them, and the harder the task of restoration becomes, the stricter will grow the demands which are associated with the super-ego. [p. 269]

The successful resolution of these early eating problems depends upon the working through of the child's destructive and hostile impulses towards the loved objects and the "combined parents" as a loved and loving couple, within both the paranoid and depressive positions.

CHAPTER THREE

Loneliness: schizoid and depressive components

The loss of the object, the giving breast, provides children with a deep and enduring sense of loneliness. If the child has the phantasy that somehow he has exhausted the breast or has been so bad as to be undeserving of the breast, then the child needs to be alone in order to avoid any feelings experienced as a result of relationships. The child feels alone and is lonely but cannot move to anyone and rejects any potential relationship.

I think that part of the rejection of relationship is due, not only to this loss of the giving breast, but also to the feeling that to take too much is to suffer or cause "hurt". The early relationship to the breast was bound up with persecution—that is, the phantasy that the breast never gave all that it could and kept most of the "good stuff" for itself. This occasioned projection of hostility to the breast, which was then felt as if the breast would become hostile to the child. Later, when feelings brought out by relationships emerge in the child, then these feelings are felt, as they were earlier, as persecutory. To avoid this phantasized persecution (the projective hostility), the child remains alone. It is as if the child feels better when he does not have these inner angry and destructive feelings because the world becomes more frightening and dangerous as a result of the destructive feelings being projected onto the object in the external world. Instead of the child feeling as if he will destroy the mother object, he fears that this object will destroy him, and so he is very frightened and must remain lonely. In my observations I have noticed several children who seem to show this loneliness.

As I watched four-year-old Tommy playing by himself, I was struck by the way in which he seemed to be so oblivious to anything that surrounded him. He did not seem to notice the young boys and girls that brushed by him, so absorbed was he in pouring the dry sand into the funnel and letting it spill out onto the sand-table. When one young three-year-old accidentally pushed him and said, "I'm sorry", Tommy did not seem to be aware of him and he continued to pour the sand through the funnel. After about 15 minutes, a young girl approached and started to play next to him. She did not try to engage him in conversation or play but just stood next to him, digging in the sand. Tommy looked over at her with what seemed to be a vacant look and then dropped his funnel and wandered off, leaving the girl to play by herself.

As I continued to watch Tommy, he moved to the blocks, fingering them, but not building anything. He finally settled in an area where he could construct a "house", as he called it, out of a blanket and a couple of chairs. Tommy put the blanket over the chairs, put a pillow under the blanket, and went inside the structure. He emerged after 20 minutes, looked around, and took a crayon and some masking tape from a nearby table and then went back into the structure.

I moved over to his house and said that I was outside the house and would like to talk with him. Tommy did not answer. I accepted this silence as an indication that it was all right for me to continue talking. I said that I noticed that he had been in his house for almost half an hour, that before that he played with the sand by himself, that he was now by himself and that he seemed not to want anyone to know that he was in the room with the other children.

At this point Tommy said that I should "shut up". I did just that for five minutes, during which period of time we were both silent. After he grunted, I continued and said, "I think you want things to be okay and that you think you should always feel okay". Tommy answered, "No, nothing is good". I said, "You want to feel good always, and I think you are having a very hard time feeling good". Tommy answered, "You think you know everything". I responded, "No, I don't think so, but I think you want to know everything and have everything perfect". Tommy emerged from the house, looked at me, and wandered off. He eventually returned to his house with a cushion, put it on the floor of the house, and went in once again. This time he said that I could go away now because I would not be coming back anyway. I told Tommy that I would be back but that I thought I could understand how lonely he felt, even though there were several people he knew and could be with.

Tommy's loneliness appears to be an inability to deal with the changes and risks that are inherent within relationships. That is, if Tommy were to try to be friendly with another child, then he might suffer from several possible reactions, such as being rejected or being asked to give too much. Such experiences might then force upon him the arousal of hostile feelings. Therefore, in keeping to himself, Tommy kept his hostility at bay. Tommy seemed to need a safe haven where no one could or would disturb him. He was able to accomplish this by getting a soft pillow to lie upon. I think the soft pillow represented the good mother—the perfect object, which would be continuously giving, soft, and non-rejecting.

Tommy seemed to fear that his perfect pillow/mother would be disturbed by others. However, it is not that others would disturb the perfect mother, but, rather, that his feelings, which would be provoked in relationship to others, would disturb the perfect mother. This mother was to remain passive, yet giving. Tommy's behaviour seemed to demonstrate that if he became angry, or sad, or unhappy, he would upset the status quo, and then his own internal state would be disturbed by the phantasy that the perfect mother would be ungiving.

I think that Tommy seemed to be a very sad boy. He was very frightened of his feelings and attempted to maintain an alone state so that none of his feelings would be provoked. He seemed to imagine that if he experienced no feelings, then he would not upset the balance that he was trying to maintain, and then his mother would not be upset with him. He acted as if he believed that if he made no demands on his world, then he would not have to experience any feelings. Later on, Tommy refused to drink a glass of milk at snack time, saying that he was not thirsty and that maybe the staff should put the milk back into the refrigerator so none "would be missing". I think that this behaviour gives a clear expression of Tommy's fear of undoing the balance that allows him to maintain himself.

Another four-year-old boy, Daniel, seemed to be having a great deal of difficulty playing with two other children, a boy and a girl. He threw the crayons at them, spat at them, and then started to kick at them while squirming along on his back. The other children backed off, and Daniel stayed by himself on his back for a while. Daniel might have stayed there longer if I had not gone over to talk with him. At first he told me to "get away", that he did not want me, that he would "crush my face", and then that he would spit on me and make me "die". I continued to sit there and told him that I thought he was a lonely little boy, that he had a difficult time with other "kids" because he was afraid that they would make him feel upset and angry. Daniel agreed with me but added, "You talk crazy". I laughed, and he sat on his haunches looking at me in a very vacant way. We sat together, not saying anything, and then Daniel said, "I know these robbers take stuff out of the oven, robbing the oven and the nurses have the babies but the nurses leave the babies and the robber takes the babies and takes them out of the ovens".

I told Daniel that I thought he might think he takes too much from his Mummy and that she might then get angry with him. Daniel answered that she does get angry and he is afraid of her, but he quickly added, "She feeds me good stuff". I agreed with him that it was hard to think of Mummy as getting angry, but maybe he got angry with Mummy, and he was afraid she would not feed him enough "good stuff". Surprisingly, Daniel agreed and asked if I would play a game of drawing with him. I did, and we ended up making some squiggles together, which he decided were "always fancy cakes". He decided to take all the "cakes" home and give them to his Mummy.

Like Tommy, Daniel is worried about upsetting some magical balance. For Daniel this will mean that he is taking too much from his mother and that he will in some way be punished for doing this. Thus, any situation that makes him feel emotions is perceived as dangerous, since the emotions mean that he has lost some control over himself. Whether he feels angry or happy, sad or loving, the important thing is that he will be feeling something. These feelings will make him sense that he will have to take something from mother, which, in turn, will make him feel that he should not do this, or possibly that there is just no more "stuff" available for him. I think that for Daniel the latter is more plausible, because he needed to take the "cakes" home to Mummy, as if to try to fill her up—that is, to make her the inexhaustible object he needs her to be.

Even in children who are described as "normal", a feeling of loneliness will often be present. The loneliness will occur when the sense of a good-enough internal object is disturbed. This disturbance makes the child distrust his capacity to trust himself and results in a projection of persecution onto the external parental object and subsequent feeling of being alone, even when "Mummy and Daddy are there".

Just such a situation occurred with a very "normal" two-year-old. He was trying to get a bottle of milk from his mother, who was talking on the telephone. She smiled at her son but did not make any move to give him his bottle. The boy said, "want bottle" several times, but he only received a smile from his mother. While this seemed all right at first, the child started to whimper and then to cry loudly. At this point the mother hung up the telephone and told him that she was getting the bottle for him. The child, crying, wandered off and refused to take the bottle. When she tried to put the nipple into his mouth, the child grabbed the bottle and threw it across the room.

It was quite obvious that the child was angry, yet he wanted the bottle. He seemed inconsolable and wandered off, refusing his mother's care and consolations. He would not take anything from anyone, would not talk to anyone, and obviously wanted to be alone. After a few minutes of loud wailing in the next room, he came back to the kitchen and took his bottle, which was waiting for him on the chair. Soon he was his contented, happy, talkative self.

The child had momentarily lost his sense of a good internal object and lost the trust that he had, not only in himself, but in his mother, that he could get the food and the continued good object when he needed it. This frustration led him to distrust his capacity, and a feeling of persecution and anger invaded his sense of self. The result was a feeling of aloneness, now not just internally felt but enacted as well, by walking away and not wanting anyone nearby.

This sense of trust in one's self and in one's goodness and integrity is precariously maintained in infancy and childhood and does require that the parents be giving, accepting, and consistent. However, this is not to suggest that parents need to try to be perfect, for they cannot know what phantasies their child has, and these phantasies are sufficient to make the child feel frustrated and thwarted, even when the parents try to meet their child's "every need". They need to become able to distinguish between the angry child and the sad child.

There are some salient theoretical points to discuss associated with the beginnings of and the emergence of loneliness. At birth the infant's ego is protected from its own aggression by splitting off these feelings and projecting them to the object, which sustains and maintains life for the infant. This object, the breast, becomes the recipient of the infant's good feelings as well as its angry feelings. However, while the infant always wants to be maintained in a state of comfort and ease, the breast is not always present to prevent discomfort and unease. The subsequent feelings of anger, because the breast was not there to prevent these feelings, are projected to the breast, which must then be split into the bad and good part. The bad part becomes the receptacle for the infant's bad feelings, while the good part continues to nourish the baby. The good part of the breast and the beginnings of trust in a good breast and a good ego are protected, because any anger is projected and, therefore, not part of the good breast or the ego. With this state achieved, the baby will be happy and not lonely and be able to participate in a relationship with the mother.

As the ego matures, the sense of taking from the good breast becomes heightened, and the baby now attempts to cope with the conflict of wanting, needing, fearing, and being angry. The baby still wants the good breast but is afraid that it might take so much that there will be nothing left and that the mother will be angry because she needs some "stuff" for herself, and/or that someone else is taking the good stuff and not leaving any, or at least not leaving enough for the baby.

It is at this point that the baby needs to integrate the good and bad parts of the breast and to view the "whole object"—that is, that the breast is whole and not split into two parts and that it is part of the whole containing mother. This integration proceeds as the infant is able to accept its own feelings of anger, love, and emerging disappointment. However, the infant is only able to do this if it has been able to trust its developing ego and its capacity to gain needed nurturance and care. Anger need no longer be projected to an external object but is accepted as one's own without subsequent feeling of death. The ego can integrate the angry and destructive feelings with the good and loving feelings. The split-off bits are not rejected, because they no longer arouse too much pain and anxiety and they now contribute positively to the richness of the child's phantasy life without making the child feel inadequate, disoriented, or out of touch with reality. No longer does the child lose bits of his feelings by projection. Now the child feels in charge of himself and can control himself in relationships. No longer does the child need to be alone and feel the loneliness of and sadness "yearning for an unattainable perfect internal state" (Klein, 1965b, p. 300).

Thus, we see that loneliness is not that state of feeling lonely because you are not with anyone. Rather, loneliness is the feeling that, even though you are with other friends and or family, you still have a sense of being alone.

Some children need psychotherapy to help them with deeply rooted problems associated with loneliness. One four-year-old girl, Zelda, was sitting at the table eating dinner with the rest of her family (two older brothers and her mother and father). I was present at the dinner and noticed not only how difficult it was for the child to eat her food, but also how painful it seemed for her to talk to and look at the other people. Everyone else seemed to be happily eating and chatting, and I wondered why Zelda was having such a difficult time. Her behaviour continued throughout the meal, and after dinner she left the table to go to her bedroom and was seen only once again when she came to say good night, without much enthusiasm and with few words and no kisses.

I talked with Zelda's mother and enquired whether my presence at dinner had created any pressure for Zelda. The mother told me that she had been quiet for about 12 months, and she had been asking to eat alone, without wanting many food varieties. Her mother noted that Zelda had very few favourite foods and wanted these repeatedly on a daily basis. There was a slight departure from Zelda's preferences at dinner, although there were several of her desired foods available. Zelda has been eating less and less. I asked if Zelda also seemed sad and upset about any other experiences, and her mother responded:

> Zelda has been sad for over a year now, and we've been worried about her. She seemed happy enough when she was an infant, but we noticed that she seemed to be a much quieter and easier baby than my other two. I thought that this was just because I had more experiences as a mother, but now I wonder whether Zelda is suffering from something that we don't understand.

I responded that I thought that Zelda was indeed a very sad little girl and perhaps they might like to talk with someone who might be able to help them. She responded positively, and I gave her the name of a trusted colleague.

Discussion with my colleague has led us to think that Zelda is a very lonely little girl, who is trying to be very good and not take very much from her mother. She tries to be "nice" and non-demanding and to make sure that she does not give her mother "extra work". Zelda explained to her therapist that her mother has enough to do, and she does not want to be "any trouble to her", so she eats very little, tries to have few choices, and does not talk very much. She reported that she just tries to be "quiet and nice, so Mummy doesn't have to work too hard".

Later therapy sessions provided material that suggested that by behaving this way Zelda phantasized that she could save her mother from her dangerous feelings of aggression and demands and that by being alone she could stop herself from being dependent and taking too much. Within the family Zelda phantasized that she was an unwanted child, and she saw herself as someone who was weaker than her brothers and who would want to take more than they did. Therefore, she stopped herself from taking very much. Yet, with her strong feelings of dependency and needs for nurturance she also experienced anger at not gaining the satisfaction she needed. The conflict of not wanting to be dependent (because she imagined she was unwanted, and thus if she did not ask for much she would not be rejected), along with the anger at not gaining satisfaction of dependency needs, created the need for isolation. This conflict also created loneliness at not being able to achieve the perfect internal state in which she would feel accepted. Her need for perfection appeared in her limited choice of foods, her few words, and her attempts to be "good" and undemanding.

Zelda was afraid that her anger would destroy her mother whom she phantasized as not wanting her. This potential destructive outcome was avoided by isolation and loneliness. The more the mother and father tried to coax her to eat by offering a variety of tempting foods, the more Zelda retreated and focused upon her limited food palate. The more they said how good she was and that she did not have to be good all the time, the more she retreated to her bedroom and to the loneliness she felt. She was sure that if she was with them, she would neither be able to maintain the "perfect state" she demanded of herself nor their acceptance of her. Perhaps Zelda also felt that this acceptance would release her aggressive feelings, and then she would experience the very thing she so feared—they would not want her, because she was a "bad", angry girl.

The split-off (angry) part of Zelda's ego helped her to avoid the anxiety that would be aroused by her aggression directed towards her mother and herself. By splitting this part off, Zelda was unable to work through some of the anxieties of the paranoid–schizoid position. This left her with a residue of persecutory feelings, which were aroused whenever she tried to cope with her depressive feelings related to the later depressive position. By this I mean that whenever Zelda began to experience the sadness aspect of the depressive position, this was accompanied by the need for integration of the object (goodness and badness had to be recognized as arising from the same mother object). She feared that her anger would overwhelm her loving feelings and destroy the object altogether. However, Zelda was psychologically unable to integrate these feelings, which would have allowed her to relate more effectively to her mother. She still maintained strong projective defences and

still saw the breast as persecutory. These defences were revived whenever the family situation seemed "too good" for her,
because she felt that she did not "deserve" the goodness; she
imagined herself to be really a bad girl. The activation of the
anxiety of the depressive position by the goodness of the family
relationships forced her to regress to the paranoid position,
and this seemed to be the roots of her loneliness. Zelda was
alone with the bad parts of her ego (Klein, 1963b):

> It is only step by step that integration can take place and
> the security achieved by it is liable to be disturbed under
> internal and external pressure; and this remains true
> throughout life. Full and permanent integration is never
> possible for some polarity between the life and death in-
> stincts always persists and remains the deepest source of
> conflict. Since full integration is never achieved, complete
> understanding and acceptance of one's own emotions,
> phantasies and anxieties is not possible and this continues
> as an important factor in loneliness. [p. 302]

[Klein's quote ends a bit sadly and perhaps hopelessly. But
might it lead to the tolerance of chance losses versus aggressive
destruction? Perhaps some idealization may become part of the
integration, and relatively completed mourning may develop
without leading to mania. By relatively completed mourning, I
mean completed to an extent that the person does not remain
lonely, but at a state where the person tolerates the doubt of
whether it is going to happen again or more certainly that it is
going to happen again. (Clifford Scott, personal communication.)]

There are other aspects to consider about loneliness. One of
these may be understood in relation to the splitting and projection aspects of the ego. When these mechanisms operate, then
the object that receives the split-off projected bit cannot be
tolerated. This would then imply that the object has turned
bad, is persecutory, and must not be associated with. I think
that this explains, in part, the need for certain people not to
associate with others, and it operates as a "prejudice" to keep
them apart. In children and adults, the split-off projected bits
make them feel that in order to be safe and to keep their fragile
inner feelings of control (to maintain a feeling of perfection of

internal objects), they must be alone. Even though loneliness is a painful feeling, it is nevertheless safer to endure than confronting either the integration of good and bad or the split-off projected bits of the ego.

With excessive projection, an individual is unable to distinguish between good and bad and may confuse himself with others because he has projected so much of his ego to others. This individual must maintain an aloneness. He cannot "understand himself nor trust himself" (Klein, 1963b, p. 304) and cannot gain dependency satisfaction from others because he is not sure whether he can trust himself to perceive others as not potentially dangerous and harmful to himself. Projection acts to keep him alone and lonely, and when he tries to reach out to others, he is forced to withdraw because he perceives and feels his own projected hostility.

Our loneliness can also be experienced in a number of ways and as parts of ourselves. Thus, we may suddenly experience a loneliness when we encounter a certain scene, a certain smell, or a certain food. These encounters seem to take adults back to a state in childhood where projected parts of themselves were never entirely integrated. For example, this can occur while watching a film and seeing an infant quietly lying in its cot while its parents busy themselves, or while seeing a photograph of a child sitting in a classroom surrounded by other children, or watching a child play in a meadow, or playing in a sandbox. These views provide us with reminiscences about our own childhood, which include needs that were never entirely satisfied, or split-off bits that were not entirely integrated. These scenes, and others, put us into a position of feeling that we were not able to sufficiently "integrate the good object as well as parts of the self which are felt to be inaccessible" (Klein, 1963b, p. 309).

I am reminded of a four-year-old girl whose mother had just left her at the nursery school. The child climbed to the window and, looking out, said, "No, don't go, don't go, don't go. I want you to be here." The child then moved away from the window, looking sad and saying nothing. Then she stuffed her mouth with a handful of beads she picked up from a nearby tray of beads and wandered off with her mouthful. She then said she wanted to paint, picked up a brush, made a wash, and appeared very listless. She looked around, dropped the brush, sat on the floor, and for 30 minutes just watched, not moving. She watched what appeared to me to be the chair that she used to lift herself up so she could see out the window. Even filling her mouth with the beads could not stave off a feeling of loneliness. Perhaps she felt that by staying in one place and in one position she could hold back her feelings of rage and grief at having been left behind. Perhaps her emotional energy was being used in this way to hold on to as near an internal good object as possible, and this left nothing over to engage with others or to work at tasks.

Thus, we see that loneliness is an overpowering feeling, and it seems to rob us of the ability to do much about it, often poised between rage and hopeful grief. In order for us to recover and be revived, we seem to need someone else to come and tell us that we are liked, that we are loved, and that we are appreciated. However, none of these methods always work. We need to be able to trust ourselves and be sufficiently integrated so that splitting and projection are not major defences of the ego. While the external world can do something to help us, it is our internal phantasies that force us to interpret these external happenings. If our phantasies are such as to view the world as persecutory, then very little can be done to counter our loneliness until we begin to understand our internal world. The attempts to accept objects or situations to use for reparations take time.

CHAPTER FOUR

Toilet-training
and related problems

Toilet-training and separation from mother often create a great deal of difficulty for young children. At about the age of two years, children are generally encouraged to try to be without their nappy and are introduced to the idea of performing their bowel movements on the adult toilet or on their own "potty". Sometimes children are very eager to try this. However, in some cases the process is too difficult for them, because they have too many "accidents". While some children persist despite the "accidents" and eventually are toilet-trained for their bowel movements and urination, others have more trouble.

For these children the toilet-training is usually difficult and anxiety-provoking. They become upset by their "accidents" and look for signs in their parents' faces to see whether they are upset, disappointed, indifferent, or calm. The children either continue on with the very difficult training process or give it up for a while, depending not only on what they perceive on their parents' faces or even upon what their parents say, but also to a large extent upon what they imagine that their parents are feeling and thinking.

38

If they continue on with the toilet-training, these children usually have to let "something else go". Parents report that while toilet-training, and particularly at difficult times, their children seem unusually "touchy", ready to cry, or become "upset at just about anything". They may develop eating problems, such as becoming "finicky eaters", wanting to be fed, wanting to eat special foods, or not wanting to eat with the rest of the family when previously they had enjoyed this. Children may also show sleeping problems, such as not wanting to go to sleep even though they usually had "easy regular bedtimes", or wanting to sleep in their parents' bedroom.

Thus the toilet-training situation creates considerable difficulties, not only for children but also for the parents. Parents often make a rush for the nearest pamphlet or book on "How to toilet-train your baby" or on "What to do if your baby balks at toilet-training". Most of these books give some advice such as on when and how long to sit the child on the "potty". Usually, if the pamphlets are any good, they will attempt to calm the anxiety of the parent, telling them to "hold off for a while and let the child calm down". Some pamphlets may suggest that there is something wrong with the relationship between child and parents, but without recognizing how much more pressure this will place on the parent to discover the right answer, the right way to go on with the training. Such statements also do not provide any real understanding about how the child feels about this whole business of toilet-training.

I know a two-year-old boy, Adam, who had recently been weaned successfully and was now trying to cope with toilet-training. He had decided that he would not wear nappies any longer but, rather, that he would wear only a shirt and nothing else. The parents allowed him to make this decision and encouraged him by telling him that "air" was good for his bottom. Adam accepted this. He wanted to make sure that he got enough "air" on his bottom, and so he took off his clothes whenever he could.

As it appeared to the parents, Adam suddenly decided that he was not going to go out of the house any longer. He refused to go to the park, to the library, to the gym, or shopping with his baby-sitter—a woman he had known all his life and who was his only baby-sitter. Adam wanted to stay at home, watch television, and have a bowl filled with Cheerios—a toasted small round cereal shaped like an O. As Adam sat on the chair with no nappy, eating his Cheerios, he insisted that the bowl be refilled as soon as he had eaten one or two Cheerios. Thus his bowl had to be constantly filled. His baby-sitter did this without any hesitation or complaint, and his mother, when she was at home, did this as well. Adam always had enough to eat and his bowl was always full, even though he was eating the Cheerios.

Within a week, Adam became less concerned that his bowl be filled and was able to eat several Cheerios before he insisted that the bowl be refilled. As this began to happen, Adam also seemed to be less concerned about leaving the house and wanted to go to the park, the gym, the library, or shopping. As it became easier for him to leave the house, his Cheerio-eating also changed. He would allow the bowl to be quite empty before he asked for it to be filled again. Now when he was asked if he wanted some more cereal, he replied that he still had some left and that he would ask for more when he needed them. At the same time he returned to asking for a nappy for his bowel movements. When Adam sensed that he had to make a bowel movement, he asked to have his nappy on, and when he "did his b.m.", he wanted the "b.m." to be put into the toilet.

Gradually, Adam returned to the toilet for all his bowel movements, removing his nappy and having his "b.m.s" in the toilet. He was very pleased with himself and seemed to want his mother to tell him what good "b.m.s" he had made, how pleased she was with them and with him, and how glad she was that he was such a big boy. Adam still enjoyed going about his house without clothes, but he no longer needed to have a bowl of cereal to eat as he watched television.

Adam unconsciously projected the good part of his ego into his mother. Excrement represented good parts of his ego and were expected to make sure that his Mummy loved him and would continue good object relations with him. Adam needed this state of affairs in order to help him maintain the degree of ego integration that he had achieved. However, his mother was going to work and left him with a baby-sitter. Adam phantasized that his "b.m.s" were either not good enough or else harmful to his mother, and that was why she was not with him. By making sure that he had his bowl full all the time, he made sure that he was not harming or damaging his mother. He could eat these little bits, and since they never decreased in number, there would never be any attacks on him for taking too much from her.

In other words, the anxieties associated with the depressive position were suddenly too great for Adam to contain and therefore he regressed to the paranoid position. This regression activated the suspicion that his mother had become a persecutor because neither he nor his products (his "b.m.s") were sufficiently good to keep her at home. Separation from his mother had created the difficulty that now he not only had to try and cope with toilet-training and weaning, but he also phantasized an attacking mother who had left him because he was not good enough. Adam's response to his phantasy was to make sure that he did not leave the house. I think his hostility to his mother for leaving was so great that he just could not leave the house because the outside had become too threatening for him. In phantasy, staying at home became symbolic of staying with his mother. In an effort to make sure that staying at home represented staying with his Mummy/house, he insisted that the bowl of cereal never show any depletion. If he could be filled by the cereal—the good Mummy objects—and they never disappeared, then the Mummy/house would remain safe and good. Adam could re-establish his depressive position and could feel once again secure, loved, and cared for. As this happened, Adam could then continue on with his toilet-training process.

Adam's anger with his mother for leaving him alone, as if she did not think he was good enough, forced him to regress, and in so doing he utilized more the projective identification processes and defence mechanisms. This left Adam feeling as if he were empty and bad. That is, he had projected into his mother his good parts—his "b.m.s"—which were not sufficient to keep his idealized object/mother at home, and so Adam felt depleted and that he had little left to give. With his good parts insufficient, his ego felt impoverished, and he needed the food to fill himself up again. He did not eat greedily but slowly and definitely, and he needed his bowl to be continually filled, perhaps so as not to recognize that he was taking in the very food, love, and care he needed. To recognize this at first would be to suffer persecution, because, in his phantasy, his mother would stay away longer if he allowed himself to know that he was taking in this food which he must have phantasized as stolen from her. As Klein (1946) goes on to point out

One characteristic feature of the earliest relation to the good object—internal and external—is the tendency to idealize it. In states of frustration or increased anxiety, the infant is driven to take flight to his internal idealized object as a means of escaping from persecutors. From this mechanism various serious disturbances may result: when persecutory fear is too strong, the flight to the idealized object becomes excessive, and this severely hampers ego-development and disturbs object-relations. [p. 9]

Adam was unable to maintain an idealized internal object and felt that he was now of no value. The stress of weaning, toilet-training, and separation from his mother was just too great for him. However, because his mother and father were able to recognize their son's stress and did not at all reprimand his behaviour but gave what he seemed to want without any restrictions, Adam was able to regain a sense of goodness and an internal good object. By remaining calm, caring, and gentle his parents provided him with the opportunity once again to feel wanted, loved, and not persecuted. Unfortunately, most pamphlets on toilet-training do not recognize these persecutory effects of tension upon the young child, particularly when the training becomes associated with weaning. If this occurs, then both events create a concern and anxiety about separation from mother. Thus toilet-training should await success at weaning and the development of some ability to feed without the breast.

Jane, a 27-month-old child, decided one morning that she wanted her pyjamas and nappy off and that she was going to find her "poo–chair" (her mother's term), but which the child had decided that morning was to be called her "boat". Jane announced that she wanted to go for a boat ride and tried to put her boat on the floor but found that the movements she made created a very unsteady boat. Her mother then suggested that she could go for a "boat" ride with the "boat" placed on a cushion. Jane put the boat on a cushion, and with both feet in the "boat" she sat down and told her mother "Look Mummy—boat ride." When the mother noticed that Jane felt shaky in the boat, she suggested that she would feel safer if she took her feet out and sat on the "boat". Jane did this and sat down. Then she stood up and sat down again and repeated this several times. Finally, Jane sat on the "boat" for a bit and asked for some toilet tissue. When she was given the toilet tissue, she rolled it into a ball and wiped herself and then dropped the ball of paper into the "boat". She repeated this procedure about three times and then asked for more paper. She repeated the same procedure a few more times (rolling it into a ball, wiping herself, dropping it into the "boat", and then taking it out and rolling it again, wiping herself, and dropping it into her "boat").

When she asked for more toilet tissue, her mother suggested to her that she had enough paper. Jane accepted her mother's suggestion but continued to roll the paper into a ball, wipe herself, and drop it into the "boat" (the potty). Jane repeated this several times and then looked at the paper balls in her "boat" and said, "See Mummy". Jane repeated the action a total of seven times, bringing her potty/boat over to her mother each time to peer into. When mother said that she saw the balls in the potty/boat, Jane looked very pleased.

Her mother said, "That's nice Jane, very nice", and Jane once again started to pick up the balls of paper and drop them into the potty. She repeated this several times and then sat in front of the "boat" and began to talk to the balls of paper in her boat in what her mother described as a "loving little voice". Jane then carried her potty around, calling it "baby" and talking and cradling it. At this point she found a popsicle stick, put the stick in with the paper balls and covered the potty with paper. Jane then found a horse, took the popsicle stick to the horse and then took the horse, a cow, and a sheep to her potty. She put all these into the potty while saying, "Mummy, Daddy", and being very delighted with herself.

Jane continued her play but now began to pour the contents out and then returned them to her boat/potty. She carried the boat/potty to her "car" and put the contents into the "boot of her car". She then put the potty away under a chair in the next room, and sat on the car and drove it. She finished this play by coming over to her mother to ask what she was doing. In going over to her mother, she hit her hand on the door and wanted her mother to hug and kiss her. After the hugs, Jane went off to watch television.

Among some of the trends that Jane demonstrated was the obsessional nature of her play. Anal and urethral anxieties were combined with genital concerns. In order to play, Jane needed help from her mother. Jane rolled up her balls of paper, wiped herself, and dropped the balls into her potty, but not before her mother had made a very shaky seat somewhat firmer. Jane had projected her fear and anxiety to her mother and the mother was able to contain Jane's anxiety and, in turn, had been able to help her daughter to begin to cope with her concerns about toilet-training. The phantasy that Jane may have been experiencing was the sense of potential loss of good things from her body, as well as the anxiety as to how these things would be accepted by her mother. In projective identification these phantasies are projected to her mother and are object-related—that is, mother is the one who in phantasy may or may not accept her daughter's anxieties and may or may not be able to think about them in such a way as to "defuse" their frightening quality. In defusing these qualities, Jane would then be able to introject her projections and feel as if she had more control over them and that they, therefore, would not be as overwhelming.

Obviously toilet-training was difficult for Jane, but she decided to try the potty, removed all her clothing, and was now playing out her anxieties. Her mother, aware of the child's concerns, could make it safe for her by putting a cushion under the potty. The unsteadiness was Jane's way of saying that she was afraid of being independent, of being separated from mother. Although she had made the decision to try the training and removed her clothes, the anxiety was great enough to try to prevent it from happening. This was represented by the unsteady potty. The danger, experienced as a persecutory anxiety, was perceived by her mother, while, at the same time, the child did not totally disown or split off parts of herself. She could accept her mother's suggestions, which I think is indicative of Jane's empathic capacity, a capacity that would not be present if she had split off and projected her anxiety fully. Since her mother was able to remain open to what her daughter was feeling and experiencing, she accepted the projections. Her understanding of this was reflected in her remaining close to her daughter, being able to offer just enough toilet tissue and being able to accept the repetitiveness of her behaviour. Jane's projective identification to mother did not empty her, nor did it destroy her purposive play at toilet-training. Rather, she continued to play in an integrated manner and went on to test further her new-found sense of protected separateness.

Jane was pleased with her play, and, as she could demonstrate the obsessional characteristics of her play, which expressed and "made safe" her anal and urethral anxieties, she went on to explore the genital aspects of her phantasies. Jane began to talk to the rolled papers in a "loving little voice", calling them "baby" and cradling the potty. When she put the popsicle stick and the horse, cow, and sheep into the potty, poured them out, and then replaced them several times, she kept repeating "Mummy and Daddy". Later she brought the potty and its contents to the "car" and poured the contents into the "boot" of the car and put the potty in the next room and drove the car. Jane's anxieties now arose from the phantasy that she had not only attacked her mother's body and taken the babies from it but she had robbed it of the father's penis as well. She was not just driving away from the scene but was now involved in phantasy, masturbation, and sexual activity with the father's stolen penis. Not only was retaliation phantasized but guilt was now experienced as well. When she had finished driving, she went to see what her mother was doing and it was then that she hit her hand on a door.

Jane's paper balls became her babies. She had created them, perhaps indicating her growing desire to make reparations to her mother—to have babies for her—and in this way to restore her for the goodness she had given. But, interestingly, she introduced a popsicle stick—the phantasized penis—to the potty. She was afraid to see what might happen to the babies when the penis was introduced, so she covered it over with paper. I think the domestic animals she later introduced represented the non-aggressive, caring mother (the cow and the sheep) as well as a non-aggressive, strong father (the horse).

However, while she was delighted with her play, for a short period of time it did not continue. In pouring the contents into the boot of the car and driving it, Jane tested her own capacity to cope with the phantasies of masturbation and Oedipal genital desires. The anxiety evoked by these phantasies was of intense paranoid persecution, accompanied by the fear of retaliation and revenge. Jane's good objects were not sufficiently established in her inner world. To maintain a relationship with her parents, Jane needed to grieve and make up in games of babies that she can have only when she is as big as Mummy and Daddy. She must be able to phantasize more reparative experiences. In phantasy, Jane did not only hit her hand on the door; rather, her mother hit her hand for touching herself and for her sexual phantasies. In phantasy she was being punished. Her reparations were undone, and she had regressed. She now needed the real mother's overt protection from the feared attacks of a dangerous internalized mother. Jane needed her mother to take care of her as a much younger child for a few minutes.

The projective identification was of a suddenly experienced, predominantly aggressive inner world controlled by persecutory fears. Mother's countertransference was of the need to protect and care for a very young child. Jane's concerns could be introjected after being defused by an understanding container. In this instance the mother did not say, "You've been such a grown-up girl. You don't need me to kiss you right now. You do it yourself." Rather, the mother supported Jane's fragile ego in such a way as to help Jane cope with her anxieties. Jane could now regain her ego integration and begin to recognize her impulses and feelings as her own. No doubt this is a process that will go on for years but, hopefully, with increasingly less projective identification.

The following is a very interesting example of the attacking aspects of projective identification projected to the child from the mother, with the child experiencing the countertransference. A young mother told me how her daughter started to gag and behave as if she were going to vomit whenever she began to change the daughter's soiled nappy. Her mother told me that the smell of the bowel movement made her feel as if she was going to gag and perhaps even vomit, but she never did and always managed to withhold any gagging. However, I think the child was gagging and "almost" vomiting on behalf of her mother, because she never gagged when her father or someone else changed her nappies and only did so when her mother did. The uncomfortable, tense feelings that were experienced by the mother were acted out by her 24-month-old daughter.

The bowel movements must have been phantasized by the mother as her own aggressive impulses, which she had some difficulty in accepting. The baby could express her rejection of these feelings by gagging or vomiting them out for her, both an aggressive act as well as an evacuation of the aggression. The child's mother was about to block the child's countertransference by giving her books to look at while she changed her nappy. This would have been less helpful than her usual reaction, which was to ask her daughter questions such as, "How many ducks do you see? How many horses can you count? Do you see a red colour? Do you see a pretty house?" etc., etc. I think these questions helped both mother and child by acting as repetitive (obsessional) verbalization, which could be answered correctly (perfectly), the answers serving to modify the persecutory and depressive aspects of the anxieties of both mother and child.

I would like to illustrate issues related to constipation by the case of a three-year-old boy, referred for play psychotherapy because he began to withhold his faeces. No underlying organic factors were discovered upon medical examination. Jimmy just said, "I don't have to go to the toilet", and he did not "go". He would withhold his faeces for seven to ten days at a time, at which point faeces might leak onto his underpants and he would begin to "dance around", as his mother called it, yet he continued to deny that he had to go to the toilet. She finally put him on the toilet and he would pass his stools, but with some difficulty and pain. Jimmy would complain that he really did not have to go to the toilet and, when he finally passed his stool, he did not seem particularly pleased or happy. It was as if he had to comply with the demands both of his mother and of his body, but he did not like this loss of control over what he later told me were his "bad feelings".

Jimmy had not had any toileting problems prior to the separation of his parents. Their separation and later divorce had been a stormy affair, with his mother and father accusing each other of not being sufficiently caring or attentive parents. In particular, Jimmy's mother accused his father of being away from him far too often, of lying to him, and of not being a fit father because of what she said was his drug problem. The father, in turn, accused Jimmy's mother of demanding, aggressive behaviour towards him and of caring too much for their son. Their situation had reached an impasse, and they separated after several difficult disputes, including one where the mother accused the father of hitting her. Jimmy's response to this very problematic environment had been to develop a constipation problem, which verged on encopresis—that is, constipation with overflow of faeces.

When I first met Jimmy without his parents, I was very impressed by the "old, serious" look that he had. He came into my office looking very worried and serious and not saying much at all. He did not move very much and sat on the edge of the couch with his hands on his lap and his head bowed. He certainly appeared as a very depressed little boy. When I suggested that he thought not much could be done about his family, he immediately agreed and said that it was good that I knew that, because he thought about his family a lot and didn't know how to talk about his parents.

Much of the first few sessions were taken up with Jimmy sitting on the edge of the couch, looking very sad and not saying very much. I interpreted this as not just his sense of despair, but also his sense that someone, such as I or his mother, was now supposed to change this situation and make things "good again". Jimmy accepted this interpretation by demonstrating a sudden interest in the room and began to talk about what I had brought in for us to play with. He noticed the crayons and the pile of white paper, the marbles (some in a bag, others on the floor beside the bag), and a game called the "Happy Hippo". This game has four stereotyped hippopotamuses whose mouths are controlled by a lever. When this is pushed down, the head shoots forward, the mouth opens, and a marble may be "swallowed" when the head is on top of a marble and the lever is released. The marble then descends into the body of the hippo and passes out of its side into a slot. I chose this game because of Jimmy's constipation problem. The game included the aggressive banging down of the lever, the gobbling of the marble (food), and then the passing out of the marble (the faeces).

Jimmy said that he liked the crayons and that he might use them some time when we were together, but "not right now". Again, I interpreted his desire for someone to make his poo "fixed up" for him, but this time I added the factor of his anger at his parents. My interpretations were based upon the countertransference feelings that overcame me when I sat with Jimmy for even just a few minutes. I felt that I was supposed to make things better and tell him that everything will be fine now, and I felt the need to talk. I felt that Jimmy's sadness was not just that he could not verbalize his feelings, but that he was very afraid of his impulses to attack and destroy his mother. His projective identifications to me of hopelessness and sadness were an attempt to avoid discomfort and pain. He did not know what was going to happen to him with the present state of his family, and he thought that he would be lost, with no one to care for him (Joseph, 1988, p. 138). My countertransference was to try to make things better for him and to talk to him about how to handle his constipation and his parents. However, my interpretations were aimed at trying to help him recognize his feelings and the associated hostility. I talked in a quiet manner, as if I were thinking out loud about his feelings, as in a verbal reverie—that is, taking in his feelings and trying to make sense of it for him.

Jimmy said that he wanted to make some drawings and asked me to give him the crayons and the paper. I did give him these materials, with the quiet statement, "I think you want me to do everything for you, to make you happy because you don't trust yourself to do anything". Jimmy responded by telling me that I had to make a drawing first, and that he would copy my drawing on his sheet of paper, like copying my speech and introjecting a containing and understanding mother. Again, Jimmy was not able to do something "first" or for himself; he needed to copy my drawing.

I made squiggly drawings of angular shapes, which Jimmy copied. His copies usually "over-flowed" the paper or the design, and I pointed out that his drawings "leaked". Jimmy said that they were still on the paper, and I agreed. He said that he just made more lines, and I agreed again, noting that it was like his "poo", that sometimes his poo just leaked out and maybe it was like his feelings, which sometimes leaked out and frightened him. Jimmy was quiet at this point, and, perhaps because of countertransference, I added that his sadness was to try and stop his feelings from showing. Jimmy attempted to prevent his faeces from coming out, but when some faeces leaked out he became frightened, quiet, and sad. At such times, I think he felt that he was losing control over his aggressive feelings, and the resulting sadness and despair demonstrated the strength of his feelings of love and aggression, related to the superego and control over aggression. Sometimes he loved mother and sometimes father, but he couldn't love both now as they did not love each other now. At this point Jimmy said that he did not want to play this game any more. He said, "Let's just sit here and you don't say anything—nothing at all". We sat together on the couch for about 30 minutes, not talking. When the session was close to ending, I asked him if I could say something before he had to leave. Jimmy said, "No", and the session ended without further comments.

Jimmy arrived at his next session looking much "easier" and certainly less sad. In fact, even my secretary noted that Jimmy smiled at her. When we were in the room, Jimmy became quiet and projected his sadness and despair once again. I noted the difference between inside and outside our room, and Jimmy's startling answer was: "I was just pretending [and, I thought, pretending for the secretary, but not pretending for me]. My mother thinks I should pretend and then I'll just always be happy." I noted: "If you pretend long enough, the happiness becomes part of you." He agreed but said that he didn't feel happy inside.

As we talked about his insides, Jimmy let me know that he was very sad, that he thought that his father should not have left home, and that when he went to visit him and be with him for a few days, he was always very happy. (His father also noted that he did not have any bowel problem when he was with him but went to the toilet without any difficulty. Jimmy's father said that it was probably "just his mother's over-concern and giving in to Jimmy that created this problem for him".)

I suggested to Jimmy that he was angry with his mother and that he was afraid that she might leave him also if she found out how he felt. Jimmy then said that we should play the Hippo game and added: "Would you get it, please?" I agreed, offering an interpretation that he needed someone to think about and work out his problems. Jimmy said, "Yes" as he chose his hippo.

At first the game was slow and quiet. Jimmy did not put much pressure on the lever, nor was he very competitive in grabbing for the marbles. When he did gain a marble, I pointed out how the marble went into the hippo's body and came out, like "poo" comes out of us. At about this point he looked very sad, and I added, "The 'poo' won't hurt me, I won't be spoiled by the 'poo,' I'll be okay". Jimmy then banged down on the lever, tried to grab a marble, and was smiling. We played the hippo game for the rest of the session, and he said, "We will play this next time, so it must be here". I noted his taking charge and commented that he could see that I was fine and not hurt and that I felt good that he could show me how he felt.

The next month's sessions were taken up in an almost repetitive pattern. Jimmy was bright and smiling as he came into the room. He became "downcast" in the room at first, particularly while he did drawings. However, now I had to copy his designs, and then, after we had done four or five drawings, he said that it was time to play the hippo game. He played with considerable aggression, trying to take all the marbles. At first, when he said, "You only have one", I said, "That's all right". I was pleased that he was winning and not afraid to win. It seemed to me that Jimmy was able to communicate his despair to me and was now actively trying to do something about it. He could become aggressive in the game, and, while fearful at first that I might retaliate, he was able to accept his feelings and impulses as his own when he saw that I was not upset, nor unaccepting of his feelings. Jimmy was gradually able to see his "insides" as not always unhappy and despairing because of his aggression, but now could experience his insides as happy, aggressive, and creative.

At about this time, he thought that he wanted to look out of my window, to see whether he could see where his mother worked. He climbed on the window-sill and pointed out "her office building"—a very tall structure, which, he said, was "safe even though it was so big". I interpreted this to him as meaning that his aggression towards her for not keeping father had not meant that she had lost all her inside penises. We talked about how sad she was at times, that she was tired and even "looked like she would cry". Jimmy said she got very angry with him when he wouldn't go to the toilet and when he talked about how his father had given him such a nice time. I think these conversations aroused anxiety in Jimmy, which had its origin in the phantasized aggressive attacks he made upon her to get her inside penises, perhaps to keep them, or more likely to give to his Daddy to make him strong, because his mother had told him what a weak man he was. Jimmy had to control these impulses and to maintain a close, vigilant guard over his aggressive feelings. Keeping things in was expressed by keeping his faeces in, representing his conflict between his ability to take father's place with mother—as he can take mother's place with father.

Jimmy later talked about his constipation problem, telling me that "it wasn't a problem any more", because usually he could go to the toilet. He couldn't go when he felt very upset and "very sad". The sadness was interpreted as feeling badly because he was angry and he was afraid that, if he hurt his mother, she would leave him and then he would have no one to take care of him. Jimmy needed an object that would take him in and relieve him of the enormous burden of his anxieties. It was difficult to trust his new object, myself, and at best I think he felt ambivalent towards me during the middle part of his play psychotherapy. He loved me and he hated me, but loving me allowed him to introject a caring, dependable, and non-retaliative object and to learn to trust this new object. Trusting this introject gradually allowed him to express his aggression and understand his faeces problem. Jimmy came to his sessions skipping down the hall, looking for my secretary to say hello to, and he expressed much pleasure at being in our room together, as if now he was free of the concerns that had held back, not only anger, but also love.

It seemed to me that Jimmy's mother could not be an understanding mother with the capacity to experience and retain her son's anxieties. Her own problems were too massive to allow this and so she could not retain the "balanced outlook" (Bion, 1988a) she had for him when he was a baby. Now she was almost intolerant of his feelings, and, while she tried not to be annoyed with him, she gave me the impression of someone who was defeated, yet still fighting, but feeling that the fight would not be successful. While she was usually not angry with Jimmy, she seemed to become "hard and demanding"—that is, she tried to insulate herself from Jimmy's difficulties by setting out a strict routine and maintaining it. She became easily "panicky": she expected things to "break down" and felt she would be left "holding the bag". She was very angry with Jimmy's father and accused him of being the cause of their problems—in other words, she attempted to project her difficulties and control them by maintaining an accusing attitude towards him. I do not mean to imply in any way that only the mother was at fault, but, rather, I see the events as Jimmy reported them in and between both parents as supporting his phantasies and his difficulties of separating what is in each of them and between them leading to the development of his problems.

For example, several months into his sessions, and after he began to feel better, Jimmy went to visit his father for a weekend. He had to sleep in the same bed with his father and his girlfriend. Jimmy told me about this, giggling, but very upset, because, as he said, he had no room to move in the bed, and he even felt "wet". He felt that he didn't sleep well, that he was angry because his father wasn't there for him alone as he spent "so much time with her". After this weekend Jimmy's bowel problems were exacerbated, and he looked once again like a sad, dejected little boy who could not do anything about the bad and frightening events that were happening all about him. The sense that I received from him was that everything was bad, and he was so completely left out of the caring relationship that he needed.

This projection of "everything bad" into the mother would ordinarily make his mother feel desperate. She felt immobilized and that anything she did just did not help Jimmy or herself. She conveyed to Jimmy her own sense that "everything was bad" and in a state of despair. My countertransference to Jimmy's projections was that I could not get his father to care for him properly, I could not get his mother to feel less despairing. Nor could I do anything for Jimmy. In this way he introjected both a real and a phantasized weak despairing object, which could not control the unfolding of very unhappy events and experiences. I said, "Jimmy, it's like we were beginning to understand why you are so sad and also so angry, and then along comes last weekend and everything seems bad again. It's like you think I can't help either." Jimmy agreed and said, "You didn't anyhow". I replied that neither of us could tell his Dad or his Mum how to feel or do things and that they had to want to do things for themselves and for him.

Jimmy just looked sad at this interpretation. I waited for a few moments, and then I thought that I should not push him to do things, nor think things out for him. I said that it was okay if we talked about his feelings and played at our games of hippo and drawing. I added that I would try to understand how sad and also how angry he felt. I thought that Jimmy was saying as well, that he was afraid to feel, and he was even frightened when he did have feelings because he understood his feelings to be an attack upon his mother who had already presented herself as sad and weak and who needed the support that Jimmy was trying to give by being "good".

Jimmy seemed to feel a bit better at this point and wanted to play the hippo game. He banged the levers with great force and tried to take all the marble/food in a greedy way. I said he could show me how angry he was and yet remain unharmed. I interpreted to Jimmy, "It looks like you can get really angry, just like the angry 'poo' that comes out of the hippos and you are okay". Jimmy smiled and replied, "Yeah". By this statement I had tried to help him recognize that his leaking "poo" and withholding his faeces was similar, one the concrete act, the other the symbolic form of the feeling to prevent him from feeling and expressing anger. Faeces came to represent his aggression towards his despairing mother as well as his father. I think Jimmy could experience me as a "safe" person—one who would not be devastated by his projections of despair and anger but continue to remain his container. As this occurred, Jimmy felt a bit better, and he began to introject a more caring, dependable, and strong object.

Some children's experiences of real or phantasized separation from their love objects compel a regression, usually in an attempt to control the feelings of anger that such frustration creates. In regression to toileting problems, the child attempts to express and control, to withhold—as in withholding "angry" faeces—by asking to wear a "holding" nappy, or even, at times, by hurting himself. In doing this, the child attempts to cope with the persecutory anxiety by experiencing depression and despair more acutely. I am not suggesting that all children who experience separation or real or phantasized loss express the resulting feelings of aggression through bowel difficulties. However, I suspect that when toilet-training has been of some early parental concern, then this provides the foundation for its later appearance, when regression is the only way that the child's ego can handle the stress of separation and loss experiences.

However, even when there have not been earlier toileting problems, parents of normally healthy, happy children have reported toileting problems when their children experienced stress of separation and/or loss. Stephan, at age two years and ten months, had been completely toilet-trained for four or five months. His grandmother arrived to visit and stay with the family for three weeks following the birth of Stephan's brother. Within a few days of her arrival, Stephan's behaviour deteriorated. He and his grandmother had frequent "shouting matches", and he began to soil. He was no longer interested in being "clean", he needed to be close and alone with his mother, and he was often discovered attacking his brother by pinching him or pulling at his skin. Meanwhile, his mother noted that he and his grandmother "seemed to be yelling at each other all the time and about every small thing that happened, like even how fast he did things".

Stephan's rage at his brother's birth, his phantasized loss of his mother, and the arrival of his grandmother seemed too much for him to bear. I think he imagined that he was now to belong to his grandmother (because she seemed to take over for his mother in matters relating to Stephan), and his mother was going to look after his brother exclusively. Depression, characterized by soiling and yelling at his grandmother appeared as his phantasized and, at times, real separation and loss of his mother. Toilet-training was begun when Stephan was nearly two years old, and he seemed "receptive and easy to train", but, as his parents then noted, "perhaps we started too early and maybe wanted too much from him".

Glen was almost four years old, and he had been toilet-trained to urinate in the toilet but had not been bowel-trained. His parents attempted bowel training by various means such as "stars" and other rewards. Bowel "problems" had emerged following the birth of his brother, eight months previously. Glen became afraid to sit on the toilet, saying that all the pipes and water and "things under the toilet" will "swallow me up", and he finally refused to sit on the toilet seat. Eventually, Glen told his mother that he was afraid to let his "poo" go into the toilet, because he would "lose it" and he would "feel funny". I interpreted this to mean that the loss of his "poo" is phantasized as an emptying of or losing his insides, including his baby. Glen withheld his faeces and refused to have a bowel movement for several days in a row. His parents were now concerned that this "constipation" would make him ill, and they wondered why this happened to him. They felt that they had not put any pressure on him to be toilet-trained. However, in conversation with them, they noted that they had expected him to be trained at "about two years of age, when most children are trained", and while they put him to bed without a nappy on to help "remind him to stay clean", they nevertheless put one on him once he was "fast asleep".

In discussing Glen's toilet-training with them, I suggested that he may feel left out of the family, as both parents seemed to be so busy with his baby brother. For several hour-long visits over a period of several months, I had been able to observe his mother being exceptionally attentive and caring of his brother and making brisk demands on Glen whenever he seemed too slow in responding or in getting ready to leave to return home. I further suggested that Glen felt very angry, and yet he had great difficulty expressing this anger. In his play he knocked over other children's constructions, he flitted from activity to activity, and he was a very receptive foil for an aggressive boy who had Glen do all his "dirty work". Glen's parents seemed to understand and accept these aspects about their son, but they did not know what to do to help him feel closer to the family. As they pointed out, whatever they gave him did "not seem to be enough". I indicated that I thought Glen felt empty and needed a lot of care, and perhaps they could start a collection of pebbles with him. They could collect them at the water's edge, sort them in terms of shape and colour, and count them frequently, placing them in small boxes and in his bedroom. I also suggested that they provide him with a lot of food—an almost "never-ending source of good supplies"—particularly at meal-time.

I thought that if Glen felt "emptied" and afraid that he might not get enough to fill himself again and if his "constipation" was the result of his attempts to withhold his anger, yet if he could express these feelings under direction and advice of another, then having a source of good supplies of food and a collection of pebbles could help him to feel full again. The emptiness resulted from his phantasized and real separation and loss of his mother and her over-attentiveness to his brother. Yet, if Glen became angry at this loss, then he would experience a feeling of further loss, if not overt rejection. The pebbles, symbolic of small faecal boluses, could be kept counted repeatedly and saved in boxes, essentially as Klein (1952b) points out:

> If anxiety of a persecutory and depressive nature is re-inforced, a regression to the earlier stages and to the corresponding anxiety-situations takes place. Such regression manifests itself for instance in the breaking down of already established habits of cleanliness; or phobias apparently overcome may reappear in slightly changed forms.
>
> During the second year, obsessional trends come to the fore; they both express and bind oral, urethral and anal anxieties. Obsessional features can be observed in bed-time rituals, rituals to do with cleanliness or food and so on, and in a general need for repetition (e.g. the desire to be told again and again the same stories, even with the same expressions, or to play the same games over and over again). [p. 84]

Glen's "good" source of food and the repetitive nature of the pebble play may have helped him along, with the less persecutory aspects he had been experiencing from his parents because of their anxiety concerning his development. Glen became interested in trying toileting again, not on the toilet seat, but on a colourful potty/chair, and, as this occurred, he became more active in playing with other children. "All aspects of development contribute towards the process of modifying anxiety" (Klein, 1952b, p. 81) and guilt when there has been a loss of control after it has been learned. The anxiety is often about the ability to make a new start or obtain control again.

CHAPTER FIVE

Sleeping problems:
depressive and superego aspects

C hildren of about two years seem to go through phases where sleeping, eating, toilet-training, cleaning up, and helping parents become problems. Most of the time these difficulties are short-lived and child and parent overcome these difficulties with patience and understanding on the parents' part and with a recognition of the continued love of the parents to the child, as well as the acceptance of love from the child to the parents.

One of the difficulties that two-year-olds seem to go through that accompanies their greater sense of independence, which is marked by their skills in walking and talking, is the anxiety bound up with the depressive position. The two-year-old child is able to go from one place to another in the house, to talk about how he feels and what he wants, and also to begin to understand more about the feelings of others, particularly the feelings of his parents. Within this depressive position, the anxiety that he has done some damage to his parents—particularly to his mother—is his foremost concern, and he needs to make sure that he has a continuing, really loving relationship with her.

Most children are able to explain this loving relationship with mother, they are able to have the feeling that they possess a trusting, reliable internal guardian, and it is this feeling that allows them to be brought to their bedrooms and to fall asleep alone. However, if the child's feelings are disturbed in relation to his feelings towards mother, then one of the consequences may be a sleep problem. The child may begin to express a feeling of loss of a good external mother, brought on by various loss experiences with her, as, for example, when the mother is so busy that she has to rush a bedtime, or when she and her husband become particularly "sharp" with each other, or when the mother is complaining that she had a hard day and she is not prepared to have a difficult evening, or if the mother has not given the kind of affection, attention, and care to him that she ordinarily gives. All these and no doubt more situations and events that both parents go through contribute to this uneasy feeling that the young child has that mother is either angry or disappointed in the young child.

This special feeling activates the child's depressive anxiety. The child fears that the mother is angry because the child has not done enough for her or has taken too much from her. The child unconsciously phantasizes that in some way he has damaged mother and now she is retaliating by not providing the reliable, secure love relationship that the child has been able to have in the past, but which is now threatened. The child is so interested in mother at this point in his development because the child is so much more capable of independence and also more capable of phantasizing a changed feeling in the mother. The child responds to all of this with increased depressive anxieties when there is a change in his usually safe, secure surroundings. Sleep is a problem now because to go to sleep is to be alone and to have his phantasies both exaggerated and carried out. Furthermore, the child may have been left alone without the internal guardian he had before. This is because the internal guardian is affected by the child's sense of having done some damage to mother—and this is at its zenith when depressive anxiety, independence, and empathic perception are mobilized at the point of going to sleep and to "the land of dreams".

Allan is a two-year-old child who usually goes to bed easily. He enjoys having stories read to him, he enjoys telling his parents what he likes about the stories, and often he wants to have the same story read several times rather than have different stories. However, one evening Allan "changed". He was obviously having a difficult time going to bed. He insisted that he was not going to go to bed "now", and he wanted to stay up and be with his parents. He told them, "I'm not sleepy", and for Allan that was that! He resisted the bribes his parents offered him to go to his bedroom with either of them, such as being told his favourite story or making a picture before going to bed. He just wanted to stay with his parents and watch them as they busied themselves with their evening work.

As Allan wandered about following his father or his mother, he would be all right for a few minutes, and then he would start to cry and insist upon being consoled. When his parents picked him up, cuddled him, and then suggested that it was time to go to his bedroom or started walking towards his room, Allan became angry and began to yell, "I'm not going. No, no bed. Not go to sleep". It was quite futile for either of the parents to pursue trying to put him to bed. Allan's bedtime routine was disrupted for more than a week by his refusal to go to his bed at the usual time. He refused to go to his bed and to sleep until about 11 p.m., three hours after his usual bedtime. By this time Allan would be cranky, fussy, very tired, and usually uncontrollable. Finally, his mother usually picked him up, carried him to bed, and put him into bed. This usually caused some more crying. Allan finally went to sleep, but not before he had made sure that his mother told him that she loved him several times. Allan would usually hug his mother and tell her that he loved her and insisted that she respond by telling him that she loved him. Allan either asked his mother to tell him that she loved him, or he kept repeating "I love you" several times until she said, "I love you too, Allan". During his intense love remarks Allan looked sad and seemed desperately to need his mother to tell him that she "loved him". When she did so, I could see the suffering that was evident in his face disappear.

Allan's behaviour during that difficult week of not wanting to go to sleep was marked with angry outbursts, clinging to mother, a greater fussiness, and a greater demand than had ever been experienced before for mother's undivided attention. His parents also noted that Allan seemed to be less "social" than usual. He did not want his parents to bring other people into the house, and when they did, Allan was even more clinging and tried to interrupt and distract his parents when they were in conversation with the visitors. Allan had suddenly become a sleeping problem, whereas, in the past he was remarkable in that sleep was never a problem for him. Now Allan was presenting an unusual difficulty for his parents.

In Allan's experience, both his parents had become very busy with their own work, and while they were at home with him just as much as in the past, they were more involved in other than home activities. I think Allan was able to "pick up" their mood of bringing their work to the dinner table and to the evening activities. They were just not able to respond to him as they had before, being more tired, more preoccupied and less communicative to each other because they were thinking about their respective day's problems and what needed to be done. Allan was now more able to perceive and be empathic to these things that went on around him. While he was acquiring the confidence that he could do things—walk around, ride a bicycle, switch on the television and talk about what he was watching, and even begin to make jokes—his capacity to feel that he had control over all of this was primarily based upon the continued reliable, safe internal guardian, the good object he had internalized from the good care-giving that his parents, in particular his mother, had given him.

Allan had been able to make use of this internal secure object in the past. This was evident in the way he had come to trust himself (i.e. the goodness of his self), and in the confidence that was observed ordinarily by his overcoming difficulties and problems as they appeared daily. For example, Allan learned how to draw lines, repeatedly made lines and looked over at his mother for approving glances, which reinforced the mutual goodness of their relationship and his capacity to continue trying to draw the kind of lines he seemed to want. However, the point is that he continued to try, and he did not lose the feeling of goodness internally. Yet, now, when his parent's were suddenly too busy, Allan felt this excess busyness as a loss of the safety and security of his mutual good object, and he did not want to be alone. He needed to reassure himself that he had not put his mother in danger, that he had not lost confidence, either in himself or in his mutual object. In order to do this, he needed to remain with her as long as possible.

I suggested that mother tell him how much she loves him but, also, that the parents should "try to leave their day's problems at the door-step" and concentrate, at least for a short time, on Allan and his play, talk, and experiences. As the parents did this, Allan's bedtimes resumed their ordinary "easiness", and I think Allan once more became convinced that his mutual goodness, as well as his capacity to feel "in charge" of his feelings, were re-established. Allan seemed to become a happier child and seemed, with his parents' support, to have overcome some of the depressive anxieties. As his phantasies became less fearful, his ego was able to pursue further development and interests. Allan began to become very interested in reading and learning letters. The name of the city where he lived, his street address, and his telephone number became new interests to be followed. As Klein (1952a) points out:

> . . . the ego's striving to overcome the depressive position furthers interests and activities, not only during the first year of life but throughout the early years of childhood. Although the crucial experiences of depressive feelings and the defences against them arise during the first year of life, it takes years for the child to overcome his persecutory and depressive anxieties. They are again and again activated and overcome in the course of the infantile neurosis. But these anxieties are never eradicated, and therefore are able to be revived, though to a lesser extent, throughout life. [p.113]

Sleeping problems can also develop in younger children. After the child reaches the age of about nine months, a change in the child's sleeping patterns seems to take place. Now the child can actually try to stop himself from going to sleep, and problems may develop. Earlier in the child's life, when mother decided that it was time to sleep, or when mother was aware of her child's needs for and patterns of sleep, she was able to put him into the cot and even be assured of a few hours of rest and calm while her child slept. However, at about nine months, the child may fight to stay awake, may become very tense when being put to bed, and may even become fearful of the dark or of something in the room, like a special picture or a chair, or even of having the light switched on in the room. Problems over going to sleep are not uncommon in the nine-month-old. Some of these may be overcome by special rituals that the parent and child develop to help the bedtime procedure.

Rituals are experienced as events that seem to provide the child with a continued feeling of comfort—originally a comfort derived from a safe and reliable mother, gradually internalized as a good object. This object helps the child maintain a sense of well-being, a sense of internal control over emotions of anger, fear, and even love, when the real external object—mother—is not present. The bedtime ritual helps the child to cope with separation from the real object by reinforcing the goodness of the real object through the presentation of rituals.

When ten-month-old Sandy went to bed, her parents would start the bedtime procedure by telling her that it was now time to begin to say good night to all the things inside the house and outside the house. Her parents would tell her that she had had a good dinner and that the food was now inside her "tummy" and would be able to feed her all through the night. After this, one of her parents would then pick her up, bring her into the kitchen, and say good night to her chair and table, to the stove and to the sink. They would then move to another room to say good night to the sofa, the lamp, the stairs, etc. Finally, they would move to her bedroom to say good night to the trees, the flowers, her bureau, and her toys. The parent then put her into her cot, all the while telling her how much her parents loved her, talking about the nice things they had done during the day, that it was now time to say good night to her and that her Mummy and Daddy would be in the kitchen clearing up after the dinner meal but would soon go to their bed. Sandy would respond with smiles and vocalizations, and usually, after her parents left her room, she would continue to vocalize and gradually fall asleep.

Before ten months of age, Sandy just "went to sleep"—she did not need any bedtime ritual. However, it seemed to her parents that suddenly she was no longer willing just to "go to bed and fall asleep". She resisted going to bed and seemed to need something added to her sleep time. The ritual became the parents' way of helping Sandy. It worked for her, and, although she insisted on having the same ritual for a few years, she gradually changed it, insisting that she be the one who would do the "good nights" to the things about the house. Perhaps Sandy was unwilling to separate from her mother and did not feel secure in her own internal controls—but the bedtime ritual provided her with the continued feeling that she was safe, even if separated from her mother and father.

The obsessional characteristics of the bedtime ritual enable the child's ego to maintain control over anxiety associated with, in Sandy's case, the depressive position. When the normal child within his first or second year is separated from the parents, even for the purpose of going to sleep for the night, anxieties relating to an inability to maintain control over certain impulses and phantasies become uppermost in the child's mind. These impulses and phantasies are associated with aggression and dependency and involve the possibility that the child's superego will not be sufficient to control the child's external feelings of aggressiveness and demand for care. The aggressiveness is related to the sense of anger towards mother for the separation, while the nurturance demand is a feeling that the child will not have enough food (good internal objects) to sustain itself alone—one reason why so many children seem to ask for "yet another sip of water" and "yet another mouthful of pudding". Both demands may be too great for the child's' superego to control, and the overriding anxiety for the child is that he may do some damage to the parent in making these demands. Anger may be too strong and may do some harm to the mother, as the child may "wear-out" the mother by wanting too much care. The superego is the agent that controls these demands in order to make them less dreadful. However, the child may sense that the demands may overpower the superego, with the result being internal chaos—that is, the internal safe, good object may turn bad because there is not enough good available, and the demand will then be for more and more. In such a situation, some kind of experience must occur to strengthen the superego.

The obsessional bedtime ritual acts in just such a way to help the superego organization to gain in strength and, in this way, prevent fearful feelings from actually emerging into consciousness. As the bedtime ritual becomes an ally of the superego, the ego organization gains in its capacity to feel safe and secure in just being able to say "good night". Where the child's ego becomes sufficiently capable of inhibiting impulses and phantasies, then this ritual to support the superego is no longer needed. The ego now has a greater understanding and acceptance of reality—a better appreciation and evaluation of the external world—as well as an increased ability to integrate internal phantasies with external reality. I think that supporting the superego in early childhood allows for a continued sense of internal control and, as well, a reduction in the sense of guilt. As this occurs, the ego continues to mature as it now has the opportunity to recognize and externalize less harsh phantasies and so reshape the unconscious phantasies to fit more adaptively with reality. As Leach (1984) has so clearly pointed out:

[1] Many mothers find that the deliberate ritualization of their good-nights, their curtain-drawing, the amount they leave the door open and so on helps the infant to release them gradually, rather than feeling that the mother has walked out on them, leaving them emotionally in mid air. [p. 341]

Putting a baby to sleep with these rituals does maintain and, perhaps, enhance the internal feelings of being able to contain and remember the good object that they took into the land of dreams. The ritual supports the superego to keep impulses and needs in check without becoming the over-demanding, strict, and punitive superego seen in children who have sleeping problems. In this former situation, the obsessional characteristic of the ritual allays anxiety originating within the depressive position. The baby's ego is safe from assault, both from its own superego and guilt and from retaliation from a phantasized revengeful parent. (I think bedtime prayers provide the same ritual function for older children. The prayer supports the suppression of aggression, relieves guilt and anxiety, and allows the child to fall asleep without the fear that some dangerous event will happen to him. The prayer supports the cultural feelings of goodness by protection from a deity.)

When the superego is harsh and overly strict, sleeping problems are apt to occur. If support for the ego is not provided, then the consequences may be refusal to go to sleep, nightmares, and night terrors. One baby of ten months cried, fussed, at times vomited, and kept himself awake for several hours every night, refusing to be in his bed unless he was able to hold on to his mother's arm. She eventually decided that she would bring a chair to his cot, put her arm through the cot bars, and allow him to hold her arm—almost as if he were holding on to a bar. He grasped her arm with both hands, wrapping them around her arm and drawing the arm close to his chest. With this accomplished, he smiled peacefully and went to sleep. This refusal to sleep was overcome by his mother's actions, and the baby soon slept throughout the night, even after she had withdrawn her arm. This sleeping problem and more or less extreme ritual continued for the following three weeks, and then, as suddenly as it seemed to start, it ended.

Another young girl of two years was awakened every night by nightmares. She would awaken, start to moan for her mother, and accept her mother's comfort. She told her mother that she saw "funny things" in the dark, that the "funny things" were "always bad", and that "they wanted to make her bad and take her away". She expressed the fear that the darkness meant "going away" and she added, "I don't want to go away". Her mother told her that she loved her, that she was safe with her mother and father, that her parents wanted to protect her and make things good for her. With the soft repetition of this ritual the child returned to sleep. However, she awakened two or even three times a night, and she continued off and on with this behaviour for about four months. Perhaps suggesting a happy dream, a dream full of warmth and light, and that it will be morning when they awaken, might help.

Another example of severe sleep problems is that of a four-year-old boy who told me about a recurrent dream. Tom said that he knew "the dead people come out at night and could make you dead if they touch you". He told me that when he woke up from such a dream, he had to make sure that his Mummy and Daddy were well. He went to their bedroom, or to wherever he could find them, and when he saw them he went back to bed and to sleep. He later told me that the dead people in his dreams were "real" and that he was "sure they could come during the day too". His play was preoccupied with building roads and garages. He talked about the roads as "safe roads", which could lead you away from danger, and the garages were places that fixed cars. However, there were some cars that could not be fixed as they were "too old", or they had "too many accidents", or they were "all scratched up" and had "even lost a door". When Tom described these cars, which were not repairable, I suggested that maybe there was some way we could work together to make them better and that we could help the garage people fix these cars. Tom reluctantly agreed—but he added, "I don't think that they'll get fixed in my dream." I asked him if he dreamt of cars, and he said that he did, that the "dead people would sometimes come in these cars", and he knew that they did not get fixed because they were "special bad cars for the dead people".

We began to help the garage people fix the imaginary broken and spoiled cars. We also talked about the dreams he was having—the frightening feelings and the feeling of not being able to do anything to help either himself or the cars. I suggested that it was because he was not sure whether he was hurting or damaging his parents that he needed to make sure they were well, and so he sought them out after his nightmare. Naturally, he would do this, not only in order to gain comfort from them, but also to see that they could give him comfort because he could see they were physically well. However, Tom did not let his parents know that he looked for them and then went back to bed. He needed only to see them, and that was sufficient to calm his turmoil—but he needed to face the fact that everyone will die at some time.

I interpreted Tom's dreams as a sense of guilt about his angry and aggressive feelings towards his mother. Tom took one of the bright painted cars, a red car with gold stars, and said immediately, "This one is the mother", and "We'd better clean her up and make sure the car goes forever". I interpreted this as a fear that his aggression was related to his sense of having taken too much from her and that he would make her old and dead. Tom simply agreed, but he insisted on having me help him wash the car with a special "soap" that he made—a concoction of water, soap, oil, and sugar. We washed that car many times and it did gleam (probably from the application of the oil), but for Tom it was "proof", as he said, that we could "fix the car and make it go back on the road" (which he had built).

In these three examples, the superego, the internal structure that acts as a critic and a control over fearful and dangerous feelings and impulses, operates in conjunction with unconscious phantasies. In these children, the phantasies seemed to be of attacking, damaging, destroying, and killing the mother. The child experiences feelings of guilt, and, when offered an opportunity to make some reparation for the imagined damages the child has done in phantasy, the harshness of the superego abates, or reparative capacities increase. The impulse to attack the mother is strong, either because she is withholding the desired safety, security, or protection, or because she has the desired objects and is using them for herself, or because envy is so great that the child has to destroy what he needs. By destroying her, the envy would be gone, because those desired aspects of the mother would no longer be there—she would not have what is desired, and, therefore, she would not be envied. Whatever the reason, the child's impulse is to attack, to project anger and aggression—feelings that the child cannot contain despite the anxiety of retaliation for this attack. Klein (1955) has clearly pointed out how Trude attacked Klein and then "showed clearly that she was very much afraid of being attacked by me . . . phantasies of attacking and killing her mother which gave rise to fears of retaliation" (p. 134).

The strong fear of retaliation for the damage done to the loved parent is experienced as guilt. The strength of the guilt is an indication that it comes from the superego. If the child is provided with the opportunity for reparation of the mother, "he undoes the harm which in his aggressive phantasies he is inflicting on her" (Klein, 1960, p. 272). Klein (1963a) goes on to explain:

> I found that the frequent nightmares and phobias of young children derive from the persecutory parents who by internalization form the bases of the relentless superego. It is a striking fact that children, in spite of love and affection on the part of the parent, produce threatening internalized figures; as I have already pointed out, I found the explanation for this phenomenon in the projection onto the parents of the child's own hate, increased by resentment about being

in the parents' power . . . the child's hate and aggressiveness projected onto the parents plays an important part in
the development of the super-ego. [p. 278]

The good object, which is introjected within the first few
months of life, is felt as changed when the infant's demands go
unsatisfied, and then the infant responds as if it is persecuted.
As the infant matures and as the persecution diminishes when
satisfaction is provided, anger is moderated by continued love
and gratification, thereby reducing the sense of internal intimi-
dating objects. The paranoid position gives way to the depressive position. At this point in the young baby's life, a feeling and
a sense of needing and wanting mother is strong and ever-
present, yet linked with a feeling of making too many demands
upon her. The phantasy is: "I may wear her out, I may take too
much and make her sick, and she will get angry with me, leave
me or, worse, destroy me."

Guilt—a stormy internal pressure—urges the child to make
reparations in order to restore the damaged mother. To be
able to make these reparations provides relief and a sense of
hopefulness on the child's part, reducing the malevolent and
harassing superego (Klein, 1963a):

If the depressive position is being successfully worked
through—not only during its climax in infancy but
throughout childhood and in adulthood—the superego is
mainly felt to be judging and restraining the destructive
impulses and some of its severity will have been mitigated.
When the superego is not excessively harsh, etc. each
individual is supported and helped by its influences, for it
strengthens the loving impulses and furthers the tendency
towards reparation. A counterpart of the internal process is
the encouragement by parents when the child shows more
creative and constructive tendencies and his relation to his
environment improves. [p. 279]

"*Pavor nocturnus*" [night terror] is not a nightmare—it is a
much more alarming night-time problem. Some of the characteristics associated with night terrors are: crying very loudly, or
screaming; extreme fright with children not recognizing the parents, or calling the parent a "witch", a "bad man", a "robber",
etc.; sweating, at times accompanied by a fever; and vomiting.

Such children are very difficult to calm, and sometimes they will not allow the parents to comfort physically or hold them. They may struggle to get away from the parents' arms, screaming at the parent to "get out" or "get away". Night terrors are not only frightening for the child but very frightening for parents to deal with. They usually occur within the first few hours of sleep, and some children experience two or three night terrors in one night. Neither awake nor asleep, they seem to be in a delirious or dreaming state, screaming, frightened as if they had been attacked, and quite inconsolable.

When a child experiences a night terror, I have recommended that the parent go into the child's room as quickly as possible, switch on a room light, and begin to talk softly to the child. I have suggested that they repeat, in a soft, sing-song voice, that the child is safe and loved, that his parents are safe and well, that the room is his bedroom and that it is a safe room. Often the child is not really awake, yet is thrashing about, or walking about the room or house. I have asked the parents to follow their child to make sure he is not about to be hurt and to continue talking softly, trying to guide the child back to the bedroom. The parent could gently stroke the child's arm or back, or cuddle him, if allowed to do so. I think it is also important to point out to parents that, while the child may express violent thoughts, they should try to contain these feelings and impulses rather than make any comments other than that of safety and love. Parental patience and presence is important at this time to reassure and prevent the child hurting itself. The problem is how to talk about sleep, waking, or dreaming when the child is doing all of these. As Scott (personal communication) points out, it is best to stay with the child until it goes to sleep or wakes up fully, or becomes "wide" awake and has begun to deal with a dream not as a hallucination, but as a memory.

Often the child returns to an ordinary sleep and awakens the following morning without any recollection of the evening's distress. If the child awakens and begins to talk to the parents as loving parents, I have suggested that they tell the child that he has had a dream and that everything is now all right, and that he can go back to sleep. If he wants a drink, or to go to the bathroom, I think that the parents should be as helpful as possible—getting the drink or going to the bathroom with the child. Then they should help him back to bed and, hopefully, to a restful sleep.

One young boy of four years started to experience night terrors after his parents had announced, in a kind and simple way, that they were going to go on a holiday for two weeks and that his grandmother, whom he knew very well, was going to take care of him. She was going to move into their home on the day they were going to leave. Tim's first night terror occurred in the evening after the parents told him about their holiday. Tim began to scream, thrash about, and shout out, and he seemed to be asleep. He would not let either of his parents touch him, and he kept shouting, "Get out", "You're bad", "You're mean", "Don't touch me", "You scare me". This episode lasted for about 20 minutes. The parents tried many supportive moves: to leave him alone, to be there together, to be there in his room individually—but nothing worked. They tried to awaken him, but he just screamed all the louder. Then, as suddenly as the episode had started, it finished, and Tim returned to sleep without "ever being awake".

Tim had another episode that night and his parents called me the following day. I gave them my recommendations for the night terror and told them I could talk with them at further length, should they wish to make an appointment. The parents felt that they could solve the problem with the recommendations I had made and thought that they wanted to try without any appointments. With some concern, I agreed, but I asked them to call me the next day. They called to report that Tim had had three episodes that night, but they felt calmer and more in charge of their own feelings. They did say that they were frightened, but they did not feel as helpless as they had the night before. They did not want to make an appointment but did agree to telephone me after a few days.

When they did telephone a few days later, they reported that Tim had been experiencing night terrors every night, and they were concerned about him and their impending holiday. They told me about the arrangements they had made with his grandmother, and I suggested that she come to live with them at least two days before they were to leave. They agreed to this. Again they did not want to make an appointment with me but did want to talk with me on the telephone. I agreed to this and now felt that I should try to help them understand why Tim might be experiencing the terror at this point in his life. I suggested that Tim was unconsciously responding to his mother's imminent departure and the phantasy that something dangerous or damaging might happen to her. In turn, this would threaten the goodness of his internal object, because he would no longer have a supply of goodness coming from her, and whatever "badness" or internal persecutory objects existed in his phantasy could "take over" and destroy him. My language was simple and, I hope, clear.

My recommendations were that his mother help Tim to see how much supply she was leaving for him—that is, she was to pack and freeze meals and various specials foods for him, to label them with the contents and his name, and to show him where she was putting these many small packages in the freezer. Further, I asked that she make a photograph album of herself, his father, and Tim in various family activities, to be looked at daily. I also suggested that she leave fourteen notes with the grandmother, telling him how much his mother and father love him and how pleased they are that he has his grandmother, who loves him, to take care of him, and that they are pleased that she is doing this for them for a short time. The grandmother should give Tim one note daily. As well, I recommended that his grandmother give him glue, paper, crayons, pieces of Styrofoam boxes, paper rolls, etc. and help him make constructions—"things" for himself and his parents. I suggested that she put these in a "safe" place, but that the safe place should be easily accessible and viewable.

Essentially, what I hoped we would be saying to his phantasy was that mother's goodness remained, as exemplified by the food packages, that she and his father could be easily brought to mind by the photographs of them, and that they were transferring his safe-keeping to his grandmother for a short time. They were giving Tim "permission" to accept the grandmother as a temporary container during their absence. Further, the constructions might act as aspects of reparation for the phantasized damage he might do to her in his dreams or night terrors.

Tim continued to have night terrors after this telephone conversation, but the parents indicated that they were much less frequent—in fact, some nights he slept peacefully without interruption. Upon their return from the holiday, they reported that Tim had a few night terrors and that the grandmother had handled them without any "problems". Now that the holiday was over, they thought that Tim had "settled" and that his night terrors would not recur. Actually, they did not, and Tim and I never met.

I think that the depressive anxieties Tim began to experience upon learning that his parents were going away triggered his phantasy that he harmed his parents, especially his mother, and that she was going away because she was angry with him. Tim, in turn, was angry with his parents for leaving him, and his anger made him feel that his phantasy was correct. What he experienced was tension, distress, and a general feeling of discomfort which he could not verbalize. His fears that he had harmed her because of his anger were confirmed by the fact that she was leaving him. In his mind, she must be leaving in retaliation because she did not love him any more and was angry with him because of his feelings and phantasy.

Anxiety and guilt as a result of superego harshness was, in Tim's case, expressed as night terrors. Tim could not express his feelings—even the ones he might know about—because there was no person available to help him verbalize these and to interpret his anxiety of retaliation. The recommendations I gave to his parents did seem to provide a container for his feelings, by telling them what to do as well as a way of dealing with Tim's phantasies, in some ways, at least. I suspect that the daily notes, the "reparative" constructions (gifts), the food packages, and the photographs were "obsessional mechanisms" enabling Tim's ego to keep his anxieties at bay, temporarily at least, until his parents returned, safe and sound and loving (Klein, 1952b):

> the demands of the super-ego to keep out of consciousness certain impulses and phantasies, both of an aggressive and libidinal nature, are more easily met by the ego because it has progressed both in integration and in assimilation of the super-ego. [p. 86]

Of course, one danger that always exists with obsessional mechanisms is that, if they are the ego's principal defence, then a severe obsessional neurosis is evolving. It is because of obsessional aspects of other defence mechanisms that support the ego in that phase of development when the superego is harsh and demanding that the ego is allowed further opportunity to mature by working through some of the anxiety created by aggression. Interestingly, Leach (1984) says

> the tired infant who will not allow himself to go to sleep is reacting primarily to separation from his mother. To allow himself to pass into sleep is to relinquish her altogether. Rather than do this, many babies will cry and scream until she returns, be delighted to see her, accept any entertainment she offers, and then start again as soon as she goes. Others will lie as long as she is in the room, but snap fully awake as soon as she creeps out, settling again when she resignedly sits down once again. A few infants, especially those who have been actually smacked for crying after they were settled for the night, will sit silent in their cots, listening for the sounds of the rest of the family moving around in other rooms. [p. 339]

Much seems to depend upon the way parents, especially the mother, create experiential opportunities for a favourable partnership relationship between herself and the baby (Klein, 1936):

> A really happy relationship between mother and child can be established only when nursing and feeding the baby is not a matter of duty but a real pleasure to the mother. If she can enjoy it thoroughly, her pleasure will be unconsciously realized to a full emotional understanding between mother and child. [p. 300]

CHAPTER SIX

Rigid parenting and perfectionistic children

Children have to endure a particular kind of pressure from their parents to behave, to think, to feel, and to respond in a "parentified", conforming manner. It is as if the parents must be in control of the child's feelings and actions and consider that they not only understand their child's needs but also know what is best for him. Often this is not done with any discussion, questioning, or actual observation of their child's needs; parents just swoop down and make *a priori* decisions in the best interest of the parents but usually with the rationalization that it is in the best interest of the child. For example, I have heard parents tell their children the following:

- "You go to bed right now, or I'll leave the house and leave you alone."
- "You get sick, and I'll just give you to the hospital."
- "If you vomit, I'll be furious with you."
- "If you touch yourself, I'll have to take you to the doctor."
- "If you don't go to school, Mummy will get very upset."
- "If you don't go to school, Daddy will get very mad."

75

- "If you don't come and sit down right away, I'll throw your meal in the garbage."
- "I don't know why you are such a nasty kid—I don't deserve this at all after all I've done to make things nice for you."
- "I can't take you shopping because you always get so upset and scream and want everything you can't have."

Sheleff (1981) addresses this issue.

Mixed with the love that a child may show his parents is the frustration they engender in him as he seeks his own independent way of life, his growing awareness of a distaste for various aspects of their behaviour, his resentment over the controls they impose upon him. Mixed with the love of a parent for his offspring is the burden that their upbringing will place on him, the anxiety that each stage of their development arouses in him, the fear that they will reject his guidance and abandon him in his old age. [p. 42]

As I was listening and watching children and their parents at a day-nursery centre, I observed many examples of parental control and children's reactions. I was quite stricken by the manner in which both parents and children participated in the dance of denial and resentment. Parents said to their children:

- "You be good, or I'll have to send you away."
- "You will eat everything the teacher gives you for snack, or you will never get any more."
- "You will be able to play with all these children, and you won't even miss me."
- "We never get mad at anybody. Just walk away when someone is mad at you."
- "You have to learn to share your toys, so I'll just have to take this one and give it to your friend over there."
- "You have to learn to play by yourself. There are so many toys here to choose from. You must not cry, because boys never cry. I'll just be in the other room, and you stay here for five minutes."

Children about two to three years of age said to their parents:

- "I don't care. You have to be here. You can't go away. I'll love you if you stay here with me."

- "I want more cookies. You said I could eat them because I'm hungry. Why can't I have more cookies?"
- "I just want to go home. It's no fun here. I'll throw the dolly at you."
- "I'll hit you on the head with this [hammer]."
- "You are a son of a bitch."
- "I don't care. You're not my boss. I don't have to listen to you."

I also observed the play of these children. There were times when they played independently and were able to show sustained creative play. However, when they tried to play together, the play deteriorated to an aggressive episode when one child tried to hit the other or take toys away from another. Typical of the play of two- to three-year-olds, they played at separate events, one pushing a car along the rug, another zooming an aeroplane, another trying to feed me play-dough cake, and still another pushing a doll into my back. They played in close proximity to each other and at times to me. However, when they got too close to each other, their play deteriorated to hitting others, destroying their train tracks, or taking away their toys—the children demonstrated considerable aggressiveness. Their play was quite different when they played alone—they were peaceful and quiet and, in fact, it seemed to me, quite composed.

I entered the play space of a few of these children and discovered that they frequently aborted their playful emotions. In one case the children said that the baby (doll) was hungry and started to feed the doll. Suddenly the play changed, and the child said, "You're not hungry", and threw the food away. In another instance a child was hitting a pole in the room, and, when I asked if he was hitting the pole because he was angry, the child answered that he did not hit the pole and walked away from me. One child was watching some other children playing with an adult. When invited by the adult to join in, he walked away as if he did not hear the invitation. It seemed that these children denied the emotions which they were experiencing. This was very unlike the situation when they talked to parents, at which time they were quite aggressive and demanding and displayed their emotions. However, at play the children were developing strategies for shrugging off their feelings, as if their feelings were becoming very dangerous for them to experience.

I observed a very different approach to a child's needs taken by parents of a 30-month-old who was in the process of trying to gain bowel control. He had sat on the toilet and defecated on several occasions. He was very pleased and proud of himself when he did this, and his parents expressed their pleasure, love, and happiness for him with hugs and with words of praise at his success. They did not insist on bowel movements in the toilet, but they asked if he would like to have his "b.m." in the toilet. If he was prepared to do this, mother or father took him and stayed with him, telling him how his "b.m.s" made a special noise when they hit the water, and how "good" his "b.m.s" were. When he completed his "b.m." and he was ready, he flushed the toilet, but only after mother or father said, "What a good 'b.m.' you made today". The toilet flush was accompanied by a happy smile and a "Let's play the music".

One evening, this child was straining as if he were having a "b.m." in his nappy, and when his mother asked him if he wanted to come with her to the toilet, he said, "No" very insistently and directly and even with an angry face. He stopped straining for a few minutes, then went on straining again, as if trying to have a "b.m.". Again his mother asked him if he wanted to have a "b.m." in the toilet. He replied "No", sharply. She did not pursue this issue but continued with her work; all the while her son remained close to her, straining and grunting, stopping for a moment and then starting again. Mother asked him a third time, and he quickly and angrily said, "No" again. He stayed close to her, looked at her often as she continued her work (showing neither anger nor impatience), and suddenly the child said, "Me go to the toilet now" and went with his mother to the toilet. He had not had his "b.m." in his nappy and defecated in the toilet. He was extremely pleased at doing this. He even tried to wipe himself and chattered happily to his mother while doing so. After this he went to play with her again, happily talking.

This sensitive mother realized that her son was not ready to do what she wanted when she wanted and gave him the opportunity to make these decisions for himself. She was available for him, and he stayed close by her—perhaps to see whether it was safe for him to experience certain feelings towards himself of independence, and towards her of aggression and, perhaps, withholding. The child did not have to close off feelings that were perhaps dangerous and threatening both to himself and his mother. He could assess the situation fully and he could test out how long he could hold back his "b.m.", how long he could be angry at her, and how long he could be independent. He managed successfully because his parents (father responded similarly) provided a setting wherein they did not insist upon promptness or taking control away from the child, and their patience allowed the child to experience his physical and emotional feelings safely and to express them when he felt prepared to do so. He maintained his own internal assessment and was able to recognize the limits of his own independence.

Such parents do not seem to experience the ambivalent feelings noted by Sheleff (1981) of loving their child and rearing him, and they are able to recognize the need the child has to exert his own controls and his frustration when prematurely asked to do his "b.m." in the toilet. Such a child has the opportunity to know how he really feels and does not have to know what "you are not supposed to know and feeling what you are supposed not to feel" (Bowlby, 1979, p. 403). This child is able to know and feel and does not have to shut out information. While his feelings may be threatening to him at first because of their power and strength, he nevertheless is able to know them. He is free to know and to feel and to know what he feels and feel what he knows. He becomes able to become reflective.

When the child is not supposed to know and not supposed to feel—even though he does know and feel—then his reactions are at first to get angry and to have the real feelings, but then these feelings and knowledge become too dangerous to "keep". If this is happening in young children's lives, their play shows the development of ways in which they learn both how to deny feelings and how to unlearn and block off knowledge as seen in some of the nursery children. For example, a child may walk away when confronted by an adult, or may say the "doll is hungry" but never answer the crying doll, or may have difficulty maintaining interest in play, or being curious about how toys work, or may refuse to look at picture books, or may withdraw and become apathetic and listless.

Parents so often tell children, "You don't feel bad. Just go outside and play"; or, "You're too soft. Don't let anyone bother you. They don't matter"; or "You have to say thank you. Even if you don't mean it, just say it." It becomes the child's role to accept the expected conformity to these rules, but the price is high and, as Bowlby (1979) suggests, such conformity may play a significant role in the development of psychopathology:

> How large a part pressures on children to shut away "impressions, scenes and experiences" play in generating psychopathology, is a matter for empirical research. [p. 407]

> Parents who seek to disconfirm their child's observations of events, to disapprove or condemn their natural emotional responses to distressing situations, and who discourage their children from registering aspects of their (parents') personalities and behaviour [p. 408]

. . . seem to discourage their children from being able to contend with their real feelings and knowledge and force them either to deny or to become ignorant. The child must try to remain the nurtured, cared-for one, (at least until an age when he can manage effectively on his own). To do this means to accept the position of feeling and knowing while not feeling and not knowing. Gradually the child does not feel and does not know and conforms to parental demands. All this becomes close to being lied to and learning to lie to others.

These demands are not necessarily of a conscious matter. Unconscious phantasies on the part of the parent often direct their "ideas" about how they want their child "to turn out". In one case, the parent seemed quite unaware that she was not allowing Frank, her son of four years, to "grow up". She said that he was just a baby and needed all the help he could get from her. She insisted on feeding him at meal-times, insisted that he tell her whenever he had to go to the toilet, insisted that he always wear enough clothing so he would not be cold, and insisted that he never go to bed alone (in fact, she must be in the bed with him). Frank was examined because of his obesity, his sleeping problems, his refusal to be toilet-trained, and his fine and gross motor clumsiness. Frank was very fat—so fat, in fact, that his eyes were "slits" and his mouth and nose seemed to disappear in his face. However, he smiled and seemed "happy". At play with an adult he had difficulty running, picking things up, and throwing and catching a ball. While he did seem to have motor problems, a medical examination revealed no motor or other physical abnormalities. When a separation was effected between mother and son and Frank was able to play with other children, usually by digging holes in the sand box, he became interested in playing with the ball again. At first he could not catch the ball, even when his arms were fashioned as a basket close to his body, but gradually he became a "good catcher" and was finally able to catch the ball by putting his hands out. At first when he tried to throw the ball to someone he threw the ball up in the air. Then he threw behind him as he looked at the other person. Finally, with both hands he threw the ball to the other person, and very shortly he was throwing the ball accurately and with one hand. This change occurred over a period of only one week—what a remarkable change in a boy who was described as having a fine and gross motor problem!

Frank was able to begin to demonstrate what he knew and could "do", which at first was very unsafe for him to show. If he did show his skill, he felt that he would no longer be loved and nurtured. It was as if his mother had shown him what was safe and desirable to feel and to show. When he experienced feelings that he was not supposed to experience, he withdrew and appeared clumsy and disinterested. To respond with his actual feelings was too dangerous.

Sometimes the situation presented to children by adults almost verges upon child abuse. I know a seven-year-old girl, Ella, who is very seriously emotionally disturbed. She had been making good progress, both emotionally and psychologically, for two years when she was involved in a day treatment centre. She was living at a foster home with her brother, and while they were both problems to the foster parents, it was Ella who presented the more serious difficulties. She was very exhibitionistic (she would try to remove her clothes at any and all opportunities, and she masturbated openly and frequently). She would also scream and become violent, throwing herself about, hitting others, throwing things, and yelling obscenities. She seemed to be a bright child, but she would show her capacities very fleetingly and then suddenly withdraw into a "fog". A "cloud" seemed to envelop her and she suddenly knew "nothing". Her speech and her motor behaviour deteriorated. She visibly regressed and became a little girl so obviously in need of care, yet at the same time a furious, raging child. Such oscillating progress and regress is often a sign pointing to abuse.

One day on the way to the centre this rage came out. The city had been covered by a major snow-storm the night before, and the school bus trip, which ordinarily took half an hour, took three-and-one-half hours. Ella seemed to be all right for the first 30 minutes, expecting, no doubt, to arrive at the centre in the usual length of time, but, since the bus moved so slowly and she had to sit in her seat with her seat belt done up, she began to fidget. The bus "child-care worker" tried to invite her to play games to distract her, but Ella's rage began to mount and she finally had a vigorous tantrum in which she pulled the driver's hair, pulling out handfuls of it, and she caused considerable panic and havoc, with danger to herself and to all the other children on the bus. Ella was not permitted on the bus again. She could not get to the centre without the aid of the bus, and she was "grounded" because she had not co-operated.

One can hardly imagine asking a seriously emotionally upset child to sit in a bus, strapped to the seat, for three-and-one-half hours and not expect some kind of repercussion! The issue is that the adults in this situation expected Ella to behave "properly" because of the snow problem. They expected somehow—miraculously—that she was to rise to the occasion, that she would not show her feelings, that her feelings were not supposed to be there, and that she would be quiet and peaceful while the bus tried to get to the centre. Perhaps the bus should never have set out; perhaps Ella should not have been on the bus; perhaps Ella should have had a special worker with her on that special day; but, surely, she should not have been punished by "withdrawing her from the bus" because she showed her frustration and her rage. The adults tried to force her into a situation in which she was not supposed to feel what she was feeling and offered her no alternatives to express or cope with her frustrations or anxiety. Their actions and their punishment are tantamount to psychological abuse.

I think that children look upon the first object that they experience as potentially showing flexibility, patience, and creativity, and it is only under the influence of both their "real" environment and their powerful phantasies that this first object becomes withholding, uncaring, and rigid in its demands. While babies are aggressive, their aggression is usually directed towards sustaining their comfortable, pleasurable state. However, with the intrusion of early frustrations of their needs, their peaceful state is dramatically altered. Now the aggression becomes turned towards the very object that seemed to be able to provide all the needed satisfaction. With the continued frustration, the object is no longer providing all the desired comfort, and the baby is left, at times, still aware of the discomfort by its uncomfortable and tense feeling.

However, babies are often given "direct instructions" that they are not supposed to feel uncomfortable or tense. They are "told" that they have "just been fed", that "they are not thirsty", that "they are dry", that "they have had a sleep", and that "their bed or cot or pram is dry and warm". Such babies are "told" at a very early stage of their lives that, whatever feeling they are feeling, they are not supposed to feel—rather, they are supposed to feel comfortable and at ease. That babies do not understand the directions and instructions their parents or adults give them is all too evident by their continued crying and thrashing about. Sometimes they cry themselves to sleep, sometimes they cry "chronically" for hours and hours, and sometimes they withdraw into a biting of their fingers and hands or a thrashing about of their heads.

At a very early phase, for some often just after birth, babies have to cope with the demands of the routines being established by parents, their own feelings of discomfort, and their inability to communicate these feelings effectively, except to some understanding and sensitive parents. When babies continue to experience their pain and parents/caretakers continue to behave as though they do not understand and/or accept this and demand feelings and actions that babies are "supposed" to show, then the babies respond to this with sadism. The frustrations experienced by the babies turn the phantasized patient, nurturing, caring, and creative breast/mother into the depriving, demanding, bad, uncaring breast/mother. The sadistic responses that the babies demonstrate are attempts to cope with the feelings of being persecuted by a bad and threatening breast/mother, who did not relieve the feelings of discomfort, but, rather, behaved as if the babies did not have these feelings. The anger at this primal object is projected into the breast not only in an effort to try to make the baby feel more comfortable—because to experience this amount or kind of anger is almost intolerable—but also to attack this object for not providing what is needed. In this way the breast/mother object becomes a receptacle of the baby's anger and hate and, as well, the continued nurturing, caring object.

In an effort to make sure that good and bad do not mix too much, or perhaps mostly in an effort to avoid the bad and keep the good, this primal object is split into the good and bad object. The ego, which is immature at birth yet sufficiently capable of performing this split, does so at the service of maintaining some sense of coherence and capacity to continue to persist—that is, to continue to nurse and survive. The ego splits not only the object but also itself. The bad part of the ego containing the sadism is projected into the bad part of the breast, while the good part is maintained by the nurturance of the good ideal breast, which, in phantasy, is now offering the very care that was somehow being denied to the baby. This ideal object is the object that becomes capable of satisfying the ego's desire for survival. The bad object and the bad projected ego become that part of the object which must be controlled as the source of revengeful anger and persecution. The ego attempts to maintain the split between this projected bad and potentially persecutory part and the good part (integrated with the ideal object) in order to prevent a separation from the caring object. The way in which this split is maintained and will be worked through in the child's development determines to a great extent the kinds of relationships that this child will experience later on in life.

When the child's projections are not countered by revenge—that is, when the parents/caretakers are able to accept the baby's frustrations and anger and not deny or accuse the baby of doing/feeling what he is not supposed to do/feel—then the baby will gradually be able to reintroject these projected feelings (bad parts of the ego) and will not have to see everything and everyone in his world as a persecutor. In such a situation the phantasy of persecution is gradually diminished by the real experiences of comfort and ease. Then the phantasy of the ideal and the persecutory can integrate and merge into one object. The baby, at this point, can view parents/caretakers as not being always bad or always good, but as being both good and bad. The split does not have to be as rigidly maintained, and the breast, now the whole mother, can be felt as the creative responsive object the baby first imagined.

The whole mother is the perceived and felt integration of the bad and the good aspect. It is the person who cannot satisfy all the baby's needs at their moment of expression, and it is this same person who gives nurture, comfort, and pleasure. The baby begins to see the mother as having her own needs and feelings and as someone who experiences pleasure and pain of her very own. The baby's first love turns out to be the "real love" and is not disappointing, but is accepting and caring. The baby is no longer afraid that the good object and the good part of its ego will be overwhelmed by the bad. As the real mother proves to be good and helps the baby to feel and accept what it is feeling, reality influences phantasy. The idealization no longer needs to be as strong because the phantasy of harm and damage is considerably lessened. The baby is then able to integrate various aspects of its ego, experiencing real and phantasized pleasures with greatly reduced fears of persecution endangering the experience.

In the situation where splitting must continue because the parent/caretaker does not recognize the actual feelings of the baby, splitting leads to rigidity. The ego must now submit to the idealization of the good object. It must try to make sure that it never disturbs this phantasized quality of goodness, which must be maintained to stave off the exaggerated badness of that bad part of the split object/ego in an effort to preserve the ego.

The result is a conception of extremely bad and extremely perfect objects. Because the phantasy of persecution is too strong and suspicions of impending dangers are too threatening, the baby continues to identify with a powerful ideal part-object. (The part-object is a feeling-function part of the object. The breast as a part-object has to do "not with the anatomical structures only but with function, not with anatomy but with physiology, not with the breast but with feeding, poisoning, living, hating"—Bion, 1967, p. 102). The baby has to try to conform to the demands of this idealized part-object and to placate it whenever the threat of loss is imagined or felt. This ideal part-object becomes just as strong a persecutor as the persecutory bad part-object, and it is a very strong demanding task master, for any lessening of conformity or perfection begins to turn even this ideal part into a persecutor. The baby cannot cope with such an onslaught of persecution and intensifies its efforts to be good and perfect.

This obsessional crippling and rigid effort forces the baby to "quit feeling, thinking, and responding" and to behave as it is supposed to. The baby cannot suffer a double persecution coming from the good as well as from the bad parts, and the baby may, as a consequence, become the overly vigilant baby who scans the parent/caretaker in an effort to "know how to feel". Such babies cannot love—they are forced always to be "out of love". They are not understood, and they cannot understand their parents/caretakers. Their egos are not sufficiently strong to endure the anxieties of imagining whether they are loved or in love with their object. In other words, they cannot endure any further projections, because they might damage the existing goodness of the object. They also cannot introject goodness because it might be less good than the goodness they have at the present time.

Such babies often experience physical distress (sometimes a general physical discomfort, other times pains). I think these pains and distress are the equivalent of the phantasized internal attacks of the persecutory bad objects against the ego whenever the idealized aspects are not sufficiently protective. The consequences may be various hypochondriacal distresses.

In one such example, a three-year-old boy, who presented himself as having "rituals" for doing just about everything and rarely got anything done because he had to carry out his rituals perfectly, experienced extreme stomach-aches until he did his "job" perfectly. He cried, sometimes screamed in pain, would let no one help him, and carried on with his rituals. In this instance he had to fill up all the available play cups with balls of play-dough, then dump them into a big basket and refill the cups again and again. If he stopped or if someone stopped him, he stuck his head in the basket with the remaining balls and cried loudly that his stomach was "on fire". He worked at this for 40 minutes. Eventually, when he stuck his head in the basket, he accidentally fell over. The balls scattered, and he could then go and collect the balls and become "interested" in something else, which kept him busy for at least another 40 minutes.

If this child was unable to carry out his "rituals", he became ill. The sickness represented his death in the sense that the idealized object had let him die because he had not maintained its goodness by means of rituals. Badness had overtaken it and him, and death would be the end result. The ego, in identifying with the ideal object, had not gained the phantasized expected strength and ability to cope with the anxieties related to its own hostility and fear of persecution.

In another instance a young, hyperactive child seemed intent on making sure of several things: that he touched everything in the room, that he had his pockets stuffed with paper, and that he did not let anyone in the room work at their projects. He became frantic and "completely out of control" if an adult tried to prevent him from carrying out his rituals. His aim seemed to be to control and master all his objects, especially his bad objects, so that they would be less dangerous and threatening to him. In his case, his hyperbehaviour was necessary because I do not think he could satisfy the demands of an idealized object. Nothing was allowed to become "important" to him. The "movement"—"touchies" as he called it—seemed to create the need to do something frenetically.

Danger is imminent when we are unable to understand or interpret. We are unable to do so when our feelings and thoughts are not confirmed or are disapproved of by those whom we phantasize or imagine to be knowing and accepting.

The following example shows the powerful effect of a mother's capacity to understand and interpret to her young son his anxieties so that his depressive reactions were overcome. A happy, contented, and pleasant young child of two-and-one-half years suddenly refused to leave his home. While he had been accustomed to going to the library, to do grocery shopping, or to go to the park with his nanny, suddenly one morning he did not want to leave the house. Any promises of expected pleasures did not change his mind; instead, he took off his clothes, to make sure he did not go out of the house. When his mother told him that it would be okay with her if he went to the library with his nanny, he simply said he did not want to go out of the house. In fact, he showed that he wanted a box of his own to get into and seemed very content when left alone inside the box. He could not be encouraged to leave the box and the house. He would cry if forced to leave, and on one occasion, when he did leave without much complaint, he insisted on going back into the house as soon as he was on the pavement just outside his house. When his mother told him that she would be fine when he went out, he still refused to leave.

I suggested that the mother tell him that he does not take too much from Mummy, that she has a lot to give him and the whole family, and that she will not take anything from him and will even make him big, long, strong "fried potatoes" for himself. When she did so, he was able to resume his morning walks with his nanny. His sadistic taking of penises from his mother's body, and the dread of her phantasized revenge upon him by leaving him, forced him to become extremely anxious about going outside. Going outside meant being without mother. The house was the loving mother, and going outside was losing this mother. The loving mother, the house, would not desert him for having taken too much. Only after his feelings were correctly interpreted did he respond with his usual flexibility. When his mother responded to what he was feeling and not to what he was supposed to feel, his anxieties became manageable once again.

"Every experience which suggests the loss of the real loved object stimulates the dread of losing the internalized one too" (Klein, 1935, p. 267). In this instance the child needed to make sure that the whole good internal object was maintained and preserved along with the external mother. This child suffered from a transitory depressive anxiety brought on, it seemed to me, by imagining that if he became too attached to the nanny, his mother would be lost to him, and, along with that, he would lose the goodness of his internal objects.

CHAPTER SEVEN

Generosity and selfishness: roots in gratitude, envy, greed, and jealousy

C hildren are often generous with their toys or their "turn" at a game. In a playground setting a five-year-old boy gave up his turn at the bat for another five-year-old boy. He did this willingly as far as I could observe and took his turn after the boy had batted. Some children give away their snacks and their lunches. While I have often observed young children of five or ten years trading food items in their lunch boxes, what I am referring to is when one child gives part or even all of his meal to another child or adult. For example, two boys were sitting at the lunch table looking at their meals, which they had removed from the paper bags. One boy asked if the other wanted his peanut-butter and jam sandwich and his biscuit. The other replied, "Yes", and the child gave his lunch away, watching as the other child ate both lunches. One can imagine that such generosity must, at times, occasion hunger if not actual resentment towards the other for having accepted the gift.

I do not think that this giving away of everything one has is unusual. I have seen young children give away the doll, the ball, or the crayons they were playing with and then sit on the floor or their stool and look as if they were expecting "something" to happen, their faces showing an expectant, anticipating look, with a sort of smile combined with a curious face. They then become fearful or even angry. In this latter situation, the teacher did not know how to calm an angry child who had given away a toy, and when she offered the toy he had given back to him, he tried to kick her. The experience deteriorated further because she said that it was "bad to kick people". The child just tried all the harder to kick her and then the other children, who began to laugh and scream at him, "Bad boy, bad boy". Finally, the child lay on the floor kicking at the air and screaming loudly for his Mummy.

Another example of unappreciated generosity did not have such disastrous results. While I was observing a group of four toddlers at play, one of the girls turned to a boy and started to give him her blocks. The boy accepted the blocks, but as he was given more and more, he dropped the blocks and began to cry. The girl looked at him in what appeared to me to be astonishment and then struck him with her hand. She then moved away from him, began to pick up the blocks, and tried to interest another girl in taking them from her. This child repeated the scene, accepting some blocks, and then she seemed to become overwhelmed, as if not knowing what to do, and walked away. The little girl then occupied herself by putting the blocks into a rather large cardboard box, pushing this box around, and collecting all the blocks. She seemed contented, and for the remaining half-hour of play-time she either pushed her box around collecting toys or sat by the box looking into it.

While generosity would appear to be at the basis of these children's behaviour, selfishness, greed, and envy characterize the following situations. A child of four years insisted on taking everything away from three other children with whom he was playing, announcing very loudly to them that he "needed it all". As he proceeded to take their toys from them, they tried to play and ignored him. They seemed to tolerate him for a short while, but then the three of them just pushed him away, continuing to ignore him and to play, albeit with fewer toys to build their farm. The child continued to try to take the materials but was now successfully blocked by the three, who seemed to have made an unspoken pact to keep him out and to keep the rest of their materials.

Children who feel gratified are able to accept the enjoyment of good experiences with their parents without the interference of greed and envy. The introjection of good objects encourages the development of the feelings of gratitude associated with the ability to care for and love another person. These feelings of gratitude enable children to share their toys, gifts, and feelings with others. Gratitude and generosity are thus closely associated. It is as if these children have introjected a giving, nurturing, friendly object, which allows them to feel an inner capacity to share what they have with others. In this chapter we will examine these early origins of generosity as well as the roots of selfishness in feelings of envy, greed, and jealousy.

I think that babies phantasize the breast as an ideal object, and the breast is admired at first as the source of love, nurturance, and all good experiences. At first, then, the baby phantasizes that the breast is an inexhaustible reservoir of all that is good, and this feeling not only intensifies the baby's love for the breast but also his desire to have it for himself. Part of this desire to keep it for himself is to protect it from his own feelings—that is, if he had it all the time, then he would not have to get angry with it, and in that way he phantasizes that he could preserve the breast. Of course, the baby would also want to have all this goodness inside himself and for himself alone.

No matter how good and nurturing the mother is and no matter how often she nurses her baby, she will not be able to satisfy all his desires. His phantasy is that the breast must be inside himself, and if he begins to feel discomfort for whatever reason, he searches for this ideal breast, which is to remove any of his pain. Since the breast is not available all the time, his anger is then directed towards the only object that nurtures him. The anger is the experienced emotion of envy and is painful for the baby, and this, in turn, forces him to spoil the good qualities of the breast as already mentioned, in order to reduce the pain of anger, of envy.

However, when this happens, the behaviour that the parents then notice is the baby's general state of dissatisfaction and the difficulty that they have in calming and in feeding the baby. As the parents experience problems, the baby introjects their concern, phantasizing this as their attacks upon himself, which, in turn, makes him even fussier. It is not uncommon to hear parents talk about how, when they are upset and try to calm their baby, they "just can't do it". They have to recognize that their own feelings impinge upon the well-being of their baby, but it is sometimes very difficult for parents to understand this. They may say that they try to comfort their child, that they are not angry with their child, but then they add, "The longer it takes, the more upset I get, and the more of a problem I have with my child". They expect that the feeding can take place in an "emotionless atmosphere" and that their feelings are not in some way connected to their baby. They expect that they can comfort their baby, and no doubt they can and do, but when they are upset, they cannot.

I am reminded of the oft-told story of the parents putting their child to bed and reading to him his favourite story. After one story, the parent is usually "fine" but when the story is requested again and again, most parents begin to yawn and feel very tired—some have actually fallen asleep. I think the yawning and falling asleep are their sublimated angry feelings for having to be with their child longer than they expected. Rather than communicate this feeling, which I think they realize would be very upsetting to their child, they become very tired and may even fall asleep.

A phantasy or even a feeling of being deprived of the source of all satisfaction, the breast, increases the baby's state of envy. The breast becomes the object that deprives the baby and becomes bad. The breast is perceived as keeping love, comfort, and nurturance for itself and is then attacked by the baby in order to get all its goodness for himself. Envy intensifies these attacks, which are felt in reality by the mother as being bitten on the nipple or breast or scratched by the baby's fingernails, or slapped. This makes it very difficult for the baby to have the feeling that it will regain a good breast. If the biting, scratching, or slapping is not occasioned by excessive envy (because the mother has not allowed the baby's state of discomfort to continue for too long), then these attacks pass quickly, and the baby resumes a normal feeling of internal goodness.

The baby does not want to endure a state of loss of good internal objects and, under most circumstances, strives to regain the good object. The loss of the good internal object creates a feeling of discomfort and a sense of dissatisfaction within the baby. It is not unusual to see a normal baby cry and become very uncomfortable and fussy but quickly become the happy baby once again when the feed arrives. Such a baby is able to enjoy the breast and the goodness that is projected to it. This is the first relationship for the baby. When this relationship is strong, it endures mild frustrations and pain. The baby does not lose this early closeness and comfort easily—rather, the baby begins to trust in the goodness of this primary relationship. Babies who are well loved and experience good-enough mothering are not fundamentally damaged by periods of envy and anger. These negative feelings are short-lived, and the good objects are recovered.

When the baby is able to regain the good object over and over again, it forms an ego that is enduring and strong and not likely to crumble upon minor frustrations. Such a baby does not doubt its internal goodness. This is the baby who can be easily comforted by its parents. This is the child who can be re-directed to other activities when upset and is sufficiently flexible to accept alternatives. The ego in such children is not fragile and is able to cope with anxiety by maintaining an inner coherence and is able to trust the relationship that exists between the child and mother.

Evidence of gratitude and generosity becomes more observable when the baby is about six to eight months of age. It is not uncommon for a mother to describe her baby as "being nice to her". Mothers report such things as, "My baby patted my breast", or "My baby stopped nursing, looked at me and smiled and then went back to nursing", or "My baby tried to feed me— he put his fingers in my mouth". The baby's enjoyment of its relationship with the breast and the mother is expressed directly, not only by taking in the good feed, but also now by the actual demonstration of gratitude to the mother. The mother, in turn, "falls in love with her baby once again". This will be experienced by the baby as mother's pleasure in its growth and capacity to give a gift to her. I have no doubt that the baby senses its mother's pleasure, and this encourages the continued introjection of a good nurturing object and an increased sense of gratitude and capacity to give gifts.

Thus, gratitude is important in building up, as well as in maintaining, the relationship with the good nurturing object. Along with one's capacity to give gifts, one begins to feel a sense of goodness in oneself as well as in others. It is almost as if the internal monologue that might go on would be as follows: "I have received satisfaction and have been able not to want every last drop from the breast. In turn, the breast continues to provide for me. I feel good inside, which helps me to continue on with the breast. It didn't get angry with me for taking in some of it, so I do not feel anxious about continuing. Since I feel good, I share my goodness with others."

This effective relationship with the mother's breast becomes the core for the health and strength of the child's ego. As children are able to introject good internal objects and they are not harmed because of occasionally wanting more or even "too much", so they feel that they have introjected satisfying and loving objects. These internal objects are not damaging, even when they want more. There is no sense of retaliation even for being greedy or envious at times. The child would want to make sure that these internal objects are kept inside him and kept safe. This feeling of gratitude is now expressed as trust, not only in the child's capacity to maintain internal good objects, but also in the mother and their developing relationship, which is essentially their mutual bond.

The sense of greed or envy, which creeps in occasionally, does not disrupt this bond; rather, the phantasy that these feelings could harm or destroy the child and his object rarely occurs. The good object remains good, even though it is "tested", as in the following example. A mother had made supper for her husband and two children, six and two years of age. Usually the food was always eaten with enthusiasm by both children. However, on this occasion, the six-year-old said he did not want the food and that he was tired of it. When his mother tried to coax him, he responded with, "I told you. Don't bug me." His mother asked him what he might like instead, noting what there was in stock. The child said he wanted a hamburger—something that she did not have—and when she told him this, he said, "You never have what I want". His mother told him he could have a pasta dinner instead, one of his favourite meals. At first he said "no" but then added, "If I can have it with ketchup", to which he received a positive reply. When he was given his dinner of pasta and ketchup, he looked thrilled, then looked at his mother and said that she was a "good Mummy" and proceeded to eat the dinner. However, half-way through his meal he looked angry, and his mother and father asked what was troubling him. The child said that he just did not want any supper, because he had a "tummy-ache".

Instead of telling his parents that he felt unwell, this child had tried to get a dinner, an object, from his mother that would make him feel well. He anticipated being well because he had experienced goodness from her in the past. His demand for this "good object that would make him feel well" was not gratified because he felt ill, and so he became angry again, as the object had disappointed him. It would not be difficult to imagine parents becoming angry with their child, not only for refusing the first dinner but then refusing the second one as well. However, the important aspect here is that the parents did not get angry, and so the boy's internal object did not become damaged or retaliatory. Rather, his temporary state of greed and anger was just that—temporary—and he could regain the good object once more. The parents remained patient, they found out what was troubling their son, and they were able then to relieve his pain. The relationship by way of trust in the good internal and as well external object was thus maintained. Trust in the child's sense of ego, of capacity to communicate, was maintained as well, although it had been threatened by his illness.

It is very interesting to note that children do become angry with their parents, usually mother in particular, when they are ill. The phantasy would be that mother either did not give enough of the "good stuff" to keep them well and healthy forever, or someone else was using "it" up and not leaving "it" for themselves. As a result of this phantasy, trust in the goodness of the object is threatened, the relationship is threatened, and the end-result could be an angry interchange, which, if it occurred, would only act to further lessen the effectiveness of the trust in the relationship and the sense of gratitude in the child. The child, experiencing doubt in the quality of his internal object, brings about a sense of uncertainty in being able to trust, which, in turn, triggers feelings of greed and envy.

In some children, I think we are able to see this uncertainty and inability to trust by their indiscriminate identification with anyone at all. Take, for example, young children who have not had the opportunity to develop a bond with a single care-giver, such as children hospitalized and/or institutionalized at very early ages and for several years. These children run up to strangers who enter the ward. They want to be picked up, kissed, and hugged and to hold on to the adult's leg. I think these children experience only doubt about their internal ob-jects. They do not have a trust in themselves or their goodness, and thus they constantly experience greed and envy. This is expressed by trying to obtain some satisfaction from every adult who walks into the ward. These children also stop other children from playing. They are "bullies" and are generally destructive of other children's toys or bodies, pushing, pinching, or biting the other children and sometimes the adults. They are angry, empty children, trying to grab what they can to make themselves feel comfortable. Usually, they need psychotherapy, and unfortu-nately they rarely succeed unless they are offered it.

Recently I was able to observe just such a young boy—a child who had been living in an institution for most of six years. He would sit by himself or wander about the rooms, and, when he saw other children engaged in some play, he would come over and push one or two of them to the ground. He would kick their toy constructions and try to tear their drawings and paint-ings. The other children avoided him, and usually, when they saw that he was coming towards them, they left the area, but not before calling him names like "tease", "bully", "baddy". This child was not able to tolerate the other children's play or con-structions. It was more than he could bear to see that they seemed to be able to enjoy some activity. It was not enough for him to take their toys. He had to spoil and destroy their work. The child could be stopped from doing this if an adult saw what he was about to do and re-routed him, but he did not appear to learn from the experience of being left out, or slapped, or screamed at by the other children. His behaviour continued in spite of efforts to divert him. He seemed never to be satisfied with anything. Also, he was not satisfied by destroying one tower or one painting. It seemed that he was always on the look-out for more things to destroy. I think that he could not tolerate the perception that another child was doing something enjoyable, perhaps even desirable.

Such children are envious children. Their envious, angry feelings originate from early aggressive attacks upon the breast. These attacks are attempts, not only to take what is phantasized to be in the mother, but also to replace it with bad objects and to fill her breast with badness, to destroy its goodness, and to render it no longer capable of arousing envy.

Such a feeling of wanting to take everything that is present —the breast and all its goodness—is aroused by the baby's uncomfortable feelings, which it has endured for too long. If the baby has a very strong need for sucking or for food, or for physical closeness and strong bonding, the frustration where this is not available creates enough discomfort and pain to threaten the very existence of the child. The fear of ego annihilation due to insufficient comfort is so great that it creates not only a feeling of deprivation and frustration, but also a feeling of destruction. The baby fears that it will not be able to survive without the needed comfort, because there is not enough goodness within it to maintain the good-enough object—that is, the breast—as a comforting object. A child such as the one in the above example, then, has to destroy the goodness, because he cannot be as good as the object he sees. He cannot build, paint or create as "good" objects. Destroying the other's goodness will mean an end to the envious feelings that are experienced, which no doubt cause him pain. In a sense, then, the child has no choice but to destroy whatever he sees and/or imagines as good, because he is envious of that goodness which he was unable to gain in the first relationship with his mother.

If the baby, because of inadequate bonding, inadequate parenting, or excessively strong impulses, or a combination of these cannot imagine that he can gain the goodness of the object, then the envious feelings that arise can only be dealt with and reduced by destroying the goodness of that object. When the baby needs the object—as, for example, in needing the breast milk, the destructive quality of envy is such as to change the good object into a bad object, and then the baby cannot nurse. The breast milk has been "turned bad". The phantasy is, "I have such a great need to feed, yet I cannot gain a satisfying feeling from feeding and I remain in pain. The breast has what I need, and I want it all, yet I can't or don't get enough. So, in order to prevent myself from being so angry for wanting something I could not get and to relieve some of this pain, I turn the milk bad, and I cannot nurse any longer." In severe cases, such a baby becomes anorexic, is withdrawn, angry, and yet aloof, and the parents say how hard it is for them "to get close to the baby". The food they try to provide is rejected, as they are rejected, and unless intervention is offered in the form of recognition of the envy and its roots, the child will suffer from a failure-to-thrive syndrome, with eventual dehydration.

Doubt and a poor primal relationship lend to a feeling of not being understood or accepted by others. Such a child cannot trust, and within this poor relationship jealousy and greed are aroused. These emotions stimulate further doubt and poor relationships, because a good internal object was not established. This child does not experience an internal object that loves and protects or is loved and protected by the ego, further reducing the child's trust in his ego and in his own goodness.

Jealousy, an emotion that has its roots in envy, makes its appearance at about five or six months. At first it may be seen when the baby tries to push the undesired parent away, or tries to make sure that it has both parents together for meals, for bath-times, and for sleep. Jealousy involves the baby's relationship to at least two other people and is mostly concerned with attempts to make sure that someone else, father or mother, does not take what is phantasized as being"rightfully" the baby's. It is at this point that the baby sees another as a rival for the goodness that it needs and wants. Jealousy now arises because the baby phantasizes that the parents are enjoying each other and using up goodness that should be maintained for the baby alone. Also, the baby phantasizes that new babies will be created, which will rob it of the mother's breasts, and that mother and father experience a comfortableness and satisfaction together, which will reduce its own feelings of comfortableness. This is a fear that the baby will lose not only what it has, but what is meant for it. When the baby feels uncomfortable, the feelings of jealousy are stronger.

One toddler I knew became so upset whenever he saw his mother and me together in the same room that he cried and tried to take his mother out of the room. He did not bother with me, seeming intent upon keeping her for himself, but once when she left the room with a two-year-old he said, "Mummy loves Danny", smiled, and asked me to pick him up and cuddle him.

Jealousy is also expressed by failure, withdrawal, aggression and assaultive behaviours, whining, and in many other ways. In one example, Corey's mother discussed her son's aggressiveness and his refusal to be involved in any play with his peers. She also noted that when she took him shopping, he always created a scene, screaming, crying, and running away from her. When his father tried to help him get ready for bed, they always had a "major fight", and the father usually became very angry with his three-year-old son. Corey's mother said that he had been an excellent baby, that he had had no problems sleeping, eating, playing, or going on outings with her before he came to nursery school. He had been in day-care on a half-day-a-week basis as an infant, and then, when he was about two years, he attended day-care on a two-half-days-a-week basis. She did not describe any problems with him at that time. As she said, "It was only when he entered nursery school that he became a problem". When I asked whether there had been any changes in the family at about the time he went to nursery school, she said that his sister was born a few months before that. Eventually in our discussion she was able to trace much of Corey's behaviour problems to the birth of his sister, not to schooling. She noted, "Corey has always been nice to his sister, and he is never angry with her. He just seems to be so mad at his father and me." After a bit more discussion, she said, "Come to think of it, Corey is starting to get mad at his sister, because she now mouths all his toys and grabs them from him."

I think Corey is jealous of the goodness that he phantasizes his sister is taking from his parents, which he perceives "rightfully" as his. He is angry with them, not only for making another baby, but also for enjoying each other and keeping him out of their activities. I suggested that the mother provide special times for Corey every day, that she put him to bed every night, and that she make sure that he has more than enough food at mealtimes—not packed on his plate, but, rather, in front of him in bowls. She agreed to do this, and Corey's behaviour changed dramatically. Corey was once again able to enjoy a relationship with both parents. He did not need to separate them any longer because he had phantasized their togetherness as a loss in himself. He could now feel "filled-up" rather than deprived and see that there was enough for him, his sister, and his father. Because his early bond appeared to be effective (he was "a good baby"), Corey was able to re-establish an effective relationship with his parents and with his sister as well.

In some instances the child may express feelings of jealousy through a sudden change in behaviour. For example, the birth of a baby forces the older child to work through the difficulties of the change in the relationship to the mother and the need to try to work out on his own how to deal with the impending danger of feeling as if "I'm just falling to bits". One child of three years responded to the change in the family when his sister was born by collecting all his stuffed toys, placing them in a corner of his room, and sitting in the middle of them, surrounded and covered by toys. In another example, a four-year-old girl insisted upon drawing circles and tacking them up in her bedroom. A third child suddenly needed to have a towel in his bath, which he insisted must cover him while he was in the bathtub. These incidences illustrate the deeply felt changes in the family relationship when Mummy is not as available because a new child has entered the family.

The way these three children managed their jealousy was not through aggressive outbursts, but, rather, by trying to cope with the new danger of loss of mother by creating their own "second skin". Bick (1968) indicates that the "second skin" is an attempt on the part of the baby to hold itself together—that is, the baby maintains a feeling of ego coherence and integration in the face of losing mother by developing a situation in which there is a "skin". This "skin" will prevent any spilling-out of feelings that may cause potential damage to mother, to baby, and to the child's ego. Ordinarily the mother is the one who holds the baby by her sensitive feeds, her voice, her look, and her touch. When this becomes unavailable because of the birth of another child and the jealousy is making the child feel very distressed and uncomfortable, an adhesive second skin is formed.

Some babies who cannot tolerate that they do not have all of the mother and her goodness feel greed. Greed is an insatiable desire to take in everything possessed by the mother. It is a feeling of wanting more than the mother is able, or even willing, to give, and it is much more than what the baby actually needs. Greed is a destructive introjection of the goodness of the object, and its goal is to scoop out, to rob, and to devour the object.

Some children not only want "more than their share" (and they "just cannot share")—they want everything. For example, in nursery school, when the stuff (the food, colouring paper, crayon, string) is put back into the cupboard, the child feels deprived and becomes desperate and hostile. The anxiety of not having enough increases the feeling of wanting more, which increases the anxiety of the child. At best this is a vicious circle; at worst it is a setting for violent temper outbursts, accusations, and crying, but eventually the aim is to make the best of a bad job—and there are so may "bests"!

Sometimes children overeat and stuff themselves to make up for the feeling that they are not getting what they imagine they need in relationships. They feel empty and cannot get rid of this feeling, even by stuffing themselves. At this point, the child is not only afraid of what the parents may do to him for eating so much, but he has to try to grapple with a superego (composed of the introjected good objects) that demands a kind of perfection from the child in order to get further satisfactions. Stuffing himself to lessen the anxiety of not having enough only increases the anxiety of being a "bad" child. This intense conflict is anxiety-inducing, as well, and the child just cannot do the "right thing" to make himself feel better. Usually the culmination is physical distress, vomiting, or diarrhoea, and that is phantasized by the child as punishment or retaliation from the parents.

Other babies and children snatch at things. They want all the blocks for themselves, they insist on getting all the crayons, they cry loudly when others are offered food at snack-time, and they greedily grab up all the contents of the others' plates, stuffing this into their mouths. There seems to be no enjoyment in getting all these things or all this food. The conflict becomes one where the child wants and demands and builds up a phantasy of a mother/father object as having been robbed, scooped out, and ready to retaliate. This retaliatory combined parental phantasy is maintained, forming a basis for the superego. More is greedily needed to cope with this retaliation, and the conflict continues.

In a child of five with whom I was working in play psychotherapy it seemed quite obvious that his greed was so great that he could never feel pleased, no matter how much he received. In his play, he made a Plasticine tube, which he inserted into a doll's mouth and said, "I'll feed the baby", but every time the baby started to feed, the tube was somehow "mysteriously" broken. The child would drop a book or some heavy toy on the tube with his eyes closed and the tube was "wrecked". He would say, "It is no good", and, "The baby is starving." I think he demonstrated his need for love, care, and nurturance, his strong desire to be protected from his hostile impulses, and his feelings that he could never get everything he "needed", because he "didn't make the tube strong enough". I interpreted this as split-off greed (the closed eyes showing a need to be protected from his anger), along with a "sense" of not being able to make his mother pleased and happy with him—nothing he did was good, and his efforts always seemed to persecute him and create a feeling of guilt.

This child was never able to enjoy any of his accomplishments—everything he did was not good enough. He always needed something more, such as another kind of Plasticine, or better things with which to roll out the Plasticine, but when he had these things, nothing "worked" for him. The painful feeling of greed and envy drove him to spoil the good qualities of the object in a powerful effort not only to reduce his painful feelings, but also to prevent the object from creating so much dissatisfaction within himself.

I think the dissatisfaction experienced within the ego is the child's sense of not being able to love others. The greedy baby may be able to enjoy the food it receives, but when it is finished, or even when there is only a little bit left on the dish, the baby becomes fussy, irritable, and obviously dissatisfied. At this point the child wants to get more and tries to take more from the mother or from someone else's dish. The anxiety of not having enough increases the sense of greed, which increases the feeling that there will "not be enough for me". In addition, if the need for more and more is satisfied, this allows the baby to sense that it can love others. For example, a 16-month-old baby girl cried when her plate seemed depleted—she had eaten some food and had enjoyed it, but now she wanted the plate full again. When it was filled, she smiled and babbled at others, was happy, and would reach over to touch her mother with a smile. It appeared to me that when she had a "lot", she did not feel greedy, and then she felt she could love others. The greed interfered with her capacity to love others.

Only when the breast, as the first object, has been introjected successfully can the child receive and maintain the feeling of being loved and returning love in turn. Nursing times are not the only occasions when the baby feels loved (just witness the many times when the baby "lights up" when the mother enters the room). The enjoyment of her presence is not simply because she is about to feed the baby, nor is it by association that the baby smiles, but, rather, it is that the good-enough feeds by a containing and loving mother help the baby to gain the feeling of being loved, and this love is then returned in her presence and gradually extended to others in the family.

With pleasure and satisfaction derived from the breast, the baby gains an internal object that is trusted as a good object. There develops a sense of being able to "spare" this object—a concern "not to use it up", "not to harm it". Then the investment in the breast provides the baby with the phantasy of this object protecting and loving the baby. Some children leave a little bit of food on their dish and do not seem to want to finish everything. They may even insist on leaving some food. I have asked children why they do this. Some four-year-olds have answered, "So the dish won't be hungry", "Because you're supposed to", "Just in case I need some later", "But somebody else might need some too", "The plate looks sad if I eat it all", or, "I'll be sad if I eat it all", "I just got the right amount". The full plate often represents the mother's forcing and control, as contrasted with the child's taking from a big plate as much as she wants, learning not to take too much, and realizing that she can take more if she has taken too little. The parent who decides when the child is satisfied causes a great deal of confusion in the child. I think these are some examples of children who feel the love and protection of the internal good breast and wish to spare it from being depleted. Greed does not interfere with their relationship to the breast; rather, the child tries to make sure there is something for the object as well so that the object will continue to love him and even to protect him.

I think the enjoyment these children experience, not only at meal-times but also at play and with other children, demonstrates the warmth and containing atmosphere within which they are reared. These children are sure that the mother does understand them because they are able to enjoy themselves. Because the object is giving and protective, the child feels satisfied. Since he has not demanded too much, the object is trusted and internalized as enjoyable. The good internal object is lasting and maintains a love and protection for the ego, and, in turn, the ego protects and loves the object. The origin of this appears to be within the successful and happy relationship to the first object, the nurturing breast. The happiness intensifies the closeness to the object, and trust in the object provides the avenue for being understood and understanding others. This child senses a friendly world and a feeling of "internal fullness" as well. This creates a feeling of being able to "share" with others and a capacity to be generous.

There is no sense of being depleted when such a child gives toys to other children and the child is able to continue to play successfully. In contrast, some children who do not have this internal trust may give away toys, but they may then go to the teacher and say, "I gave my crayons to Jamie, and he didn't say thank you. I always say thank you", or, "I gave Mary the doll, and she won't even play with me, and she isn't nice". Other children give the toys away but want them back almost immediately, while still others try to hoard toys around themselves as they play. These children feel persecuted when giving away toys, because then they feel depleted and are quite unsure that they have enough left over "to take care of themselves". They tell us that they need something from us. They need a containing, nurturing environment that protects and trusts them.

Children need to enjoy their play and to see that the adult is also pleased with them. As this occurs, children can play with ease and not be disrupted by momentary feelings of not having enough, which sometimes forces children to give toys away in an effort to have the teacher or the adult tell them how generous, kind, sensitive, and caring they are. Pleasure and gratification from the adult who is with them and watches them makes children feel well and provides them with a sense of trust in their own goodness. With trust in themselves, they do not feel persecuted. When they have given some toys away, they realize an inner sense of richness, which allows them to do more and to get more. Then, when a child gives another a gift, it is not depleting to the child, nor merely creating or strengthening a relationship, but, rather, it is a demonstration that the child has enough trust in his good internal object. Giving a gift is only possible when we introject kind, nurturing objects and possess the feeling of enough trust in our own inner richness to be able to share and to be co-operative (Klein, 1957):

> Inner wealth derives from having assimilated the good object so that the individual becomes able to share its gifts with others. This makes it possible to introject a friendly outer world and a feeling of enrichment ensues. [p. 189]

CHAPTER EIGHT

Early defences, confusion, and learning problems

Confusion in thinking has been considered to be related to such factors as the child's "immaturity" or even "lack of intelligence". While these factors may operate at times, children and adults most often experience confusion in thinking due to such psychological factors as envy, greed, and jealousy, which are associated with the functioning of their internal objects. The following are some examples of children who had difficulties in judging, thinking, discriminating, and sometimes even in hearing what was being said by others. I will suggest how, I believe, their projections and projective identifications led to their confusion in thinking and action and how these disturbances in thinking protected the children from the hate and sadistic attacks that the child could have made on his loved internal object—the containing mother. Of course, there is the confusion the child experiences when the parent hurts the child and says, "This hurts me more than it hurts you". As Scott (personal communication) points out, the child becomes confused about the pain the parent has produced by the pain the child wishes to give the parent, both because it is being beaten and because it wants to get rid of the pain and put it back in the parent, instead of internalizing it all and having to work through the beginnings of sadomasochistic relationships.

Joe is one example of confused thinking. Four boys, each about four years old, were playing with me and building "structures". This meant that they would find a block that, they decided, would fit into the "structures" we were building and then place the block in position. My role seemed to be making sure that the structure—a tall building-like affair—would continue to stay in place and not topple over. As the boys continued to find just the right block and then fitted it into its place, I noticed that one of the boys was not as active as he had been about ten minutes previously—he just seemed to sit back, holding a long, thin block. Then suddenly, when no one expected it, he appeared to want to use the block as a battering ram and came to knock down the structure. I prevented him from doing this, saying that perhaps we could make a special structure right beside the one we were building, and he could work on that one with me. Joe did not want to do this and persisted in his attempts to try to destroy the structure. All the while the other boys continued adding their blocks to it. Joe's insistence on destroying the structure and the other boys' continued building efforts—along with, I suspect, my refusal to allow him to destroy it—seemed to culminate in his frantic attempt to throw himself on the blocks and on me. When I caught him, he moved away to my side, looking very vacant and distant. I asked him if he was okay. Joe simply answered, "I don't care", and continued looking very distant. I asked him if he felt upset and maybe angry, and he replied, "Why should I? I don't know what you're doing anyway." I then realized that Joe had suddenly become very confused. I asked him if he wanted to play with us, and he said, "I don't know what you're making".

I then said, "I think you might be confused because you're so mad at us." Joe continued to look vacant, and at my remark he got up and wandered off. He did not become involved in any other activity but just walked around the room or stood and looked about, as if he did not see anything or anyone. In fact, he did physically bump into people and things during his wanderings. Fifteen minutes later, at snack-time, Joe sat at the table, but it took him several minutes to begin to eat his fruit snack. However, as he started to eat, he became livelier and seemed his old self once again.

Joe wanted to do things his way, not simply because he had to have "his own way", but because his own feeling of goodness was being threatened by the recognition that the other children were building and participating in ways that I think he felt he was unable to do. Joe was identified with the good object, which at that moment was me, the one who was able to keep the structure from falling, the one who seemed to be the container for the children. However, this identification was sufficiently threatened by his envy (that is, his angry feelings that I had the capacity to keep things good) and his desire to have an exclusive relation with me, that he had to try to destroy, not only the structure, but me as well. And so he finally hurled himself both at me and at the structure.

As Joe gradually felt that he could not continue to build the structure, his anger, disappointment, and resentment became projected into me. The projective identifications of the split-off fragments of his ego left him confused. In his attempts to control me—or, rather, his projected parts in me—the danger mounted, as he could not spoil me, until he finally attempted to destroy me. In doing so, he was, in phantasy, destroying those aspects of himself in me that he could not tolerate, and, at this point, he could not recognize himself. He became confused and greatly depleted, so much so that he could no longer carry on the active interpersonal relationship he had been involved in only a short time before.

In a second example, Marjory, who was about three years old, was playing with a jig-saw puzzle. She seemed to be able to do the puzzle and had actually put all the pieces in their correct spaces. She watched another child about the same age, who was also playing with a jig-saw puzzle, but who was being helped by a teacher. Marjory went to the cupboard and took all the jig-saw puzzles she saw (four of them), carried them over to her table, dumped all the pieces out, and then set about to replace the pieces in their correct space. Marjory was all right at first. She replaced some of the pieces in her original puzzle, but soon she found that she just could not put any pieces into place. She looked over at her "friend" and the teacher, both of whom were very engrossed in their puzzle and doing it so well.

Marjory started to cry. She shoved all the puzzles and pieces on the floor and sobbed bitterly for several minutes. Nothing seemed to calm her.

I think that Marjory was expressing greed. While she needed to show the other child and the teacher that she could do things "better", at a phantasy level I think she wanted to take everything that was available, representing a desire to scoop out the breast and devour everything that she could find. In taking all the puzzles, she expressed this phantasy of scooping out the breast. By completing the puzzles all at once, Marjory was attempting to devour the breast. Essentially, she was attempting to introject the goodness that she unconsciously perceived within the relationship of the other child and the teacher. The introjection was destructive because it involved the destruction of the phantasized goodness within the relationship she was seeing. This led to the expression of confused destructiveness that she demonstrated. What she introjected was not the goodness she seemed to need, but the badness, which made her bad in turn and unable to show the patience that she was ordinarily able to show on other occasions. Ordinarily Marjory would be quite capable of sorting the puzzles she had taken from the shelf, but on this occasion she could go no further because her greed led to a confused state. However, greed does more than lead to confusion—it leads to confused thinking, because of the difficulties involved in selection and discrimination. While on the surface it does seem that Marjory could not sort out the right pieces for the right puzzle—perhaps because she had taken too many puzzles—she nevertheless had been able to "work" four puzzles successfully before. Greed led to her difficulty in selecting the right piece, of discriminating which piece went to which puzzle.

A third example involves jealousy and greed. When three five-year-old children were playing "hop-scotch", I noticed that one of the children left in a huff because she could not count the right squares. She was actually having difficulty counting the squares she was to throw her marker into. Yet, when we met much later in the afternoon, she had no difficulty pointing out to me all the numbered squares. I think her difficulty was the result of a combination of jealousy and greed—jealousy being the concern that the other is going to take what rightfully belongs to her, with greed entering as an attempt to get more of what she thought she needed in order to be the attractive one.

If children are involved in excessive projective identification, then their capacity to introject and integrate is limited. In other words, they will have difficulty introjecting concepts (aspects of the good object) and integrating them in their developing thinking processes, along with the functional aspects of their internal objects (seeing, hearing, thinking, remembering, touching, etc.). Their thinking remains at a primitive level associated with the paranoid–schizoid position. Language and thought may be perceived as a potential source of attack because words will express the anger of envy, greed, and jealousy, with fear of anticipated retaliation from the attacked object. Such a child cannot move to the depressive position. His psychological growth and thought processes are fixated at the paranoid level. To further their thought processes, there would have to be a reduction in projection, splitting, and projective identification processes. This would then allow thinking to develop, with greater freedom to accommodate—that is, to recognize—reality as reality and not distort it, as occurs in the process of assimilation (Piaget, 1962; Weininger, 1989). When this occurs, thought need not be attacking, it may now become pleasurable. Language may now express ideas for which approval and rewards can be received and is not seen as a potential source of attack.

However, children whose thinking shows the expected growth towards accommodation do show, as well, regression to paranoid-assimilation thought processes. This will become apparent when their previous understandings are suddenly lost, perhaps as a result of some kind of threat, either internal or external. I will illustrate with an example of such a breakdown in thinking processes representing regression to earlier mental processes. I have noticed three- and four-year-old children walk away from their group and the teacher when asked a question that they either cannot answer or answer in a "wrong" way. As they walk off by themselves, no longer talking, they have often stuck their hand into their pants and held or touched their genitals, or else put their hand on their anus. (I can only see where their hand is placed and judge by the motions what they are doing.) Thinking stops, and the phantasy of retaliation for attacks (or wrong answers) means the child now feels attacked. In other words, the aspects of the ego and object that were unacceptable and were projectively identified within the mother object (for example, sadistic phantasies directed towards the mother object) are experienced as being returned with revenge. The child now feels attacked and can only see his world as persecutory. Therefore, no longer is the link to words and thoughts safe—this link would only verify the attack—and so coherence in thought, as in ego, deteriorates (Bion, 1988a, p. 75). The child has to touch his genitals or his anus, not as in function, but now in structure, to make sure that his sadistic phantasies towards his mother/object have not "returned" and destroyed his genitals and anus. I do not think that these children are trying to take "things" in through these anatomical parts, but, rather, they are making sure that these parts are still there, as well as closing them down or covering them to make sure nothing unsafe comes in.

Excessive projective identification as originally used by Klein (1946) weakens the ego because of excessive splitting and projection of parts of itself. Thinking and knowledge are closely bound to the aggressive feelings. If the aggression cannot be tolerated and, therefore, projected, the energies of the child become bound up with both attacking others and projecting aspects of itself. No longer can the child use aggression to gather links of knowledge and express this verbally so that others are able to tell the child how good he is. This child feels that too many persecutors are ready to pounce when he makes a mistake, and so the child's thinking is arrested and remains concrete, unable to form symbols (Segal, 1981). Thinking becomes directed, rather, at trying to preserve the remaining ego capacities.

Children who come to premature conclusions, who cannot tolerate listening too long, and who need "to do it alone" are expressing the fear that their remaining ego functions will be annihilated (Klein, 1946) if they allow too much to come into their thinking. They are afraid that they will find out how dreadful will be the revenge for the sadistic projections. In other words, those aspects projected into the object arouse the unconscious fear of their ego parts being persecuted while inside the object. It is as if the child is saying: "I am afraid of understanding and thinking, for then I will find out how I am being controlled and persecuted within the object for having forcibly projected into the object those aspects of myself which I cannot hold on to myself." The object becomes the bad self. As re-introjection of these aspects takes place—particularly if done prematurely—the ego is now felt to contain those very dangerous parts of itself. This anxiety is extremely difficult for the child to bear, and, rather than suffer the dread of ego annihilation, thinking and language are "closed down".

When such processes occur in children and interfere in learning, the teacher can be helpful. In excessive projective identification, the child first empties out those unacceptable impulses and feelings, first into the mother, who then often becomes identified as the teacher. This child is afraid to learn unless the teacher makes it "safe" for the child. The teacher experiences the child's fright, perhaps by the look on his face, or even by the way the child makes the teacher feel uncomfortable. The child may be freed up to learn and understand if the teacher acknowledges the child's fears and prepares an environment that is "safe". This will be one where the teacher works alongside the child, lets the child lead the learning, goes no faster than the child's anxieties permit, and uses materials that are known to the child. This is tantamount to the interpretations offered by the therapist, which, at an adult level, put the patient's fears into words (Rosenfeld, 1988), and, at the child's level, make use of the teacher as "container" and materials as "symbol" interpretation (Segal, 1981).

By symbol interpretation I mean that the materials may be used to represent some unconscious phantasy, an unconscious wish or fear, which the child may experience in ways that are consciously acceptable. This allows aspects of the unconscious phantasy to be "worked through" to the point where some of the internal conflict may be, in part at least, resolved. This aspect of partial resolution allows the child to continue within the learning process. The symbol is needed to displace aggression from the original object and, in that way, to lessen the guilt and the fear of loss. The aim of the displacement is to save the object, and, thus, the guilt experienced in relation to the aggression is far less than if an attack were made on the original object. Thus, the symbol here is not equivalent to the original object. The symbols are also created as symbolic displacement objects in the internal world as a means of restoring, recreating, recapturing, and owning again the original object destroyed by the original aggression. However, in keeping with the increased reality sense, these objects are now felt as created by the ego and, therefore, never completely equated with the original object (Segal, 1981, p. 55).

Jenny, a five-year-old child, had been arrested in learning due to her excessive projective identification and was helped to reduce this and return to learning. Jenny always had to give things away. Whenever a classmate approached her and asked for the red crayon, or the paint pot, Jenny not only gave her the red crayon but gave her all the crayons, all the paint, all the paper—everything, in fact—and Jenny was left empty of any material. Jenny wandered around the classroom until the teacher brought her over to a table, offered her play-dough, rolling pins, and biscuit cutters, and helped her play at kneading and rolling out the dough and cutting out biscuits of various shapes.

Jenny asked many questions, such as was it okay to do this stuff, wouldn't the other kids want to do the same thing, would she feel very tired if she made all these biscuits, would the teacher think she was all right if she didn't make them all "so perfect", could she leave to go to the bathroom if she needed to. Many more questions filled the time during which she and the teacher worked together, making the biscuits. The teacher had selected a quiet spot, with materials that were "safe"—that is, the materials were known to Jenny and could be used in ways that might help her express her conflicts. The materials made biscuits, which Jenny was sure the other children would want and be angry with her for having them. When the teacher suggested that perhaps Jenny might be angry and was giving all her stuff away to keep the other kids from getting angry, Jenny relaxed and went on with her biscuit-making.

The unacceptable aggressive impulses were emptied—were given away, in a sense, to others—and thereby would not arouse their anger, which was, essentially, Jenny's projected anger. As Jenny made more biscuits she asked for a bag to put them into and said that they would keep "for me until tomorrow", and then she added, "Maybe I'd like to draw some pictures now." Jenny was able to work through perhaps a small amount of her aggressive feelings—but sufficient to allow her to return to an activity with which she had not been able to deal before. Jenny worked with the symbol interpretation of the play-dough and the biscuits, and as a result was able to reduce the strength of her projective identifications so that she could become aware of the differentiation between herself and her mother, which had been prevented by excessive projective identification. Since she no longer felt she was containing so many dangerous internal objects, she became more capable of containing her own feelings without guilt.

Perhaps an even more dramatic example of projective identification interfering with learning and leading to confusion is that of Jason. Jason was a five-year-old boy who always wanted to play games with other boys and girls, but he always lost. It seemed to me that he could never bear the thought of winning, because even when he was about to make the winning move in a game that operated primarily on chance, like "Snakes & Ladders", he managed to lose by using such tactics as tossing the dice again, explaining that he "hadn't rolled them properly". Jason also could not answer questions correctly. He would give wrong answers when in a group of children, yet he was able to answer the question correctly when he was alone with me.

After I had the opportunity of playing with Jason and talking with him over a period of several weeks, I asked him why he never let himself win the games. I also said, "You know the answers to questions when I ask you, but when you're asked the same questions in front of everyone else you don't know the correct answers. Can we talk about this?" Jason agreed with what was said and was very definitely aware of this behaviour on his part. He said, "I get very confused. I don't know what to do." After playing some more with me and talking, Jason added, "I think they'd get angry and jealous because I know the answers".

Jason was able to show me in his play that he was very angry and jealous of others—for example, of his brother, who, he thought, "got everything he wanted while he got very little from his mother". Jason did not want to recognize his anger and wanted to protect his brother and mother from this jealousy and anger. He responded to the children in the class as if they would be very jealous of him if they knew he was bright, and as if they would get angry with him because they wanted to be able to give the right answers. Jason's projective identification was evacuating jealousy and anger into his brother, mother, and classmates in order to protect them from his own anger. While winning would represent an expression of Jason's jealousy and anger, losing, aided by confusion, allowed Jason to phantasize (1) that he could not hurt his brother/mother/classmates, and (2) that he would not be persecuted as the "brainy kid in the class".

These two projective identifications, perhaps originating at different times in the past and operating at different levels of the personality, protected Jason from recognizing the intensity of his jealousy and anger. However, in order to maintain this state, further projective identifications, which clearly kept him apart from the others, became necessary. In other words, he could not recognize that he was a very jealous person as long as he could not be close enough to people to find this out. In a way Jason was forced to maintain a homeostasis by projecting "a predominantly hostile inner world which is ruled by persecutory fears leads to the introjection—a taking back—of a hostile external world; and vice versa, the introjection of a distorted and hostile external world reinforces the projection of a hostile inner world" (Klein, 1946, p. 11). Jason's confusion in thinking and behaviour provided a protective screen for his unacceptable impulses.

The mechanism of splitting, as well as excessive projective identification, can contribute to confusion and rigid, concrete thinking processes. Klein (1957) indicated that

> When the fundamental normal splitting into love and hate and into the good and the bad object is not successful, *confusion* between the good and bad object may arise. I believe this to be the basis of any confusion—whether in severe confusional states or in milder forms such as indecision—namely a difficulty in coming to conclusions and a disturbed capacity for clear thinking. [p. 216]

I think this confusion is often seen in young children who have difficulty distinguishing where their feelings and impulses are coming from. For example, a three-year-old says, "I didn't do it, my fingers spilled the milk", or "I didn't eat it, my mouth ate it", or, " I didn't pee in my pants, my penis did". These young children are having difficulty integrating their action and impulses and their imagined and/or phantasized consequences of their envy. As a result splitting occurs—a split between impulse and feeling at the service of maintaining some coherency in the ego. If this splitting is excessive, the child does not develop the ego capacity to cope with the differences between internal objects and sensations and the reality of his/her external world. The splitting is successful—but it does not prevent confusion from arising. The result is an inability to acknowledge experiences, leading to rigidity of thinking and reaction with confusional states when the child is pressured for answers and/or a logical adaptation.

Excessive splitting leading to this kind of rigidity and confusional state may lead to an increase in a certain kind of projection, which can create further confusion in some children. The child maintains the splitting of his internal object by projecting and identifying the good, omnipotent aspect as now being contained within the mother. The child then imagines himself as the mother, with knowledge of what she feels and thinks, and responds to her according to this omnipotent and narcissistic state. She becomes the idealized part of the child who does not phantasize any separate life for himself. The child does not have to become aware of any of the mother's feelings and impulses, for in the child's mind these are identical with the child's feelings and impulses. The child phantasizes that he knows how he thinks and what he wants. If the mother insists on a separateness—as for example by telling her child to go and play by himself or that she "needs some time for herself"—the child will just stand there, almost immobile, as if he cannot understand how to integrate her instructions into action, in just the same way as the child has difficulty integrating his bodily action as being part of his total behaviour. If the mother then pushes her child, she risks a severe temper tantrum because the child now feels that this good part of himself has turned bad and has begun to attack him. The child may have to attack in return. To destroy the mother would result in the child's own death because she contains his good parts. In an effort to prevent such a dire situation, the child becomes disoriented, confused, and lost.

The child is dependent upon the mother accepting the child's projections and maintaining the projective identification with the narcissistic idealized version of the child now within the mother, who the child must assume, in an omnipotent way, totally understands and accepts him. Her care of him is thus idealized because the child cannot differentiate his own sensation and actions. Instead, the child has projected this idealized aspect of his internal object into her and identified with it and in this way "knows her completely". She then becomes the child's idealized caring object, and he does not have to take care of himself. In such a case, splitting successfully maintains the ego, and the child becomes confused only when the difference between inner and outer worlds is demanded, perhaps before the child is equipped to deal with this differentiation.

Children also become confused when they have difficulty recognizing whether an adult is a good person or a bad person. They often experience this confusion when having to identify someone as good or bad without sufficient clues and signs offered by the adult. It is, for example, difficult for many children to recognize the danger in speaking to strangers, yet when they are with adults who give cues, they have no difficulty in doing so. Klein suggests that confusion results in some young children because "persecution as well as the guilt about spoiling and attacking the primary object by envy is to some extent counteracted" (Klein, 1957, p. 216). She also suggests that an impairment in maintaining successful splitting results in confusion, as noted above (Klein, 1957, p. 220).

However, I am also suggesting that when both successful splitting and also successful projective identifications are threatened and are in danger of not remaining intact, then confusion may result. Confusion, lack of understanding, and poor perception of reality may be experienced, partly to avoid the intrusion of painful emotions such as envy and hostility, and partly to avoid the anxiety of retaliation. This may result in learning difficulties. In particular, understanding of information may be impaired due to the attempt to maintain projective identifications that relate to subjective rather than objective reality.

Klein indicated that the individual who makes excessive use of projective identification may also experience confusion because "he constantly feels himself not only to be in bits, but to be mixed up with other people" (Klein, 1963b, p. 304). In this case, I think the child feels emptied—a process described by Rosenfeld (1988, p. 121) as "emptying out the disturbing mental content which leads to a denial of psychic reality". With excessive use of this defence the child sees himself in so many people that he becomes confused. This may be shown in the child's attempts to keep himself somewhat together, and the great difficulty he has recognizing himself, due to the dispersion of self bits. This often results in temper outbursts as the child is less and less successful in this attempt. Confusion also results because the child assumes that everyone will understand his needs and feelings and will be there for him when he needs someone. When no one is experienced as "being there", then temper outbursts occur.

The child will assume, also, that these others will make him feel less threatened and frightened because "The child cannot accept and tolerate his own needs and impulses—he cannot learn to tolerate his own impulses" (Rosenfeld, 1988, p. 121). Confusion as well as thinking disorders result. The child neither knows who he is, nor can trust that he has evacuated all the bad parts of himself because he still feels so terrible, nor can he trust others to understand him because of suspicion and persecutory feelings. Throughout this process projective identification continues, in the futile hope of getting rid of all the bad fragments contributing to the final resulting state of emptiness, confusion, and isolation. Rage becomes evident whenever an attempt is made to "clear up" the child's confusion.

I think as therapists we all experience these reactions when we make premature interpretations to a psychotic child who then becomes hostile because the child is sure that he cannot tolerate the pain of introjecting his impulses. After all, the projective identification was for the explicit purpose of reducing the anxiety and pain by having it contained completely by the other. Thus, the psychotic child may say, "Don't talk crazy", or

"Stop it, stop talking", or "Don't talk any more", or, "Stop moving your lips", or stick his fingers in his ears so as not to hear, or become overtly destructive and hostile to the therapist who is no longer experienced as the adequate container (Bion, 1988c).

This child attempts to maintain the splitting and the projective identifications and fights any attempts to broaden his expression of feelings and impulses and contacts with others. These restrictions are felt as safe, and the projective identifications are useful, although the mechanism may have to be used excessively and even make the child feel depleted and empty. The confusion in thinking, in taking in information, in making decisions, and in understanding is certainly uncomfortable for the child, but it is unconsciously easier to bear than the pain experienced by his "real" feelings and impulses, which must be avoided. Bion suggested that the adult patient strives "to escape the confusional state" (Bion, 1988b, p. 62). I think children and perhaps adults, use the confusion to ensure a return to the "restricted relationship" (Bion, 1988b, p. 62).

The feeling of terror and dread arising in this child when the link with the internal and external breast is attacked by the infant's envy can best be handled by projective identification. [The object-relations between mother and baby are attacked by the baby's envy, where the good object is attacked and its goodness spoiled leaving the baby with a sense of aloneness and separateness leading towards confusion, that is, considerable difficult in gaining and maintaining a sense of reality.] The mother who is unable to experience the communication of this feeling from her baby or who denies its existence because of her own psychological problems cannot provide an adequate container for her child. She is unable to retain a "balanced outlook" (Bion, 1988) and becomes aloof, if not emotionally cold and distant towards her child. The child, in turn, attempts to split off his envious impulses, but the projections are either denied by the mother through her inability to understand and receive them, or returned prematurely, and then they attack the child as introjected objects. Both mother and child become vulnerable to imagined and phantasized panic—experienced by the baby as terror and dread and by the mother as exhaustion and futility. So also does the therapist often experience this as the therapist oscillates identification with the child and identification with the child's objects.

Both are afraid of what is going to happen—essentially annihilation (a sense of fear of fragmentation and disintegration of the ego)—and the child and mother then respond with feelings of confusion. This is meant to serve as an attempt to maintain the status quo, to maintain the split and the projective identification on the part of the child and the rejection by the mother of understanding of the emotional life of her infant. Rigidity sets in. This is an inability to understand the needs of the child—even if these needs are explained and directions and instructions provided by welfare workers or consultants. The rigidity of thinking and behaviour is, I think, a response to the confusion felt by mother and by child as well and is a way of avoiding the changes required in the container and in the splitting and projective identification. To avoid the needed changes, both mother and child now increase the strength of their rigid behaviour. Rejection, if not abuse, is the parental response, while excess projective identification is the child's response. The feeling of emptiness experienced by the child forces him to try again and again to have the parent become his container. The cycle experienced by the child is splitting → projective identification → emptiness; while the cycle experienced by the mother is exhaustion, futility → rejection and anger.

The child needs a container for projections, but the parent cannot provide this. The child's emptiness leads to the impulse to get some "good stuff" from the mother, yet the response is rejection. Confusion in both mother and child helps to deny this rejection and leads to the child trying again and again with continued rejection and denial of this, aided constantly by the confused state (Bion, 1988b).

We so often see this in young children who return time after time to their abusive parents, not because there is no one else, but because the confusion helps to deny their parents' abuse, and the rigidity of thinking and behaviour continues the cycle. To intervene with information or even "modelling" is usually futile. Rather, parents' need to understand what it is that prevents them from being adequate containers for their children.

CHAPTER NINE

Rivalry and its origins in pre-Oedipal and Oedipal relations

Rivalry usually implies that a relationship exists either in reality or in phantasy and that someone else seems to be "getting the better", either in terms of strength, love, friendship, or success.

I overheard the following conversation as I watched two four-year-old boys playing with Plasticine:

BOY 1: I am making a flying saucer.

BOY 2: I'm making a flying saucer. I'm making one like yours but it's better.

BOY 1: I'm having a console on mine.

BOY 2: Mine has 100 thousand people.

BOY 1: I think I'll cut mine into two. [This play changed to munching the Plasticine after Boy 2 cut his flying saucer into two pieces.]

BOY 1: The cookie is food.

BOY 2: Mine is a cookie—good, good, good.

BOY 1: Here, take this knife [a piece of wire].

BOY 2: No, I want the sharp one.

BOY 1:   Well, this one is sharp here [pointing to one part of the wire where it was bent].

BOY 2:   This one is sharper.

BOY 1:   No, you take this one. I want that one.

BOY 2:   Well, it's mine.

BOY 1:   You want the sharp one, so here is the sharp one. I need that one.

The boys poked at their piece of Plasticine, each holding their "knife" so that they jabbed the wire knife into the Plasticine leaving little holes. The first boy poked the wire knife into the Plasticine and then left. The second boy picked it up, looked at it, poked into his Plasticine, looked at it, poked his own wire knife into the Plasticine, looked at both wires in the Plasticine, pulled out the first boy's wire and replaced it in the other child's piece of Plasticine. Then the first boy returned, this time zooming a stick around the air, and the second boy joined him but used his arms as wings as he zoomed about the room.

Rivalry, expressed as attempts to "outdo" the other, is quite obvious in the above example, with one child having to have a better flying saucer, a sharper knife, and a better zoomer. The other child attempts to rival his opponent but is never entirely successful.

Rivalry does not occur just between boys. The following example is between a girl and a boy, both five-year-olds:

GIRL: You want my car?

BOY: No, I want a difficulter one.

GIRL: Mine has a gun at the back and over here [on top].

BOY: Mine has guns all over and is better.

GIRL: This one has six guns right over here. You can't have it.

BOY: Mine has special guns.

GIRL: If there's any trouble, this is a good one. It is a ship and looks like a racing car.

BOY: This one goes on and this one goes in space [another boy joins them].

BOY 2: Tell us what to do.

BOY 1:   We will make war and one guy will direct it.

BOY 2:   Ready for war?

BOY 1:   No, not yet—soon now, but there's no time. We will make a sign not to touch this, and we will save it right here [the boys make a sign that says "stop, leave", and they move away].

Interestingly, in this example the girl–boy rivalry escalated up to a point where the boy seemed to have to try to "outdo" the girl; he had many guns on his car and his was better, he had "special places" for his pieces, his could go on land, and he suddenly acquired another one to go into space. Then another boy happened along who seemed very willing to follow the first boy, so the girl was ignored, the boys said a few things to each other, and the play ended.

Rivalry seems to be evoked when a child begins to feel that what he is doing is inadequate or the person with whom he is playing is outdoing him or making him feel less successful. While both examples contain aggressive themes, it is the sense of not being able to maintain a lead role that seems to dominate the play. It is almost as if the child must feel that he is in charge of his feelings—particularly feelings of aggression—and that he will be able to do whatever he wants to do.

This feeling of being in charge and in control over aggressive and probably destructive feelings is essentially expanded towards the parents, who are both loved and hated. Rivalry is the oral-sadistic impulse directed towards mother and father, who not only are in a position to control and direct the child, but are also giving nurturance to each other. The phantasies that a child has are of two people who stop him from getting what he wants and demands, but who also point out that they have what he wants and, furthermore, are giving it to each other and not to him. The conscious image is one where the child has to obey. When I asked what they had to do at home for their parents, one five-year-old told me, "Do as you're told". Another four-year-old said, "Not take too much candy". A four-year-old stated, "Give some of your crayon to your sister", and yet another five-year-old stated, "Try to be quiet when you're baby brother is asleep". The children also said that they had to clean up, pick up their toys, wash dishes, set the table for dinner, mind their baby sister or brother, take out the garbage, and several other chores, which indicated to me that they were "outdone" by their parents. Rivalry is a family affair and is an expression of aggression towards the parents who seem to "have it all". A seven-year-old mentioned that his parents "have it all, they can do what they want whenever they want to. They can even go to the movies and to the restaurant if they want to. I can't. I have to go to bed at eight o'clock and even switch off the light. I can't read in bed either."

Rivalry is not just an unconscious aspect of behaviour. There seems to be a very conscious element to it as well. As the child becomes more aware of his aggressive feelings, aroused because he does not feel that he is getting what he wants when he wants it, the child's rivalry is evoked towards the parents (although this is usually expressed towards other children and, at times, even towards animals or inanimate objects). It is not uncommon for a parent to tell me that their child has broken their favourite vase or piece of china, or kicked and dirtied their best chair. Nor is it uncommon for the parents to say that their child seems to be openly aggressive towards their dog or cat, even teasing, pinching, or snatching its food away.

Sometimes these feelings of aggression and the resultant rivalry are very difficult for the young child to handle, and it is at such times that the child may try to have the parent with him. These feelings are painful because they are directed towards the very person who can comfort and satisfy, and so the child may try to make sure that the parent is ever so close by. At such times the child may be unable to sit in a chair but seems to slip off the seat, or is clumsy in bringing the spoon to his mouth, or may even ask to be fed. These attempts to bring the parent close are to ensure the child that not only is he not deserted but that his painful aggressive feelings have not harmed the parent.

In phantasy, rivalry is marked by a sense of omnipotence and control, by a sense of being able to get whatever is desired and consciously to win at "one-up-manship". However, the strength of these feelings carries with it a sense of potential danger. Triumph means that "you will be alone", that "there will be no one to take care of you". The child cannot be entirely transparent, and I think that is why the children in the above examples wandered off instead of completing their triumphant rivalrous relationships. When the relationship is not rivalrous, the play may continue or it may end but the ending is not disorganized, as in the following incident, where four 5-year-old boys are playing at "talking".

BOY 1: They have playfulness.

BOY 2: I'm a battleman.

BOY 3: You have strength.

BOY 4: Do you know where the dinosaur is?

BOY 2: We're players over here and that's the base over there.

BOY 3: Can the spaceship go faster than anything?

BOY 2: Of course, it's always the fastest. Okay, now follow me and I'll lead the attack [picking up a long block and pretending that it is a spaceship].

BOY 3: They go 100 miles per hour. These go very fast.

BOY 2: That's not fast—not 100 miles per hour. Maybe 1,000 miles per hour or even 5,000 miles per hour—that would be fast.

BOY 4: Mine goes 300 miles per hour, but why do they go so fast?

BOY 2: [Just laughs and continues flying his space ship.]

[At this point the group splits into two.]

BOY 3: We're playing our own game.

BOY 4: You're not the boss of us.

[Boys 3 and 4 continue to play at spaceship.]

BOY 3: This is a regular space-flight trip now.

BOY 4: We will have regular stopovers. Let's get the outer spaceships over here. [These boys continue to play in a co-operative, non-rivalrous style, while the play of the other two boys has changed and they now push chalk into a groove in the floor.]

BOY 1: Do you care if it rains?

BOY 2: No, I don't care. We can play here all the time.

Parents often suggest that rivalry makes its appearance when their baby is about six months old, or upon the birth of a second or third child, and that its appearance is usually associated with the expression of aggression. Starting at about six to nine months, the baby begins to show rivalry with the father. For example, when the mother is holding the baby and the father comes over to hug them both, it is not unusual for the baby to push the father away or to snuggle closer to the mother. If the father persists in trying to hug them both, the baby may cry and push the father with greater vigour or try to drop out of the mother's arms altogether.

The baby at this age is becoming aware of the mother's relationship with other members of the family, and, while the baby expresses a possessiveness for the mother, it is also aware that there are demands made upon her. It is as if the rivalry with the father reflects the baby's fear that, if too many demands are made upon the mother, there will not be enough for the baby. Associated with this is also the baby's attempt to extend relationship boundaries—that is, to extend the boundaries of the baby's love, towards toys, siblings, aunts, uncles, and grandparents. However, it is interesting that, in spite of its attempts to do this, the baby still does not extend this consistently towards the father. There are certainly times when the baby is loving towards the father, but I think that these are times when the baby feels that there are enough "supplies" obtained from the mother, and so the baby can now risk being with the person who is perceived as the baby's main rival for mother's care, nurturance, and goodness—in short, her "supplies".

If the baby experiences these supplies as inadequate, then the danger would be a fear of being unable to control anxiety. In other words, these supplies provide the ego with a sense of well-being, of being in charge of relationships, and of being able to handle one's own greediness. It is at such times that the baby has enough "supplies" not only to accept the father's love for its mother, but to be able to be kind and soothing to the mother herself as well. The baby can pat her cheek, put his head softly on her shoulder and smile. The baby can, in this way, feel, "I'm not taking too much from her. I'm going to give her some back." This also reinforces the feeling that the baby will not lose the mother, that she would want to be present for the baby, and that, in effect, the baby can give something to the mother, as baby imagines, consciously or unconsciously, that the father is doing for mother. Again, the rivalry is stimulated. Thus, even when the baby is loving towards the mother and the father, the situation is short-lived. The baby will push the father away, because the father might take what is due to the baby, and because the father's presence and his "giving" to the mother is a rivalrous relationship for the baby, as it evokes an Oedipal reaction.

The boy baby phantasizes that he wants to take all of the mother's "insides" for himself, and he tries to do this by making many demands upon her, such as not letting her "out of his sight" and, generally, by being very upset when she does not seem to give in to him and understand all his desires. Much of this desire is to take, in an aggressive way, to grab, even to pinch or pull at her, to get whatever he phantasizes she has. Associated with the urgency of his demands is the danger that she will become angry and retaliate. Because the phantasies are mostly unknown if not understood by the mother, no mother can provide satisfaction for all these desires. Frustration is an inevitable consequence, and this frustration leads to further aggression and rivalry with the father, who is also presumed to take the "supplies" from the mother. Under the influence of fears of retaliation by the mother as well as attacks by the father, the boy lessens his demands. In phantasy, he is afraid that his body will be harmed and mutilated, an early expression of castration fears brought on by this "couple"—the phantasized reaction of both parents to his demands.

This phase of the Oedipal relationship has been referred to as the feminine phase, "characterized by anxiety relating to the womb and the father's penis" (Klein, 1928, p. 190). The greater the capacity of the baby's ego to withstand this anxiety, the stronger will be his ability to achieve this phase of development. The ego's strength is provided by the care and nurturance with which the baby is being reared. While the baby may feel very demanding and very angry with the mother for the phantasized withholding of "supplies", the strength of the ego will help to maintain a positive relationship with her. With less ego capacity, the anger towards mother often impairs the boy's relationship to her and his ability then to accept "supplies" from her. In other words, if he is angry with her, then he is afraid that if he takes anything from her, she will retaliate and destroy him. So he phantasizes that he has very little, is angry for having little, and cannot accept much from her because she would not give to an angry child and she will harm him for wanting. These phantasies, in effect, are the basis of a developing sadistic superego, which will impair further sexual development by a phantasized image of the father/mother as a harsh, demanding, devouring, mutilating couple. The father is phantasized as being within the mother, and every time the baby tries to take "supplies" out of the mother, the father is there to damage him. In a way, then, the boy has to try to keep the father away from mother. While the rivalry seems to be with father for mother's supplies, it is really the desire to take mother over, and the real rivalry is then with mother, who keeps her "supplies" inside herself.

Rivalry of some men with women is, therefore, an aspect of their unresolved feminine phase, where they phantasized that they were not able to gain their mother's inside goodness. Their later rivalrous attacks on women may be vicious because they still unconsciously view them as containing the "supplies" that would make them great or greater, if women would relinquish these supplies to them.

Baby girls also phantasize taking and demanding their mother's "supplies" of goodness, care, and nurturance, and if the ego is not sufficiently strong to endure the anxiety of their sadistic demands, then further sexual development is hindered as well. The frustrations experienced at the oral phase of development, from the desire for the breast or an always giving object, pushes the girl to look for another object of satisfaction, and she turns towards the father. For a short while she seems to be content with this relationship. It is less anxiety-provoking than the previous one with her mother. Father should be able to give her the "supplies" she needs, and it is at about this age (six to nine months) that the baby may prefer to be held and fed by the father and may cry when he leaves. However, in reality and in phantasy, the baby girl recognizes that it is the mother who nurtures the father, and she, the baby, must change her perception of her father as nurturer to one where he is to be her lover. Now the "complex unfolds further in the development of the child's rivalry with one parent (the mother) for absolute possession of the other (the father)" (Britton, Feldman, & O'Shaughnessy, 1989, p. 100).

If the relationship that the baby girl had to the breast was nurturing, loving, and grateful, then the relation to the father (and his penis) is phantasized as "a source of happiness and good gifts" (Klein, in Britton et al., 1989, p. 73). Gifts are to provide her with continued gratification for nurturance and for "motherhood" as well. "Motherhood" will provide her with the sense of "well-being" within the inside of her body. The girl experiences intense doubts as a result of her sadistic impulses towards her mother for a phantasy of withholding goodness from her and, instead, keeping it for herself or giving it to the father. Her anxieties about her own insides increase, not only because of having taken too much from her mother, but also because she is trying to "have a baby with her father to prove to herself that her insides are undamaged". This longing to be sure she is all right corresponds to the strength of the internal persecutory mother (which is based upon the degree of sadistic impulses to her mother and subsequent anxiety about retaliation and damage). The expectation is that the father will be able to make up for any hurts. However, this expectation is disrupted by the frustration of the Oedipal relationship. The little girl does not achieve a sense of internal well-being from the father and, within this frustration, she is forced to see her mother not as a rival but as a "co-object". Mother becomes a visible object confirming the girl's well-being. As one five-year-old girl said to me, "I know that I'm all right because my Mummy is all right. She is a strong lady and she knows how to work and make supper and have babies and when I grow up I'll have breasts just like her and we will both have breasts. My baby brother won't even have breasts. He has a penis, but I can have babies, because I'm a girl, and my Mummy's a girl too."

> If the internalization of a good mother, with whose maternal attitude she can identify herself, counterbalances the persecutory fear, her relation to the good internalized father becomes strengthened by her own maternal attitude towards him. [Klein, 1945, p. 414]

The boy can see that his penis is there. He can touch it and watch it grow and, if necessary, continue holding it. The girl does not have any such external example of assurance that she is well and functioning. Compared to the boy, she needs to be much more concerned with her insides—that is, with her internal world—and, since she cannot see but can feel this directly, she takes support for her well-being from the well-being and strengths of her mother. As the girl sees herself "more like her mother" and identifies with her, she is able to accept the rivalry for father between herself and mother. Young girls often demonstrate this rivalry by saying, "I'm going to make special cookies for Daddy"; "I'll give Daddy his bath tonight"; "I'll tuck him in bed"; "I'm going to clean up his car so it will be a fancy car"; "I'm going to make my Daddy a big heart (a drawing) and give it to him when he comes home". But the rivalry does not disturb her relationship to her mother—even though the girl sees herself and mother both competing for him. The girl's superego is benevolent and continues as a nurturing, giving mother aspect as well as an "admired internalized penis of her father" (Klein, 1945, p. 414)—that is, a conscious sense of being able to achieve her wishes.

Rivalry between siblings is yet another example of this revival of early infant–parent rivalries. When mother arrives home with a new sibling, and for several months thereafter, the older child will be dispossessed of his portion and will have to deal with a severe loss of affection from a mother and father, who are occupied with an infant. There will be a sense of rage at having an interruption in the ongoing relationships within the family. However, apart from these feelings, the older child must also try to deal with feelings that are revived from earlier times. For the boy, the sense that his mother and father made another baby, and also that it was not he who made the baby with his mother, forces him to realize that he does not have a "special" love relationship with mother. A seven-year-old girl expressed this loss of specialness to her mother when a baby sister was born: "How come you let her do what she wants? You're the mother. You're supposed to tell her what to do. She's not supposed to tell you what to do. She's the baby, and you're the mother. Oh yeah—just cause she is little and she cries. You don't let me cry. You get mad at me. You don't get mad at her."

Gradually, with parental support and understanding of his feelings, the boy's image of himself as being little Daddy comes to the fore, and he imagines himself as being able to make a baby just like his Daddy did. For the girl, the rivalry with a new sibling becomes resolved by her image of herself as someone like her mother who can make babies inside her. She loses the rivalry with the new sibling and begins to be as caring and nurturing to it as she imagines and sees her mother to be.

The girl's self-perception as someone who will be able to become pregnant and have babies implies that her insides are all right and not damaged, and that the relationship to her mother was sufficiently good. This self-perception also implies that her sadistic feelings were not overpowering, and that her sense of relationship with mother was primarily resolved before the birth of the new child. However, this birth occasions a revival of the feelings that mother may have kept too much for herself, and/or that she may have damaged the daughter for taking too much. These feelings are helped when the parents are understanding of the rivalry and do not see these feelings as unusual. Understanding, patience, and support from both parents enables the girl to begin emulating the role of the mother as a nurturer. She now nurtures the baby as well and, in this way, strengthens the identification with her mother and demonstrates the presence of a benevolent superego.

Rivalry with a new-born sibling may, however, be an expression of the parents' own rivalry projected to the older child. In such a situation the older child is then rivalrous because there seems to be so little available for him, and the parents insist on the child taking over duties that are inappropriate for either his maturity, age, or ego strength. In such instances the rivalry is fostered and encouraged by the parent or parents and would be an expression of their own unresolved feelings of rivalry towards their own parents, who kept too much of the goodness to themselves. These parents then feel that they have not got "enough" to give to their children. They have the older child nurture the younger, recreating in this child a sense of deprivation. If the parents have been unable to resolve some of these feelings, then they will be unable to help their child to deal not only with his own developmental rivalries but with the sense of being deprived as well. Then, of course, this older child will be all the more rivalrous and even hostile towards the new sibling.

CHAPTER TEN

Thinking, learning, and the internal container

Projection, an early mechanism of ego defence, is necessary when an infant cannot tolerate the anxiety created by frightening and angry impulses and feelings. These anxiety-producing impulses are split off and projected to the mother, who, under ordinary circumstances, is able to accept them, returning these feelings and impulses to the baby when the baby's ego is more capable of handling the anxiety that always accompanies these feelings. However, it is not only the aspect of fright that creates anxiety; it is also the unknowingness of these feelings. Anger is felt by the baby, and this emotion creates sufficient anxiety for the baby to try to get rid of this feeling. However, in order for the mother to understand, recognize, and know this feeling for the baby, it is not only this "getting rid of" that is important, but also the fact that the mother acts as a container for this feeling. As the baby realizes this, it becomes clearer that this internalization helps the baby to know that it can do a bit for itself.

Bion refers to this as the mother's "reverie"—that is, her willingness and ability to think about and learn to know her baby and its impulses, needs, and feelings. Thinking about, being interested in, and trying to be aware of her baby's impulses provide the avenue by which it will gradually be able to accept, become aware of, acknowledge, and know its feelings, impulses, and the experiences that generate these. If the mother is able to be the adequate container and to think about her baby and its impulses, the baby can then identify with her because it is no longer so anxious that it must avoid or withdraw. The baby is now able to experience the mother's thinking and begin to introject this as its own without the anxiety that was previously attached to these impulses.

Babies and toddlers go through these experiences of projection–introjection continuously. If the container is adequate, then the baby, freed from anxiety, is able to continue exploring its external as well as its internal worlds. No longer is the baby restricted to explore only the known and safe; it can now extend its vistas to new and perhaps even dangerous experiences and feelings. It is not uncommon, then, for babies and toddlers who have such safe containers to attempt the feats they do—like jumping into mother's arms from what must surely seem a great distance or even a great height. But the baby does this unhesitatingly, not just because it is "in-one" with its container, but because it trusts its container to hold the more frightening aspects of its brave feats. Gradually, then, the child can jump without the mother's outstretched arms. The child gradually internalizes a capacity to think for himself, to recognize what he can do and what he wants to experience, and to differentiate which aspects have to be projected to his container. Gradually, the child is able to perform this differentiation of knowing "what I can do and what I need help with".

The child who is unable to differentiate like this does not have an adequate container and does not have the opportunity of being able to manage his anxiety by projection. The two-year-old who tries to do so much for himself and who wants to be independent and refuses much of the help mother and father offer is able to tolerate the anxiety of his impulses to be independent. But he is only able to do this because he can tolerate anxiety. The ego of this child has developed to the point where it can tolerate anxiety and has introjected an object that earlier had the capacity to contain, to think, and to hold. This internal object performs the beginning function of helping the child to think about events, experiences, feelings, self, and others. This thinking part of the ego is the result of mother accepting and thinking about her baby and providing the opportunity for her baby to continue exploring without being stopped by excessive anxiety. "Her thinking transforms the infant's feelings into a known and tolerated experience" (O'Shaughnessy, 1988, p. 179).

Recently, I had the opportunity to be part of a small group of parents and their babies and toddlers. We discussed aspects of day-care for very young children. As we continued our discussion, most of the parents expressed the view that it was very important for them to be able to continue with the careers they had started before they began having babies. Both mothers and fathers said that nursery and day-care were very important to them, but they all wondered what might happen to their babies and toddlers if they were involved in care for eight hours a day, four to five days a week. As we talked about these urgent aspects, their children kept coming over to them, asking to be picked up, wanting to play with their parents, or trying to drag them off to another section of the room in order to be alone with them. The children were persistent. If a parent refused to be involved with a child or tried to talk to another adult prior to answering the child's request, the child might cry, or look into the parent's face, or, in frustration, try to pull the parent's face to his own. Finally, most parents provided the needed interest for their child's important question or statement. Some did not reply to their child's request, and these children either walked away looking very tired and withdrawn or began to cry vigorously, pulling at their parents' arm.

For most parents, the thought that their children needed them was very acceptable, but they did not seem willing to cope with the idea that their babies needed them as much as they did. The parents were asking for "time for themselves", away from their children; they insisted that their children would become more adequately socialized if they were with other children their own age rather than with them for most of the day. As we talked, I tried to point out that I thought that their concern about socialization was not as important for two-year-olds and that usually it was at three years of age that children are able to play with other children in a parallel if not a co-operative way for short periods of time. The parents' response was that they needed their children socialized at earlier ages, as this might provide them with more time to pursue their own interests and/or careers. I sympathized with their remarks but reiterated that babies and toddlers (if not children) are very demanding of parental interest and involvement, and that this was a necessary involvement to allow their thinking and problem-solving abilities to develop to the potential that I believe possible.

As I expected, the response to this was quite strong, and they were amazed by my linking a child's involvement with parents to the development of thinking skills. As I tried to clarify by making use of some of the concepts that attachment theory offers us, annoyance in the parents changed to concern about how they might be damaging their babies. This was not the point that I was trying to make, but guilt was quickly aroused, and the parents said they felt caught: on the one hand, "society" and some researchers were suggesting that such care for babies and toddlers was without harm; on the other hand, I was presenting a view suggesting that babies and toddlers, until at least the ages of two to three years, needed their parents much more than parents were willing to accept.

I presented an interesting example derived from an interaction between a father, his baby, and a woman who was a stranger to the child. The father placed his four-month-old baby daughter on the lap of the "strange" woman sitting next to the father. The child looked startled and began to "pout" and to make noises indicative of "I'm about to cry." The father picked her up but very quickly "needed" to put her on another person's lap—another "strange" woman. This time the child pushed away from the stranger, arched her back, and refused to be held. The adult said, "You'd think I did something to hurt her". I considered this to be a projection of the child. Father was the "safe", familiar, good person; the stranger was the unknown one. The child's anger towards the father for placing her onto a stranger's lap was projected and felt by the stranger as if she had done something wrong to the child. She had become the bad and dangerous object.

When the father took his daughter back, she looked at him as if she did not know him—with a sort of vacant look, to which he responded, "It's okay, I'm your father; you're safe with me." She didn't cuddle immediately, but, rather, she seemed to need some time to make sure he was not angry with her. Her anger, displaced and projected to the stranger, was meant for the father, who left her with this stranger and created for her a sense of discomfort, tension, and frustration. The child's capacity to handle frustration was limited, and I think her response to the second adult was not to regard her, not to take her in, and not to know her. The child's frustration had reached the point where she was quite unable to take in any information about the goodness of this stranger. The projections had made her bad, and her discomfort would not allow her to be taken care of by this stranger. I think that the vacant look she gave her father also represented some difficulty in knowing due to both the projection and the feared retaliation, which, together, created a sense in the child of not being able to take in information or knowledge in the situation.

This difficulty in taking in information and the problem of thought development—i.e., recognizing father as the good father without the anticipation of badness coming from him— seems to be due, at least in part, to the poor ego capacity in infants and babies to tolerate frustration and the attempt to avoid frustration. Seen in this light, the attempt to get away from the stranger was not just difficulty in toleration of the stranger, but the evasion of frustration. The good internal father object was becoming a bad object. Projection of this badness to the stranger might have been the child's attempt to prevent the father from becoming bad—yet retaliation for the projection of anger prevented her from acknowledging father. The thought process of "this is my father" was disturbed, and the evasion of frustration meant, then, that she could not recognize father immediately. The father was evaded in order to allow him to become the good father once again. This event did not happen immediately—it took time to occur, because the thought that could be present in her mind was that "he was a bad object". However, as the internal objects become bad, they have to be evacuated. Information and knowledge are then treated as bad because the recognition of the stranger forces recognition of the badness of father, and this must be evacuated. As Bion (1988c) points out:

The end result is that all thoughts are treated as if they were indistinguishable from bad internal objects; the appropriate machinery is felt to be, not an apparatus for thinking the thought, but an apparatus for ridding the psyche of accumulations of bad internal objects. [p. 308]

I was able to observe another young girl, two-and-a-half years of age, the child of a mother attending the above group. Celia was intent on having her mother come and watch her while she played. Her mother would come with her to the play-room, supervised by a teacher, stay for a few minutes, and then leave. Celia, who would become involved in playing while her mother was present, would walk out of the group as soon as she noticed that her mother had left, despite attempts by the teacher to get her involved in activities. Celia went to fetch her mother, and her mother returned. Celia's play would start again—usually doll play in which Celia dressed and took a doll for a walk in a baby pram. However, when mother left, Celia stopped playing and again went to get her mother. If her mother did not want to come with her to the playroom, Celia would refuse to leave her side or sit and cry loudly.

Celia could not tolerate being separated from her mother at the playgroup. She seemed very unhappy and withdrawn when forced to stay in the playroom without her mother. She cried until her mother came into the room. Celia's mother com-plained, "She never leaves me alone. She makes me feel fright-ened for her. I don't think she'll ever be independent of me." I think that Celia's projections and projective identification were too difficult for her mother to contain without anxiety. This was expressed by mother as "I don't want my daughter because she isn't a big enough (good enough) girl" and interpreted by daughter as "I can't be alone. I'm afraid of my anger. The room with the other children makes me worried that I won't get what I need. They will get it all. My mother is to protect me from my envy and her presence ensures the goodness of the room and of her as good internal object."

The mother, unfortunately, could not accept these projec-tions and was all too ready to give them back to Celia before Celia was ready to re-introject them. Celia was referred to by her mother as a "leech", "a greedy, sucky baby", and, in a sense, she was right in terms of the understanding of the feelings that her daughter gave her. Yet there was nothing she could do to contain these projections and nothing the daughter could do to contain her phantasies. Celia's ego was sufficiently fragile to need the containment her mother might provide.

When Celia was with the "play-teacher" and was introduced to materials with which to paint or draw, she seemed quite unable to make use of these materials, and then, if the issue of making something was pushed a bit, Celia became terrified and ran out of the room, crying for her Mummy. Nothing could be good for Celia; whatever goodness or activity the teacher might introduce became bad and threatening. In phantasy, her internal object could not accept goodness, but, rather, the goodness was experienced as badness and threatening. Only mother could save her, and yet mother could not accept her projections. Celia interpreted her mother's pushing her away as retaliation, as if she were bad. Since the child's projections were not accepted by mother, who demanded that Celia become her own container before her ego was sufficiently able to cope with these projections, Celia had to introject her projections to mother. This made her feel continually fearful, threatened, and frustrated, and unable to accept direction or information from the teacher. Thinking could not advance from the primitive state of trying desperately to have her mother hold all of her painful bad feelings.

Celia's mother made her feel that she was being given back her frightening feelings. Since Celia could not accept them, her fears became quite unmanageable, and she could neither be without her mother nor gain the containment she needed from her. Celia continued to project her feelings, always at the service of trying to maintain her fragile ego. Since mother could not receive these but always gave them back, Celia could only interpret the teacher's requests to play as denied projections, and she phantasized that she was being given her frightening feelings back again. She could not then participate in any play with the teacher, because the teacher was asking her to do something rather than simply following what Celia seemed to need at that moment. A chart of these dynamics is given in Table 1.

Another mother/child interaction provides an example of the mother as a more adequate container. I was observing a four-year-old who was lying on his stomach, playing with

TABLE 10.1

Mother	Daughter	Teacher
1. unable to be container for daughter	unable to tolerate her feelings of aloneness because of anger projects to mother	tries to help her stay in the room and do things
2. demands that daughter not project	experiences mother's anger and frustration	attempts to keep her playing and be pleased
3. accuses daughter of being a baby	feels threatened by mother's demands to re-introject her projections	at times seems to be demanding by insisting that she stay in the room
4. leaves her alone in the playroom	fearful that projections will destroy her and so she looks for a comforting container	
5. when pulled back by Celia, she sits there until Celia seems distracted	returns to mother to find her unable or unwilling to accept the fearful projections	
6. returns to her previous activity looking withdrawn and annoyed	teacher's suggested activity for Celia is phantasized as demands to introject the feared painful feelings and so she leaves	
7. when Celia comes back she tells her to go back and play: "can't you see I'm busy"	no information can be given to her or accepted by her	
8. with obvious annoyance she is dragged back into the room		

several blocks, a few small cars, and some train tracks. As he assembled the blocks and the tracks, his mother, who was sitting close by, said that he might want to push the cars on the train tracks. The boy looked at his mother and began to destroy his construction. She moved over to him and continued to tell him that he should "play nicely with the cars and the blocks", and that she would sit and watch him. The child at first lay on the floor with his head on the carpet, not moving or talking, and then, after about five minutes during which time neither mother nor child spoke, the boy went back to constructing his game.

I think that the mother's first intrusion was felt by the child as criticism, as non-acceptance of what he was doing, and as if she was "rushing" him. The child's response was aggression, and the capable mother, perhaps realizing that she had made her suggestion too quickly, sat and watched him, but now without criticism or suggestions. I think that she became the adequate container, that her presence acted to allow him to explore the blocks and tracks and cars because she could accept his projections. As soon as she showed that she would not or could not be that container, by making a suggestion that must have been one that he was thinking of but was at that moment not prepared to carry out—perhaps because it meant something special to him—he became very upset, and he stopped playing and thinking. As she became the thoughtful container by sitting there looking at and thinking about his play, he was able to resume his construction.

When the mother is unable to contain the projections, then the child does not adequately develop that part of the ego which performs the learning and thinking function. Anxiety, generated by new experiences, prevents learning; the container is not adequate. Then anger in the child prevents information being accepted from others, as this would mean for the child that "others have something I don't have". The child's envy of the mother who is phantasized as being able to contain but who did not—that is, who "has something I need"—creates feelings of persecution. By not learning—that is, by not recognizing that there is new information to take in—the child is able to deny the persecutory feelings. The envy thus prevents the child from introjecting an object that is able to think and be thoughtful.

Kenny is a three-year-old boy who has been unable to introject such a thoughtful object. His mother says that she is worried about him. She starts off her conversation about Kenny, but within a very few moments she is talking about herself, her troubles, and her very real worries about where she will live and how she will survive. As she says this, she returns to Kenny, to say, "I just can't think about him right now. He's too much for me. I don't know what I am going to do." Kenny is a very aggressive and demanding child who refuses to be involved with anyone. He wanders about the playroom, kicking over anything that he can, punching other children, and running about the room. When a teacher approaches him, he looks as if he could be manageable but quickly lashes out and behaves as if he felt threatened. He spits, kicks, and waves his arms about as if he were trying to get rid of a persecutory object. Kenny behaves as if he were always alone and, whether he is approached or given something to play with, he behaves as if he has been attacked. He hits out. Contact with adults and children evokes what appears to me as painful, threatening, and persecutory feelings which he needs to get rid of. Projection of his anger makes everyone his enemy. The children then do behave as if they were his enemy: they tease him, then try to hit him, and no doubt they confirm his feelings of persecution.

Kenny's mother is unable to be his container and has been unable to think about him since his birth. She tried to obtain day-care services for him when he was only a few months old but none of the services would "keep him". They all told her that he was too much for them and left her with her screaming, angry baby. Kenny experiences only pain and threats. He experiences a world that is hostile and about which he cannot think, nor be aware of. He splits off and projects these impulses that such a world, both internal and external, evokes, and that leave him feeling empty and devoid of love, nurturance, and support. His mother's serious difficulties left her unable to contain him and to think about his feelings—she could neither accept nor think about his projections (Bion, 1962a).

Kenny's early phantasies of a good-enough object capable of providing care, love, and nurturing were probably never adequately fulfilled. Instead, the predominant phantasy that he would have experienced was one of an external object that was rejecting, frightening, and unable to support his needs. The original paranoid phantasies of retaliation for anger would thus have been reinforced, for when Kenny was upset, uncomfortable, or angry for any reason—hunger, cold, or just the need to be held—he was screamed at, thrown into his bed, or hit! With such severe frustration and maltreatment, Kenny's phantasies of a retaliatory, hostile external world, retaliating because of his own hostile impulses towards this ungiving world, would have been continually supported. Reality was terrible for Kenny—and thinking as a way of testing reality could not occur, because there could be no modification of his hostile phantasies. Kenny always expected the world to be angry with him, and it always was.

On one occasion, Kenny was sitting beside his mother fingering play-dough. He took the rolling pin and began to press out the play-dough with the rolling pin. His mother sat beside him quietly. A teacher sat close to him, in fact touching him, and suggested that Kenny make some shapes. Kenny did not talk to the teacher but began to hit the play-dough with the rolling pin and then, suddenly, began to strike his mother with the rolling pin. She looked startled and angry and then said, "Well that's what he always does. You can't have any quiet times with him." I didn't see the situation in this way—that "you can't have any quiet times with him"; rather, I saw the intrusion of the teacher as an event that aroused envy in Kenny. Her closeness and suggestion to him made him aware of his inadequate container. The projection of hate and fear into his mother and her inability to contain these impulses made him phantasize that she kept goodness for herself, and so his attack on her at that moment was in order to destroy the phantasized goodness in an effort to reduce his envy. In this case Kenny's direct attack on his mother was his way of pointing out that nothing is good and that his anger leads to continuing persecution. The teacher represented a potential successful container, which he could not tolerate because of the envy that she aroused.

Kenny suffers from difficulties in learning as well as from several other serious problems, but it is the learning problem (which I think arose from an inadequate container) that prevents him from gaining any further understanding of his internal and external world. Kenny experiences his internal and external world as terrifying, and he does his best to get rid of everything by doing very little, by talking very little, and by not learning. To learn would mean to find out that his worlds are indeed as terrifying as he expects them to be—essentially that he can never trust others or have confidence in himself. He has become an independent, lonely isolate, afraid that everything and everyone will attack him. In phantasy, as if to try to demolish these attackers, he has fragmented them in an effort to make them less dangerous, but all he has succeeded in doing is making his attackers more numerous. Thus, he is continually "surrounded by bizarre objects" (Bion, 1967, p. 47).

In contrast to the above is an example of how a normal, emotionally healthy child, who has introjected a good container, approaches learning. I know a two-year-old who often turned to his mother when asked a question by others or sometimes by his mother and said, "You tell me". Billy trusts his container to provide him with the answer, and thus to provide him with an ego that is unconsciously internalizing an object that can think. His mother is thoughtful; she does not turn him away; she listens to him and then tries to give him as good an answer as she can. Sometimes he is not satisfied and asks for more information, and gradually he is adding his own thoughts to those provided by his mother. Billy is becoming aware of what his mother says and thinks and what he wants and thinks. He is beginning to distinguish between phantasy and reality, between conscious and unconscious processes. This will gradually allow him to recognize what he is looking at or being shown and what he imagines in his own mind, what he is being told, what is expected of him, and what he wants to do for himself and by himself. He now has the ego capacity to cope with his omnipotence—that is, to accept and think about directions and instructions from others and not to fight this all the time. His thinking process derives from the internalization of an object that has accepted his projections, thought about them in a careful way, and is then willing to return these projections, but only when the child is able to introject them without disturbing his feelings of trust in others and his confidence in himself. Because he internalizes such an object, Billy is able to learn. He can attend and try to understand, because that is just what his container was able to do for him.

Some children have not introjected an adequate container but have been able to introject a partially adequate or good-enough container. As Bion puts it, "The mother's capacity for reverie is the receptor organ for the infant's harvest of self-sensation gained by its conscious" (Bion, 1988c, p. 183). These people have not gained a thoughtful enough container that has been willing to hold sufficient anxiety continuously enough to alter it into feelings and ideas that the baby may re-introject. As Spillius (1988) notes,

> If all goes reasonably well, the infant re-introjects not only the particular bad thing transformed into something tolerable, but eventually he introjects the function itself, and thus has the embryonic means within his own mind for tolerating frustration and for thinking. [p. 155]

If the container is only partially adequate, the individual is unable to tolerate excessive "bad" feelings and thoughts. These can be aroused in such children (and adults) either by more complex thinking problems or by frustrations from other sources and can lead to certain kinds of learning problems.

For example, it is interesting that some children are able to remember information that they are given on a particular day and even seem to make use of it, only to forget it the following day, or, at best, to remember it and not know how to use it. I think that such children have difficulty accepting information from others; it is as if the child has been unable to introject a continuously thoughtful object. The original introjection of the "at times" thoughtful container is an introjection of a leaky container, one that satisfies only if the information is worked on directly by the child. But if the information is "handed" to the child, then the child will seem to understand, only to lose it the next day. Only by working on the information directly and alone—that is, by incorporating it as if it were his own and not given by the teacher (the phantasized leaky container)—does the child learn. Such children are usually lonely children, needing to work things out on their own, rather than being with others. The inconsistency and "leakiness" of their original container makes them experience excess envy and fear when they accept or take things from others. However, they were "given enough" care and nurturing so as to permit them to learn, but they seem to need to learn in situations that do not arouse their envy.

Some children demonstrate effective thinking skills in the first few grades of school, but, as the requirements for thought and abstraction become more demanding, these children begin to experience considerable difficulty. When the thoughts and ideas that are presented become difficult or complex, then what I have so often noticed is that a sense of confusion comes over the child and the child just seems to stop thinking. Teachers have mentioned that when some children are beginning to solve mathematical problems at a grade-three (eight-year-old) level and are having some difficulty, they begin to experience tension, discomfort, and anxiety. They tell their teachers that they feel upset or even that they feel ill and say, "I can't do that problem; I don't understand it; I think I feel ill and maybe I should go home."

Most of these children are bright children; sometimes they need further help in the "basics", but most often they need supportive understanding and, above all, an effective container that will be able to hold this anxiety while the child copes with the mechanics of the problem. Sometimes you can see this happening as a teacher sits down beside the child and talks quietly about how some problems are difficult and make us feel stupid, and then adds, "but what I'll do is slowly go over the problem with you as if you were reading it to yourself, only I'll read it to you". The teacher then becomes the absent mother container and willingly provides a reverie for the child which helps the child maintain interest in the material and a container for the difficult, if not intolerable, anxiety as well. The child sits quietly, listens, and then in the midst of the reading often says, "Oh yes, I think I know what you mean." These were children who previously knew what the teacher meant and had no problem with thinking and information accessing and processing. However, now, when the problems become more complex, their inability to contain the anxiety that is felt by their not being able to solve the problem as quickly and easily as they were wont to prevents them from continuing with the learning process. By stopping the learning process and the thinking, no doubt the ego is attempting to save itself from any further development of anxiety. The thought processes stop, and a sense of confusion sets in. The sense of confusion blocks out further potential ego deterioration, and the confusion is the result of not having introjected an adequate "container object" that would ordinarily be able to hold the anxiety and thereby allow the child to solve the problem. In the latter case, no confusion need result, because the child has the trust and confidence in this introjected object as being quite capable of handling difficult if not stressful learning situations.

An example of anxiety leading to confusion and cessation of learning due to poor containment by a teacher was presented by an adult who remembers when she was a child learning to play the piano. She was able to play "beautifully and skilfully" with one hand. When the teacher insisted that this seven-year-old girl play with both hands, the fear of failure led to an onslaught of anxiety, and its effects on her ego were too great for her to endure. She felt confused, upset, and very worried. She felt she could never learn to play the piano with two hands, and, because her internal "container" object was fragile, she could not endure this anxiety alone. Unfortunately, her teacher did not know how to become an auxiliary container and the girl "gave up the piano". Even though she "loved" playing the piano with one hand and could do this very well, she never returned to playing, nor did she learn to play any other musical instrument.

I watched a young child play with blocks. He built up the blocks with considerable ease and skill and then tried to build a bridge from one of his constructions to the next. As he tried to do this, he became more and more verbal, saying aloud, "How do you really do this? It really can't be done. I've put the two buildings too far apart. I need to do this. I have to do this now. I need bigger blocks. I need many more blocks. I want only a special colour. You don't have the right blocks." And with that, this six-year-old boy kicked over his structures and wandered away from the setting, to be alone.

I think that the child started with a simple construction and set a goal for himself, which was perhaps beyond the blocks he had (although the bridge could have been erected), but, more importantly, required that he experiment, that he allow his curiosity to "run freely", and that he endure the discomfort that he was experiencing. The child had to stop his building because

the thinking skills needed to construct his bridge became confused. He could not "see" what was needed; he began to become
illogical and could not tolerate this aspect of his thinking. He
could not "think" that if he allowed himself such thinking freedom he might come up with a solution. The confusion, and his
inability to contain it, the result of an inadequate, introjected
container, forced him to destroy his structure. Without the
structure present, he no longer had to think about it. He wandered off alone and when I looked at him again, he was reading
a very simple nursery rhyme book. I think the nursery book
allowed him to regain his sense of competence once again but,
unfortunately, until someone helps him cope with the anxiety
produced by complex thought processes, he will continue not to
learn.

An adult artist once told me that she was only able to do her
drawings while doing something else, such as talking on the
telephone or listening to a radio talk show. She felt that as long
as she did not have to think about the complexity of the drawings, she could continue doing them. She said, "When I'm talking on the phone, the task I have set for myself is no longer
complex. I'm just not thinking about it, and I can draw. I don't
do these complicated drawings when I'm not busy with something else that seems to take up most of my mind." I think that
the confusion that she experiences when she has to concentrate on her drawings is the result of an introjected container
that is inadequate and leaky. As long as she does not have to
recognize the difficulties involved, she can do her work. It is as
if she has to occupy her conscious mind while allowing her
unconscious mental processes to operate. Then she is able to
draw without the interference of anxiety and confusion.

In summary, the model I am proposing is that the maternal
capacity to contain the "bad things" that the infant experiences
and to hold these feelings long enough so that they are not as
anxiety-inducing and/or the ego is more capable of handling
the stress allows the infant to encounter more and more complexities of problem-solving without fearing that its ego will be
annihilated by anxiety. These "bad things" are projections of the
infant to the maternal containing person. These projections
actually set up the primary process of a communication relationship—that is, the dyadic basis of a learning relationship.

The projections are re-introjected as the baby can handle them or when they are stripped of some of their terrifying fearfulness. It is a maternal function to make these less terrifying for the baby, so that in the re-introjection of these projections the infant can tolerate the existing frustration later on and be able to tolerate frustration even when this maternal function is no longer available in reality. This function is now part of the toddler's ego, which, I think, allows the toddler to exercise skills of exploring, walking, talking, seeing, smelling, and thinking in order to learn about the world. Without this, the external world is much too frightening a place to endure; the feelings of persecution and terror cannot be projected, and the child must "close down" and not think. Bion (1988c) suggests that the

> failure to establish, between infant and mother, a relationship in which normal projective identification is possible precludes the development of an alpha function [that function which the mother performs as a container for the infant and which, through her process of reverie changes the feelings which makes the baby feel bad, and which he projects to this mother container into tolerable feelings which can be introjected] and therefore of a differentiation of elements into conscious and unconscious. . . .
> The infant personality by itself is unable to make use of the sense data, but has to evacuate these elements into the mother, relying on her to do whatever has to be done to convert them into a form suitable for employment as alpha-elements [thoughts and ideas that are available to the child to act upon] by the infant. [p. 183]

I am also proposing within this model of maternal containment that inadequate containment can result in three types of fixated development, reflected in three types of children who will experience different types of learning and thinking problems and styles.

The first type of fixated development occurs when the child is deprived of the container and its reverie function. "Reverie is that state of mind which is open to the reception of any 'object' from the loved object and is therefore capable of the reception of the infant's projective identifications whether they are felt to be good or bad" (Bion, 1962, p. 36). Then I think that the child will be psychologically bound to the paranoid–schizoid position.

Rejection will be the primary maternal attitude and will be experienced by the child as an unavailable container. This forces the child to handle its own intolerable feelings by denial, splitting, and projection, by assuming an omniscience (Bion, 1988a), and by being unable to enter into the learning process. As Klein (1921) points out,

> The important causes of injury to the impulse for knowledge and to the reality-sense, repudiation and denial of the sexual and primitive, set repression in operation by dissociation. [p. 21]

The sense of dissociation is the container–reverie process gone wrong, and the child cannot accept the communication within the learning process—i.e., cannot accept the projections of others in the way of teaching, because this only makes him less and less capable of tolerating the frustration and anxiety of not yet knowing. Dissociation results in the phantasy, "I know everything and consequently do not have to tolerate doubting or speaking or thinking because that brings out my difficulty in saying there is nothing to say because I know everything." Such an unavailable container is usually characterized by discouraging emotional dependency and encouraging early separation; discouraging interpersonal interaction and encouraging aloneness; punitiveness, promoting and reinforcing suspiciousness and resentment; inattentiveness to individual needs and impulses; and discouraging verbal exchanges but encouraging rigid and inflexible regard for existing rules and routines. The primary relationship to this unavailable container is authority–power–control by adult over child. O'Shaughnessy (1988) notes,

> Bion has two central contentions. To develop a normal mind with a sense of reality an infant must learn from experience, i.e., he must use his emotional experiences with the object to try to know them. This means to notice them, assess them, understand their nature, remember them i.e., to think. As well, the infant needs to be loved and known by his nurturing object. [p. 186]

The paranoid–schizoid child is deprived of the opportunity to learn from experience because he is not known by his nurturing object, his container. Projective identifications were not accepted, and the child had no way of handling terrifying or complex feelings and ideas by himself. His method of handling these impulses was to maintain the split in feelings and to deny the existence of terror. In this way of limiting his world and experiences, he maintained a fragile yet primitive ego. The introjected object is a non-nurturing, depriving object, a non-containing object, demanding non-alliance with others. Closeness always arouses a suspicion of danger and terror at being annihilated by a non-containing object that required independence and separation. Therefore, the reality of being with others involves a concern of being hurt and punished. This child cannot learn. He fears that information and knowledge will only bring on feelings of persecution, terror, and disintegration.

A second type of fixated development occurs when the child has a container that does not allow him to re-introject his feelings and impulses but insists on holding them for the child, implying or stating that he cannot "handle things" by himself. Such a child is psychologically bound within the depressive position. This child is fearful of expressing aggression, feels inferior, guilty, and remorseful, yet is never adequately capable of overcoming or resolving these feelings. The excessive dependency is encouraged by the overly caring and protective container by being excessively intrusive into all the child's feelings and impulses, by being overly attentive and by discouraging independent action and thought, thereby restricting and limiting feelings and attitudes. Furthermore, this container expects trouble and failure from the child, controlling the child through induced guilt and expectations of rule and routine conformity. The child is excessively nurtured and cared for and is not permitted feelings of aggression or anger, being made to feel not only that these feelings are dangerous "because you won't be able to survive them", but also that they "will hurt me terribly". As Klein (1921) points out:

> The impulse for knowledge and the reality-sense are threatened with another imminent danger, not a withdrawal but an imposition, a forcing upon them of ready-made ideas, which are dealt out in such a fashion that the child's knowledge of reality dares not rebel and never even attempts to draw inferences or conclusions, whereby it is permanently and prejudicially affected. [p. 22]

The depressive child is overly cared for by the nurturing object, which demands continued projective identification without returning it to the child in a less frightening state. This object maintains itself as the thinking object, the assessing object for the child, and requires an almost symbiotic relationship if the state of comfort is to be maintained for the child. The introjected object is a nurturing object that demands closeness to an outside person, who will care for and protect the child. In this way the internal object of the child is maintained, and then the child can learn. Without such an object, the child cannot learn; he is fearful that separation from the nurturing object will not only result in his destruction, but also will be very painful to the object itself. Guilt, mania, and depression may result, because the child fears he has hurt and done damage to the nurturing object by trying to become free of it, as is often the case when the mother dies.

A third type of fixated development occurs when the child is subjected to an inconsistent container, where the container is sometimes adequate, sometimes not present, and at other times overly intrusive and caring. This child seems to me to be the child who moves back and forth from the paranoid–schizoid to the depressive position, becoming at times poorly integrated, persecuted, and dissociated, and at other times functioning adequately and being integrated. Some characteristics of such a container are: erratic attempts to be adequate, yet usually encouraging infantile behaviour in the child as a way of "taking over" for the child; self-concerned, with little emotional energy to be adequately involved with the child continuously; highly suggestible to authoritative-like statements, as if looking for the "right way to do things"; erratic attempts to control the child and its impulses and feelings, but providing poor communication in the way of directions and routines to do so; expecting "magical help" from the other members of the family, or else that the child "will wake up perfectly fine tomorrow"; erratic expressiveness of feelings, followed by a withdrawn passivity.

The child, in response to such a container, has difficulty evaluating situations for himself, and his behaviour varies from active and impulsive to passive and withdrawn. The child tends to rely on others for direction and expression but does so in a demanding and aggressive way, clinging, dissatisfied, and

TABLE 10.2

Paranoid–schizoid child	Depressive child	Normal child
New information		
This is eagerly sought but quickly felt as dangerous, for fear that it will show him up as inadequate. The child looks for more and more information, as if to prove he has taken in the previous information. Information is not integrated, and the child tries to hide what he does not know or denies any lack of information and understanding.	The child quietly and at times smilingly accepts new information, but he does not integrate the fragments presented to him unless shown how to by the teacher. The child looks as if he knows because he looks pleased, but information is poorly integrated and remains as isolated bits, which may be appropriately given back to the teacher when asked.	This child regards questions and new information as challenging, attempts to work at them, and can work independently or with the teacher and small groups of children. The child is able to use new information and materials and creates various strategies to approach learning. If the child experiences difficulties, he is able to endure the anxiety and knows how to gain assistance to reduce the discomfort. He gains a sense of pleasure at success.
Motivation		
The child shows a high drive to master, but usually an insufficient amount of information is taken in to understand concepts, and this forces the child to concreteness in thinking—i.e. abstraction is very difficult for him.	There is a high drive to do things for the teacher, to get the "learning" finished. The child will learn for the teacher, but integration is very difficult as this will make the child independent of the teacher. There is little "push" by the child, as this is felt as expressing too much and the teacher might get angry.	This is usually good, with the child trying to learn to maintain a feeling of competence and trust in himself. His thinking is fluid in that he is open to new ideas and ready to try out things alone or with others.

Mastery

The child attempts to gain "quick mastery", even if he has to leave out details of the new information. The child seems to retain little of the information, and while practice and repetition help to retain the knowledge, he finds it difficult to repeat the same task.

The child easily feels overwhelmed by the task and/or the information, seeks much reassurance from the teacher, and seems to find it difficult to make use of the new knowledge.

The child is able to view relational aspects in his learning, and while it may be difficult to acquire this, he is able to continue working at the task and ask for assistance. He is pleased at being able to combine ideas and mastery and looks forward to further mastery.

Strategy for thinking

The child's strategies for action and thinking are usually independent of the teacher, and it is hard for him to accept information from another person. The child finds it difficult to scan concepts and looks for immediate solutions and rewards.

The child's strategy for action or thinking is based on what he thinks the teacher expects and in reality on what he recommends. He seeks out the teacher's direction, looking for cues from him, not from the material; scanning of information is usually inadequate.

The child's pattern for decision-making may be one of several choices. He may scan material—i.e. an idea about how to follow up a thought results in action, as if he were testing an hypothesis. He can follow directions and can ask for help when strategies are inadequate.

Object constancy

This child has difficulty in maintaining object constancy; he seems to be looking for something to "latch" onto; he seems to be always on the go, as if not pleased with his accomplishments.

This child clings to the teacher in an attempt almost to create a symbiotic tie with the teacher, as if the image of himself or herself were of a child who does not do things alone. This child does very little alone.

This child has a normal tie to the teacher, regarding the directions and information provided as a starting point; he tries to be independent yet can be dependent when he needs help. He can catalogue events in his mind and summarize these to enhance his learning skills.

TABLE 10.2 (continued)

Paranoid–schizoid child	Depressive child	Normal child
	Language	
Language is used by this child as a way of demonstrating the need to feel superior and control others; as long as this child is in charge of the dialogue, he functions well.	Language is felt to be a possible way of showing independence and separateness and is avoided unless the teacher provides the child with the sense that his effective language skills maintain closeness and dependency with the teacher.	Language skills are used to express ideas, to ask questions, and to help gain new information and understanding. Language develops to express abstractness, to represent experiences, and to understand differences and difficulties.
	Cognitive operations	
These are poor as the child tries to limit his environment so as to understand it totally and in that way control it. The child does not like to explore.	The child's cognitive operations are limited to gaining and maintaining dependency. Knowledge that makes him feel as if he is moving away from the teacher is avoided or redefined so as to maintain the dependency.	These are normally developed with the impulse to try to be clear and effective in his thinking.

making others feel drained. The child has difficulty attending to instructions, learning, and integrating ideas, and it may be difficult to orient him to learning except by intrusive focusing, as by intensive psychotherapy or psychoanalysis.

The child who has internalized an adequate container will be able to gain an understanding of reality and use his emotional experiences to learn. A mother described the following situation to me. Her 25-month-old boy arrived in his parents' bed very early in the morning. Ordinarily, he would ask for his bottle of juice. However, this morning he began to search his mother's body, trying to get underneath her night-gown. His mother asked him what he was looking for. He looked at her in a very quizzical way and said, "I don't know." His mother cuddled him closely and suggested that he go to sleep with her in the parents' bed and that perhaps he would now like to have his bottle of juice. He became more awake and said, "Now I know, I want to nurse." His mother reminded him that he does not nurse any longer, but the juice bottle was ready for him to suck. The child became very insistent at looking at her breasts and "minimally checking" to find out if there was any milk. At this point he said, "Find a baby nipple and put warm milk from the bottle in it for me please Mummy." His mother told him that she could not do that, but that they could have "close cuddles" with him and sleep in the same bed. The child calmed very quickly, took the bottle of juice and said, "I can sleep a little bit now."

Whatever awoke the child seemed to drive him to seek his mother, and whatever dangers were present for him in his phantasies and/or dreams forced him to seek an early feeling of safety derived from nursing from the breast. Since his mother is a caring, capable container and could accept her child's projective identifications, the child could explore not only his phantasies but also reality and find out that reality could indeed reduce the strength of whatever his phantasies were. Thus, he looked at her breasts; he "checked" them for milk; he could tell his mother how to fill them up again for him, and, because she contained his anxieties, he could accept an alternative way of being comforted. The child was able to use this emotional experience to further his knowledge of the differences between reality and phantasy and, in this way, to find reality satisfying and, with his mother, to prepare the foundation for future learning.

In the classroom, the paranoid–schizoid and the depressive child are distinguished from the normal child by such characteristics as those shown in Table 2.

CHAPTER ELEVEN

Homicide, suicide, and the superego

I was playing "trains" with a three-year-old boy when he suddenly stopped pushing the train along the track, picked up the train, and announced that the train was very sick and would "get sicker and sicker and go away". When I asked him why the train was getting sick, John said that the train was bad, and nobody could make it better. We talked about the train, and John simply insisted that the train should get sick because the train had not gone fast enough and had broken the tracks. As we talked, John pushed the other trains along the track, but without the enthusiasm he had exhibited before. I talked to John about his morning, asking him whether he had had breakfast before coming to the play centre, whether he had come to the centre with his Mummy or Daddy, and whether he felt okay. As we talked, John became more and more distant, and at one point said he did not want to play any more and that he just wanted to sit quietly beside me. I suggested that maybe he felt like the train, and that maybe he too should be sicker and sicker. John just looked at me. I continued talking, saying that sometimes we think we might be bad and we think we might have to hurt ourselves. John stood up, went to the other end of the room, looked at me, and then sat down. I waited for a few moments and then followed him and asked if I might sit down beside him. John did not answer, and I sat down. He made no motion to move away, and I sat close to him, not saying anything. John then said that he was bad, and he did not know how he could be good like his Mummy and Daddy wanted him to be.

In an interview with a young mother about her four-year-old son, she noted that when he was about two years old he told her that he wanted to go into the street and "get hit by a truck". Usually he would say this after he had been prevented from doing something that he wanted to do, such as play with the pots, or scribble on his books, or pour water into the sink.

An adult describing herself as a five-year-old child noted that whenever she felt upset and thought that maybe she had disappointed one or both of her parents, she would go onto the balcony and try to walk along the ledge of the balcony rail. She often fell off and hurt herself, yet she continued to do this for several years. She felt that she needed to please her parents, and yet they never seemed really happy with whatever she did. She thought that she could not do anything adequately and usually considered herself as the "dumb" one in the family. She only began to understand her "rail-walking" as her attempt to hurt herself when she was considerably older. Most of the time she had thought that doing this was her way of proving she could do something. Walking along the rail was not only difficult, but it was also dangerous, and the dangerous element was necessary for her. For example, she could walk along a straight line with her eyes closed, she could walk up and down the stairs without "holding on" to the banister, she "could even play games" with the older children, but none of these activities seemed to please her. She needed to walk on the ground-floor balcony railing even though no one watched her. When she fell off and hurt herself, her parents told her she was "stupid" for doing those "silly things". No one seemed to understand that it was not her attempts to do something heroic or startling, but rather, like the other children, she was attempting to kill herself.

A four-and-one-half-year-old boy whom I recently met was very interested in sticking sharp pointed instruments into electrical wall sockets. He would try to stick pencils, scissors, and forks into the electrical outlets, and even though his parents had carefully taped over all outlets and had placed various devices over others that were in use, he still managed to poke objects into the outlets. His parents said that he had been "jolted" once, but that "didn't stop him from doing it over again".

Children have attempted to kill themselves in various ways, and children as young as two years of age have crawled out onto window ledges, have drunk poisons hidden under sinks, have cut themselves with sharp knives or stabbed themselves with forks, have fallen down flights of stairs, and have done countless other acts which, I think, are designed not just to harm themselves but to kill themselves. Most of the parents of these children are careful and do not have poisonous or sharp instruments available for children's activities, and they lock windows. Children seem to find these things—even when we hide them—and the stronger the determination of a child to harm himself, then the stronger the probability that he will find something to do harm, or do something that will be of harm, to himself.

The four-year-old who wanted to go into the street and get hit by a truck was able to show by his play and by his talk that he was a "bad person". He said that he always wanted to have the "light on" at night, that he did not like the dark and he should not be afraid. He added that if he were "bigger", then he "wouldn't be afraid". He showed by his play that the doll/baby was not toilet-trained and that the parents were very upset by this. He said, "The baby should go to the toilet and not poo in his pants". I asked him if the baby felt very badly when he did this, and he said that he did, and he "shouldn't poo in his pants any more because his Mummy and Daddy won't want him". Then he suddenly said that he had a funny dream of "a radio in my room with a lady's voice that says 'No'". There were no other details that he could add to the dream.

It appeared to me that the child felt very angry towards his internal objects. The child had internalized phantasized objects that were strict, demanding, and punitive, and the aggression that was frightening to him was even more frightening when he felt that it was directed towards his parents. The angrier he felt with his parents, the more punitive did his internal objects become. In this way the child was as much afraid of the anger he experienced as the anger that he expected to experience from his parents. He imagined that his parents were always angry with him (he projected his aggression towards them), and that they could never trust him. As his capacity to form relationships with other children deteriorated, he was also aware that his parents expected him to be able to play with other children because he was "old enough", and this only added to his angry feelings towards them. As this occurred, he felt worse. In his phantasy, his internal objects began to attack him and to make him feel and think that there was nothing he could do that was good enough. In addition, he also thought that his parents were very angry with him and had given him enough evidence to make these feelings very real. However, he also had the feeling and idea that he was bad, and that he was supposed to be good and could not seem to be good, or at least he could not get rid of his feeling of being upset and "hurt inside". He could not make friends, he seemed to get into a "lot of trouble", he was not "grown-up", and he had the idea that all the frightening people "live in his head". He could no more trust himself to be good than he could trust others to love him. He felt that he must be unlovable, and the more difficulties he got into, the less he felt he could be loved. The child seemed to have no way of altering his phantasy. He projected his "bad" feelings and expected bad feelings back, and he responded to the expected anger with his own angry feelings. Even when there was no anger coming from the parents, he anticipated it; the parents went on to say that they try to be very loving and accepting, but "somehow we always manage to get angry with him".

The child's anger and the parents' anger created a circular reaction. At the base of this was the child's anger towards his harsh internal objects, which continually made him feel upset, tense, and unlovable. In trying to hurt himself (or perhaps to destroy himself by "going out into the street in front of a truck"), the child was trying to get rid of these harsh objects. His ego could not detach itself from these internal objects, which were at one point the nurturing, caring, and protective objects, because his ego was still dependent upon these objects. However, the dependence is for their loving qualities, which were no doubt present at an earlier time in his life. Now these internal objects had become harsh and stern and were demanding a kind of "good" behaviour that the child could never live up to. The conflict between needing these originally loving objects and getting rid of them now because they were so harsh becomes resolved by the destruction of the ego by suicide. In other words, if he got himself run over and killed, the child would not have to stop loving his parents (the phantasized internal parents now turned demanding), nor would he have to endure the pain he was experiencing as a result of the harsh internal objects. In this conflict resolution, the child, then, does not have to deny the importance of the goodness of the internal object or suffer from the pain of the demands of these objects.

An interesting example of hurting oneself was presented by a three-year-old, who tried to make a "thing for her Mummy". She was never satisfied with it. As she smashed the clay pot with her fist, she kept saying, "No good, now I have to make a better one". As she proceeded to make another one, I noticed that she had her foot under the leg of her chair. At first I thought that this was "accidental" and I tried to help her remove her foot from under the leg of the chair. She resisted, but I persisted and did get her foot out from under. A few moments later I saw that her foot was back under the leg, and she seemed to be sitting "very heavily" on that corner of the chair. I asked her if I could help take her foot out. She said, "No", and I said, "You want to hurt your foot". She did not reply but continued unsuccessfully to try to make her "thing". As she smashed yet another "thing", I could not help but see that she pumped down that corner of the chair and that she had tears in her eyes. I suggested that we sit on the pillow and talk about the hurt foot. She agreed after a few more attempts to make the "thing". When we sat down, we had the following dialogue:

I: You want to make a "perfect" thing, don't you?

SHE: Because my Mummy wants a nice "thing".

I: You think your Mummy won't really love you if you don't make a perfect thing?

SHE: My Mummy always loves me, but I get mad and I need to make something nice for her.

I: You want Mummy to love you, and you think she won't know how mad you are if you give her the bestest thing.

SHE [with a big smile]:   Yes, that's why.

I: Let's try to make flat pancakes and paint them just the right colour for Mummy.

The child seemed to like this, and we went back to the table. She made flat pancakes by hitting the clay with her flat hand. She seemed to enjoy this as long as I was there, but if I tried to leave she stopped the hitting and looked sad. When I encouraged her activity and remained beside her, she seemed all right. She decided that her Mummy liked flat pancakes and that she should paint them red.

Ordinarily this young child was quite unable to take anything she had made to her mother. She either said that the things she made were not good enough, or else when the teacher insisted on putting her "things" into a bag and getting it ready for her to take home, she just "forgot" to take the bag. Once when the teacher had taken the bag with her to the taxi and given it to her, the child dropped it out of the taxi window on her way home. Her mother had commented on the fact that she "never got anything that she made" and had wondered about this.

I think that the child's anger towards her mother was sufficiently strong so as to make any of her reparations—the "things" she made—disappointingly inadequate to provide her with relief from the pain she experienced. Since she did not have any relief, she imagined that her "things" were no good. In a sense they were not good or perfect enough to satisfy the harsh internal Mummy-object, and she was never able to feel part of, and united with, the loved object. She felt angry, alone, and unable to do anything about her feelings except to show us how she felt—that she could not make a good "thing", that she didn't want to take anything home to Mummy, and that she was hurting herself—as if she deserved the pain and punishment.

However, while this child, like the others I have described, have very strict and harsh internal parental objects, they seek to harm themselves rather than others because they have received sufficiently good-enough parenting so as to allow for the internalization of an internal good parent. These children are trying to preserve their good internal parents in the face of their own angry feelings. They experience their angry feelings as unacceptable, and, in projecting these feelings to parents, they experience their parents as disappointingly disapproving of them and their feelings. The projected anger exaggerates their sense of needing to do something good as well as their sense of being bad. It is this sense of being bad, and not phantasizing any further deterioration in their relationship to their parents, or in their experienced feelings of pain from their anger, that causes them to hurt themselves rather than others.

In normal development, the internal parental objects, which provide children with a sense of well-being or a sense of guilt, are the basis of the superego. The phantasy objects of the paranoid position give way to the phantasy objects of the depressive position as the ego is more capable and, therefore, uses less and less projection and, associated with this, fewer and fewer imagined persecutory threats. Furthermore, as children's parents come and go and are safe and unhurt when they return, the children gradually become aware of the feeling that their phantasies are not so powerful as to harm or destroy their parents when they get angry with them for leaving or frustrating them. As the children become aware of these feelings, the increasing strength of the ego allows them to begin to see the parents as the source of both pleasure and anger, goodness and punishment, satisfaction and frustration.

To aid this process, children attempt to weigh the balance in favour of pleasure, goodness, and satisfaction by trying to be good, if not perfect. This attempt at goodness and perfection is at the service of appeasing the internal parental objects, the superego. If the child's feelings are very angry feelings, then he needs to be extra good or extra perfect to keep these internal objects from being angry or upset with him. In other words, if the anger is strong, because of either real or phantasized frustrations, then the child has to do something extra good in order to calm a harsh superego from punishing or even threatening him. The child has set up a fantastic level of perfection which must be met if the superego is not to punish him for the feelings of anger towards the parents. It does not seem to matter why the child is angry; what matters is the strength of this anger and the sense of a phantasy of punishment from the phantasy internal parental objects, the superego, and from the real external parents.

If the real parents do not disapprove and act as a foil to the phantasy image, then gradually the child's phantasy will alter, but not without the child trying desperately at times to prove that his phantasy is correct. It is for this reason that so many parents say, "No matter how much I give her, no matter how much I tell him that I love him, no matter how nice I am to her, no matter how long a bed time I give to him, no matter how I made his very special foods, it's just never enough. The child just seems to know how to press my buttons. In spite of myself I get angry." The confirmation of the phantasy image seems so important for the child because it allows him to cope with a known and expected, rather than an unknown and unexpected, internal object. In a way, the dread of angry disapproving parents, coupled with the phantasy image, helps the child to curb the sadistic impulses (Klein, 1933):

> the real objects behind those imaginary, terrifying figures are the child's own parents, and that those dreadful shapes in some way or other reflect the features of its father and mother, however distorted and phantastic the resemblance may be. [p. 249]

> In this way each child develops parental images that are peculiar to itself; though in every case they will be of an unreal and terrifying character. [p. 251]

This distortion is a consequence of the child's own aggressive impulses projected to the parents and then feared as attacking him with just the same anger as he attacks them for real or imagined frustrations. As the child's frustrations make him more and more uncomfortable, the phantasy is then to destroy the object that does not provide enough to make the child feel comfortable. The ensuing anxiety is uncomfortable as well and forces the child to imagine further destructive impulses against this ungiving object.

However, to this desire to attack the object is coupled the continuing nurturing and care offered by this object. This care provides strength for the internal objects to become powerful and harsh internal controlling objects. Sadism towards parents lessens with accompanying attempts on the part of the child to be good and perfect in an effort to maintain the nurturing aspects of the internal objects. The superego is both protective/ nurturing and threatening/demanding. Strange as it may seem, this care acts as a needed defence for a weak ego to cope with an overly stern superego, for the effect of the superego will be to lessen the aggressive impulses and subsequent anxiety derived from them, which makes it very difficult for the ego to continue surviving.

The above is what we believe happens in normal development. However, if the child has not experienced continued and consistent good-enough care and nurturing during the first several months of life, then the anxiety aroused by the hostility towards the frustrating internal objects can only be endured by phantasizing the destruction of the objects. The superego in this case forces the child to try to destroy the object that brings about so much anxiety in itself. If the child can destroy the object that creates such anxiety, then the phantasy is that the anxiety will be greatly reduced. The aggressive impulses will be less because the frustrating internal object will be gone.

This superego is the child's projected hostile impulses and phantasies to the parents, which, in turn, become the child's internal objects. This makes the child feel as if he is dominated by stern, demanding, threatening parental imagos. To rid himself of such a phantasy the child attempts to destroy these objects to lessen the quality of threat arising from the superego. To do this, the child tries to destroy and kill the imagined external representation of the parents, which may turn out to be a real person. The child's "fear of real objects—its phobic anxiety—is based upon its fear of its unrealistic superego and of objects which are real in themselves, but which it views in a phantastic light under the influence of its superego" (Klein, 1933, p. 249).

This unrealistic superego, derived from the vicissitudes of the paranoid–schizoid position, is terrifying to the child and plays a more primitive role in the formation of his mental functioning. The primitive unconscious phantasy of dangerous and destructive internal objects introjected within the paranoid–schizoid position becomes a split-off aspect of the superego. While Klein notes that this primitive aspect is not actually the superego (Klein, 1933), my observations force me to see this aspect as a very deep unconscious phantasy. This internal object is split off from the regular superego but acts to force the superego to become the driving, demanding, harsh superego, preventing anxiety (Meltzer, 1978). Whenever the superego seems to "let go" or become kinder, this deep split-off aspect becomes more dominant and more anxiety-provoking to the child. As this occurs, the superego comes back with full force, to maintain some degree of protection for an already beleaguered ego. This ego is beleaguered because it had not been able to develop effectively an ideal in a situation where no idealized figures were available to allow the idealization of the superego as a protective barrier to excessive anxiety.

The ego in this situation bestows control to this superego, which protects the ego from annihilation by demanding excessive goodness and/or perfection as well as the destruction of any phantasized or real figures that threaten the control of the superego. This control would be threatened by the eruption of the split-off aspects of the real and phantasized terrifying and harsh introjected imago of the parents. The ego cannot gain strength for integration of feelings but continues within this paranoid–schizoid position—fearing and hating these imagos not only because of continual frustrations and deprivations, but also because of the phantasized revenge that would be meted out to the ego.

This deep split-off aspect of the superego remains unintegrated, always ready to erupt, and a dangerous persecutor. Either there is no real love object available, or the love object has been so depriving and hurtful because of its inconsistencies and lack of caring that the ego does not feel support for either reparation or integration, and guilt, which would ordinarily create some basis for the desire for reparation, is absent. The ego support comes from the harsh demanding superego and its split-off terrifying aspects. It is this latter aspect that controls and rules the destructive elements in such a child, and then extreme hostile behaviour such as killing would not be unknown.

This child's ego is overwhelmed by anxiety that can only be dealt with by getting rid of the internal and/or external pressure and tension. Often this tension becomes related to a real figure in the external world, and this figure is "marked for destruction". I think this is so because it threatens the maintenance of the splitting process, which, if not maintained, would once again threaten the fragility of the ego. The superego has become protective by becoming demanding, and the demands are now to get rid of the figure that threatens the rigidity of the split. This superego is a harsh conscience, and it functions this way at the service of the ego.

> In the early sadistic phase, which every individual normally passes through, the child protects himself against his fear of his violent objects, both introjected and external, by redoubling his attacks upon them in his imagination; his aim in thus getting rid of his objects is in part to silence the intolerable threats of his super-ego. A vicious circle is set up, the child's anxiety impels it to destroy its objects, this leads to an increase of its own anxiety, and this once again urges it on against its objects; this vicious circle constitutes the psychological mechanism which seems to be at the bottom of asocial and criminal tendencies in the individual. [Klein, 1934, p. 259]

Carla provides an example of such an intrapsychic situation. I first met Carla, a four-year-old, when she was brought to see me because of "previous emotional difficulties", which were described as being the result of "early emotional deprivation, neglect and punishment". Carla was described as demanding, aggressive, sneaky, manipulative, and very rivalrous towards her two-year-old sister. Her worker said, "You have to watch those two girls when they are together. Carla isn't to be trusted, and the younger one seems to be a trusting child."

I was struck by Carla's "easy behaviour". She came into my examining room with ease. She sat down on a chair and started to talk to me as if she had known me and played with me for months. She led the conversation and said: "You have lots of toys here; maybe I could have some of them for me." "So other kids come to play with you?" "Do you like my new dress?" "Do you want to play now?" I tried to answer her questions, but she just flitted on to another question, never waiting for an answer, and it soon became very apparent that she wanted to tell me what to do, when to do it, and how to do whatever she felt she wanted done. She was friendly and always looking for things

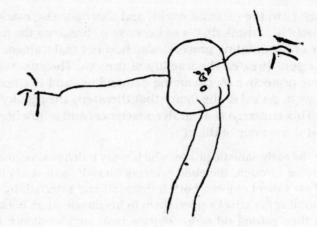

Figure 1.   Carla, 5 January 1986

she could stuff into her pockets and take home with her. When I suggested that she usually felt empty, Carla looked at me rather strangely and announced that she did not want me to say anything. She said, "I talk, you do what I say!"

Her play with dolls was superficial. She tried to dress and undress the dolls, but she usually did not complete the job. She tossed the dolls into the corner, saying, "That's enough with them. What else is there to do?" She wandered over to the chalk board, made some scratches with the chalk, said, "I don't like to draw", and threw the chalk on the floor, stamping on it with her foot. I suggested that she might want to use the pencil and paper I had to make a drawing of a person. She said, "No", but then took the paper and pencil and drew a "tadpole" person. She said that was the best she could do (Figure 1), and she wandered off looking for something to do. She rejected my suggestions. When I interpreted her behaviour to her she told me not to talk, and at this point she ordered me to sit on one of the chairs and "be quiet" while she occupied herself wandering about the room. The session ended when Carla said that she had been in the room long enough, and she left. I asked if we could meet again the next day, and she said, "okay".

When we met again, she was still interested in me and the room. This time she asked if we had some "special games" to play with. Her worker had told her that we would be "playing something special" today. I think the "special game" was to be "intelligence testing". The agency caring for Carla thought that they would be able to have her "adopted" if they knew that she was functioning within the "normal range of intelligence". While I had several concerns about adoption for Carla, I did agree to "test" her present cognitive level, because this provided me with a further opportunity to interact with her. The results of this test indicated that she was functioning within the lower range of the normal intelligence range, certainly a level that was consistent with her speech patterns as well as her well-developed "manipulative" skills.

During the testing Carla accepted the role of being examined and in fact told me that she knew "all the right answers" and that meant that she wasn't "afraid". When I asked her what she meant by not being "afraid", she said, "Of you, of course". I pursued this and asked why she was not afraid of me. Carla said, "I know the answers so you can't hurt me." I said that she thought that if she did not know the answers she might be hurt. Carla agreed, and I continued, "Who might hurt you if you don't know the answers?" Carla thought for a moment and said, "My worker—no—my mother". I asked her if she ever sees her mother. Carla said she did, but mostly in her sleep. Carla meant that she dreams about her mother and said that these dreams were of terrifying witch/mothers who hurt little girls unless they did everything that they were supposed to do. Carla could not elaborate on what little girls were supposed to do, but I suspected and asked if they were to be "pretty" and "neat". Carla said "Yes" to this. I had asked this because she seemed so careful in her play not to get "messy", and her dress looked so neat and pretty. I was not sure who had chosen her dress, and when I asked her she told me that she did. Carla seemed to maintain control internally by maintaining control externally of her appearance, her continued smile, and her "knowing everything". Carla would lie about anything in an effort to behave, both for herself and others, as if she knows "everything".

Carla talked about her sister, and while she said that it was nice to have a baby sister, she told me that she had to hurt her. When I asked her if she thought about hurting her sister, Carla said she could "put her in a fire and burn her", she "could put a cord around her neck and choke her", and then she "wouldn't be bothered by her any more". As Carla told me what she could do, she smiled and said that her "foster Mum doesn't know how bad my sister really is".

In my report to the agency I noted that while Carla can appear as sweet and kind, obedient and nice for short periods of time, her behaviour and attitude can quickly change to become sadistic, manipulative, controlling, and assaultive. I recommended that Carla could not be trusted and that unless the foster family was able to provide 24-hour observation for Carla, she should not be in the same house as her sister at this time. I recommended that Carla become involved in a residential treatment centre that was organized in small family-like groupings, each "family" having four or five children with various emotional and psychological problems and being cared for by three experienced and trained workers who became "parents" for the family.

While the recommendations were accepted, the child was not moved from the foster home. The workers decided that since it was nearly Christmas time, Carla should remain with the family and enjoy the holidays with them before she left for the treatment centre. I asked the foster mother if she would keep a short diary of Carla's activities during this time. The diary read as follows:

December 21

The social worker was out today. She came with gifts for the girls from their parents. As soon as she came in, Carla said, "I don't want to go to the dirty house". The social worker assured her that she was just visiting and that she wasn't taking her anywhere.

December 22

Carla's sister was telling me today how her old Dad used to sleep, how her old mother would make blood on her head. I always get some of the girls' other life after a visit from the social worker.

December 23

Carla is very moody today, and she is fighting with her sister all day. Carla keeps telling her sister that she is going to get new toys from Santa and that the sister can have all the old ones. We have to keep telling Carla's sister that Santa is coming to her also because she has been a good girl. The girls have started hollering at each other. They have never heard this hollering between me and my husband.

December 24

Both girls are fighting, and now my husband calls them the Martins and the McCoys. The more secure the younger one becomes, the less she will take from Carla, and this frustrates Carla. She used to be able to push her around, but now the younger one just won't be pushed any more.

December 25

You never saw so much under the tree. We brought the girls down; everything was fine until Carla realized that her sister got the same things she did. Then it started. By noon Carla had broken four of her own toys and tried to break her sister's buggy and monkey. When I scolded her, she said, "My sister always got the broken toys at the dirty house". I told her when she broke her toys she was hurting herself, because I would not give her her sister's toys. When Carla wasn't sulking, she was being destructive. We thought they would be so happy at Christmas, but Carla did her very best to make everyone miserable. At dinner Carla dumped her sister's dinner all down the front of her dress and all over the floor. When I asked her why she did it, all she would say is Santa wasn't nice. After dinner I caught Carla pulling off the bows on her sister's dress that we had given her for Christmas. The child started to cry, and she walked over and caught Carla by the hair and started pulling, and did she hang on when I tried breaking them up. The younger child was almost beyond herself and kept repeating, "Carla is a bad girl, I don't love her any more".

December 26

When I got the girls up I noticed blood on Carla's blanket and I asked her what happened. She said, "Nothing". Later

on she complained about a sore mouth, and when I looked I
could see she had been picking her teeth and making them
bleed. I called my husband over to show him. When he
questioned her, she said she did it because "Santa wasn't
nice to bring my sister a buggy. At the dirty house I always
get the new toys and clothes." Carla is so jealous she is
frustrated.

December 27

Today I had to spank Carla. Every time I went out of the
room I would hear a bang. When I asked what happened,
Carla would say that her sister hit the dryer, stove, or
fridge with her new buggy. I scolded the young child and
told her to be more careful and if she chipped the dryer I
would have to take her buggy away. The next time I went
out of the room, I came right back in the other door just in
time to see Carla give her sister's buggy a push right into
the front of my stove. When she saw me she looked straight
into my eyes and said, "Look what she did again, now you
will have to take the buggy away". I told her I saw her
push the buggy and was going to spank her for trying to get
her sister into trouble and for telling me lies.

December 28

Things are just about the same. The girls fight more, they
slap each other, and the hollering gets louder. I finally had
to put a stop to it. I told them nice girls and nice people
don't holler. Carla said, "My old Dad did".

December 29

My husband said that Carla and her sister were fighting all
the time, even outside, but he never expected the younger
one to stand up for herself and fight back. She was such a
timid little mouse when we got her, now she is like a prize
boxer. A friend of ours gave the girls a toboggan, and when
I asked the girls to thank him, Carla said, "no", because he
had given her sister a toboggan. Our friend said, "You
wouldn't want your poor sister not to have one. I love you
both." Carla looked at him and said, "I don't love you if you
love my sister".

December 30
Everything went fine today, girls both seem happy.

December 31
Girls played outside most of the day, no problems; the usual tiffs.

January 1
Girls are a little touchy today. My husband is home and both are fighting for attention. Carla keeps trying to put her sister in the background, but her sister is fighting more now.

January 2
A friend spent most of the day with us. She played with the girls and found how careful she had to be with any attention to the younger one. Carla is still fighting to be top attraction.

January 3
Carla is very moody this morning. I have noticed that her left pupil becomes dilated when I am about to have trouble with her. Troubles really broke out at noon hour. Carla broke her own buggy, and I had to take her monkey away from her; she was trying to pull its arms off. She wouldn't give me any reasons for her actions. Put them both up for a sleep, Carla wouldn't be good, had to bring her downstairs and put her on the chair. Her eye very noticeable. She wouldn't have anything to do with any of us. I tried to coax her by trying to get her to laugh. Then I tried to get her interested in a colouring book. When the younger sister started to cry, I came to see what happened. Carla had scribbled all over her sister's book and had broken most of the sister's crayons. When questioned, she said her sister wasn't going to school next year and it's not nice to show her how to colour.

January 4
We have a Quebec heater in the kitchen, and both girls have been warned not to touch it. They have never gone

*near it. I was in the front room cleaning when I heard Carla
say to her sister, "Go touch it", then in a louder voice,
"Touch it". When I came out she was trying to get her sister
to touch the stove. I said, "What's going on Carla?" Carla
said that her sister "was going to touch the stove, Mummy".
I went over to the sink, got a little water, and dropped it on
the stove. When it spit and bubbled, I told them it would do
the same to their hands if they touched it. So then the
younger one told me that Carla wanted her to touch it.
Carla slapped her, saying, "You bad girl". I grabbed for the
younger child, afraid she would fall against the stove, with
my arm and got burnt. I got them dressed and put them out
with their shovels and toboggans. I heard the younger one
screaming, and when I looked out Carla was on her
toboggan riding down the hill right for her sister who was
on the way up the hill. By this time my husband was half-
way up the hill to the rescue. He brought them both in. I
made Carla sit on a chair to think over the error of her
ways until lunch was ready. After lunch I put them up for
their afternoon sleep. When I went up, Carla had dirtied her
bed and all the blankets.*

At the end of February, I asked to see Carla again. Her
foster mother said that she was unmanageable, that she was
ready to "burst". She was afraid that Carla was going to do
something terrible to her sister, and although Carla had been
placed on "tranquillizers" for the past month, the foster mother
had not seen any change in her behaviour, nor in her attempts
to harm or destroy her sister. Carla told me that what she would
do is stick the scissors into the floor with the sharp points up
and push her sister on them so she would get the scissors in her
belly and die. I think Carla would have attempted this, and
upon our recommendation she was admitted to the residential
treatment centre within two days. She arrived at the centre
looking very pretty; she was, as she said, "All dressed up", she
was smiling and she quickly became the centre of everyone's
attention. She looked so "cute", she behaved so "beautifully",
and she smiled so "sweetly", that the staff said they could not
believe that this was the "little monster everyone had been
waiting for".

Figure 2.   Carla, 23 November 1986

Carla remained with the centre in the same family treatment home for several years. Our paths crossed but once again, eleven months later, when we met and she asked me if I wanted her to draw a person again (Figure 2). The staff described her as having had a very difficult time for several months, when she tried to destroy everyone, by fighting them, screaming at them, trying to harm them with knives, forks, sticks, and so on. She wanted everything for herself, and when she received any gifts, she destroyed them and then went looking for other people's belongings to try to destroy them. Her staff said that she is now a more settled child—however, with many upsets. The difference is that now she tells her staff how angry she is and how she hates everything and everyone. Carla drew the picture in Figure 3 about one year after I last saw her.

Figure 3.   Carla, 16 December 1987

I think that Carla is a child who experienced the introjection of a terrifying and destructive part-object, which then became split off. The introjective image of the original object, the breast, was phantasized as punitive and extremely frightening. From the description I was able to obtain, the parents were, in fact, physically abusive and extremely frightening people. The objects they gave rise to were equally terrifying as objects that were taken in, in no doubt an envied manner, and the consequence was the phantasy of an internal attacking persecuting object.

The ego, in an attempt to rid itself of the envied object, attempts to empty it, to destroy it, and to fill it with badness so that it no longer is a valued object. However, in the case of children who have been abused, the envied object is never destroyed. Attempts to destroy the envied object, both in phantasy and in reality, result in severe and unfortunately continual abuse, some of which is in phantasy, which, I think, is even more severe in its destructive character. Thus, the object never loses its character of persecutory terrifyingness, and it becomes an internal part of the psychological functioning of the child.

> The very nourishment that has been taken in, so long as it is perceived as having been part of the breast, is in itself an object of envious attacks, which are turned upon the internal object as well. [Segal, 1973, p. 41]

The infant in such a situation will no doubt feel that it has introjected "badness", rather than the desired "goodness" of the breast, which, in the expected good relationship with the breast, should relieve the discomfort and anxiety. Since the discomfort is not relieved, the breast and its goodness continue to be desired, yet the experienced breast is one of anger, deprivation, and rejection, and is certainly not a "good breast". This real aspect, derived from the real relationship to the breast, is coupled with the phantasized aspect of persecution from the breast for having taken too much from it. In other words, the breast is phantasized as attacking the baby for envying the goodness that is phantasized as being contained in the breast, an envy that is experienced as an intense need to obtain goodness from the breast. And yet, because the infant is frustrated in its attempts, it experiences only pain—a badness that continues the sense of persecution and being damaged. As the breast is attacked in phantasy, projection of the experienced pain, hate, and anxiety occurs, and the breast becomes attacking in turn, in a revengeful way.

In most infants, the defence of splitting results in an ideal part and a persecutory part of the object, the ideal part acting as a protector from the attacks of the persecutory part. In the abused and deprived child, however, the idealized part cannot ever emerge—reality forces the object of the infant's phantasy to be all bad. In Carla's case, the idealized aspect of a split-off breast could not occur—the breast was always bad—and even if the infant tried to maintain an ideal aspect in phantasy, it would become attacking as well because this phantasized split-off part did not protect the infant from abuse by the real parents. It is because of the continued abuse that no idealization can occur. What does occur is an attempt on the part of the infant to become "nice", "charming", "quiet", "calm", "smiling", in order to lure the desired object not to become persecutory. "Mother should love me and care for me if I am sweet and smiling, she should not hit me or starve me." Then, if the mother approaches, the infant tries to grab what is perceptibly and phantastically available. In Carla's case, she would try to take what she could then, and mother would become furious at her "grabbing baby".

Later on, in the foster care situation, Carla was sweet and charming, and yet, as her foster mother pointed out, she could never be trusted not to attack her sister, who seemed to have become the hated yet desirable object—a projection of the original breast. The younger sister seemed to attract people; she was given presents, and she was liked. Carla felt that she deserved, needed, wanted, in fact, craved these things, and she would have killed her sister in an effort not to experience the anxiety her envy created within her. The idealized younger sister, as the idealized split-off breast, could not be maintained; she, too, became envied and attacked, with anticipated real and phantastic attacks being made upon Carla in return. Introjection of an ideal object was impossible. Carla was continually attacking, and the object was continually retaliating and frustrating and was never kind or sensitive. Her envy, hate, and persecutory feelings led Carla to become a child who could love no one but would try to take whatever she wanted, especially anything that was given to another, her sister in particular. In this way she developed a limitless supply of revengeful, attacking objects, all of which created anxiety for her. Carla had to attack or be destroyed.

These internal terrifying objects directed and ruled Carla's ego and superego. These split-off parts must be maintained deep within the recesses of the unconscious; this job is shared by the ego and superego. The ego perceives everything as persecutory and, therefore, as objects that must be controlled and robbed of their goodness. The superego becomes an ally in this endeavour by reinforcing this sense of ego persecution, thereby keeping the split-off terrifying imagos deep within the unconscious. The superego provides the sense of comfort, ease, and nurturance whenever the ego attempts to get rid of an object. Survival of the ego is dependent upon a directing and rewarding superego. When the ego becomes less vigilant of its persecutors, the superego becomes demanding and threatening. Carla could not become good in the ordinary sense of the word; she had to see her world as always hateful and destructive, for if she did not, then the split-off part would attack her and destroy her. She had to hate and destroy, or be hated and destroyed. Her strict superego maintained a vigilant ego, and Carla survived; she was not overwhelmed by anxiety. She could not trust anyone, including herself, and she did not have the capacity to form relationships and thereby gain reassurance and pleasure. Carla had to maintain a lonely, distrustful existence.

CHAPTER TWELVE

Case of John:
an attachment failure

J ohn, aged six years two months, is living with his parents. For a period of just over one year, he has been involved with two treatment centres for emotionally disturbed children. A re-evaluation of his progress at the end of that year notes that he has "not been able to make use of a therapeutic day-treatment environment". He is a highly defended, anxious, depressed child, with an extremely low self-esteem. Self-destructive and aggressive behaviour is becoming worse, and his behaviour continues to deteriorate, despite continued environmental improvements, including admission to the day-care programme and to a "special needs" school.

John's early history included foetal distress, "failed heart", and induced labour, followed by forceps delivery. He also became moderately jaundiced at five days of age but this condition was remedied without complication.

John's early development was described as "low" average; he sat alone at 8 months, stood at 12 months, and walked unaided at about 18 months; he spoke understandably at 20 months and in phrases at about 30 months. John was irregularly constipated from five weeks to 42 months of age. Toilet-

179

training was started at 18 months, with bladder and bowel control being established at 42 months.

Generally, John shows age-appropriate gross and fine motor skills; a language assessment completed a few months before he was six years old did not reveal a receptive or expressive language problem, and an intelligence test indicated that he was functioning within the "low normal range". However, John does have difficulties in attending to and being involved in solving cognitive tasks; contributing to this is his difficulty with "taking in" directions. Even before the task is presented to him, John has often either run away or become interested in something else, and it is then very difficult to regain his attention. It does not seem to help to speak to him in a harsh manner or to tell him to do a certain task. John responds by looking blank and becoming withdrawn. His workers report he then gives them the feeling that "he's just not there, and you can't reach him".

John behaves very poorly in the classroom, and his teacher cannot seem to control his hostile, destructive behaviour. Even in a small group of children his behaviour is very difficult to manage (although he functions much better in a one-to-one situation and can be friendly as well as co-operative). With peers, John is provocative, aggressive, and assaultive, and he accepts no responsibility for his actions, denying that he hits anyone and blaming other children for difficulties or destructive acts (he lies even when caught outright). Generally, with other children John is also "sneaky, bullying, teasing, boasting, blaming;" he disrupts any activity, usually grabbing other children's toys, throwing them around the room, or holding them behind his back. He also becomes very angry if another child looks at him, or if he even thinks someone is looking at him. (The parents report that if he goes to a restaurant with them and if he has eye contact with another child, he goes "berserk", behaving as if he had been attacked, and the only thing he can then do is throw things and himself about.) Consequently, John is not a "liked child". Other children do not want John to be present and usually say that they are afraid of him. This situation creates some very negative self-perceptions in John. He says that he is "bad" and that is why he is at the day-treatment centre, that he cannot help being bad, and that he has "to be bad all the time now". He is indeed also "bad" at home with his parents, who report that he requires "very firm limitations and consistent expectations" in order to manage him. John also bites his fingers, often to the point where they are bleeding, and he continues to do so even though his mother has tried to discourage this by putting "peppery stuff" on his fingers.

One morning, while John was still enrolled in the centre, he came into the classroom and "everything seemed to go wrong right away". He kicked at other children, he tried to tear up their drawings, he laughed in a loud, staccato fashion, he swore at some of the children, he told the teacher that it was her "fault" that he was bad and that he was just going to be "bad all the time". He further antagonized the children, trying to push a toy frog into their faces and repeatedly doing this, even when the teacher "pulled him away"; John just went back to sticking the frog into the children's faces. Finally, the teacher sat him at a table, and, since she knew that he liked to draw, she presented him with a few crayons and some paper and asked him to draw.

John immediately took the crayons and paper and created a drawing, which he worked on for about 40 minutes (Figure 4).

As he finished his drawing, "snack time" was announced, and John became "bizarre"; he started saying, "Yes, I saw your father's here. He's really fat, really ugly. My father told me to kick you in the weenie." He then attempted to kick the children in the genital area.

John suddenly sat down alone, at a different table than the one he had been drawing at, had some juice, and, just as suddenly, got up and became assaultive again. He was brought into another room to be alone with an adult, and he became quieter. He stood in the room, looking around, holding blocks in both hands, but not making any effort to do anything or to move. He remained motionless for about ten minutes, until it was time for him to go home.

In his first drawing, John made a yellow rectangle with some black lines and a pink area. Over the rectangle, he suspended a navy-blue hammer-like object. In the second drawing, the hammer is still there, but the yellow rectangle has more black lines, and there are two defined orange-pink areas with the rectangle outlined in light orange. In the third drawing, the hammer is

Figure 4

still suspended above the rectangle, but the rectangle is blacker with dark black outlines, two defined orange spots, along with a long black line, coming from the end of the rectangle. In the fourth drawing, the rectangle is definitely black, with two pink spots, two black lines, one at either end, coming from both ends of the rectangle. In the fifth, sixth, and seventh drawings the rectangle becomes blacker and has more lines (now dark blue) coming from it—obviously "bars". In the eighth drawing the hammer is no longer drawn. In the ninth drawing, the black shape is larger and three-dimensional and the lines or bars are now red and have a top bar.

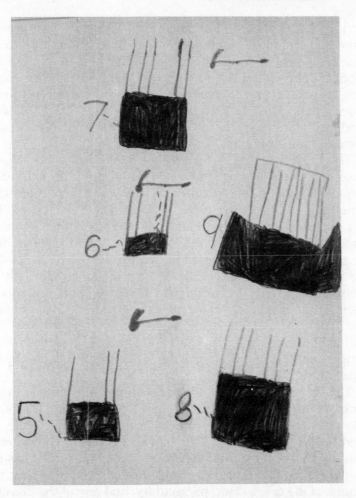

John's drawings can be interpreted as his representation of how he thinks his "jail" developed. In his first drawing, I think John portrayed his own body filled with goodness, good objects (represented by the yellowish-orange colour), but also containing the black bad bits. It is as if he is trying to keep the good internal objects safe, but, as represented by the pictorial progression, these objects are rapidly turning bad and the threatening, suspended hammer keeps on making them and him bad. The hammer is his representation of the forces working outside himself, which threaten him and make him "turn bad". Thus it is as if his external and his internal world are threatened by forces that do not know how to satisfy him and/or make him feel more comfortable, thereby enabling him to reduce his sense of frustration or allowing him to express his feelings. John would have no choice, then, but to view everything as painful and to making him feel that he is continually under attack. The jail, then, becomes his "safe" place, his self-developed container, keeping out the external forces that threaten to destroy him.

The drawings that John created demonstrate his experiences of a painful inner and outer world, and the phantasies that he developed to explain or fit this world were such that something bad is always going to happen to him. Indeed, his very early life had been traumatic, and the suspended hammer, representing this trauma, remained as a threat until he had been made totally bad and all locked up. His early discomfort and pain, coupled with continued discomfort, surely built up the phantasy that the world was an angry and destructive place. These very early experiences are related to the breast, which John phantasized as ungiving and persecutory. The few satisfactions and comforts he did receive from the breast were not sufficient to overcome the threat of annihilation by his persecutors.

The first few months of life are occupied in coping with the paranoid anxieties—that is, the infant goes through the paranoid position in which the primary concerns are anxieties related to the "bad breast". This badness is felt to characterize both internal and external life. When the infant undergoes the kind of discomfort that John went through, then the first few months of life are, in fact, persecutory, and any of the possible good that the infant receives or could receive from the breast quickly turns bad. Thus, the child's earliest experiences of painful external and internal stimuli provide a basis for phantasies about hostile external and internal objects, and they contribute largely to the building up of such phantasies (Klein, 1936, p. 292).

John's drawings, then, seem to represent his very early life, when the potential for goodness was present, but the discomfort and pain was not relieved by a sustaining, nurturing breast. Rather, he seems to have been maintained in a state of pain until at least three-and-a-half years of age when the constipation seems to have been relieved. A possible good relation with his mother as a helpful person never seemed to happen. Instead, the frustrating mother became the frustrating world. It would seem that his mother was unable to help her infant overcome these early paranoid phantasies.

These paranoid anxieties influenced and coloured John's actual experiences, so that gradually he became harder and harder to deal with, and even after a year of day-care treatment he was considered as a child who "has not been able to make use of a therapeutic day-treatment environment". John's drawings tell us that John could only perceive the outside world as threatening. His phantasy is that he has become a very bad, destructive, and sadistic child who must be in "jail"—the name he gave his last drawing (number nine). The jail might keep his sadistic phantasies in check, because he was concerned about hurting someone; it might then also stop someone from being revengeful towards him for his sadism.

The feelings of destruction did not abate in John, as they might in another child whose early experiences were not so difficult and painful. Such a child would then be able to phantasize the breast as providing more good than bad, thereby helping him/her to overcome the internal destructive rage. John was not able to introject a loved object within himself and could not find a way to love the mother, because he could never phantasize her as anything but a part-object—a bad part-object that had been unable to give any goodness. Splitting was maintained by John as a primary defence at the service of keeping some ego coherence. In other words, if he remained suspicious and defensive of everything and everyone, then there was less opportunity for him to be destroyed by the bad pain-giving breast mother. To feel something as good was dangerous, because if he "let it in", it would turn bad and revengeful, as everything had always become for John. Thus he put himself in jail—or perhaps felt as if he was in jail, but in jail to protect himself and perhaps others from his rage. Jail is a place for murderers and robbers, and perhaps John felt that he was too dangerous to be free.

For John, no good object could exist, although there once was a good-enough part-object to provide him with some small sense of ego coherence, where the ego does not fall to bits. If

John began to feel that some part of his objects might be good, then this would invite a fear of the "bad-turning" process. Splitting, then, in this sense helps to avoid the painful distress of seeing goodness destroyed (along with fragmentation of the ego), with the resulting sense of annihilation. There is no goodness, so there is no distress. This also includes a lack of hope in the capacity to acquire and keep the good object. John has given up.

The conflict of wanting to express destructive impulses towards mother and yet wanting to save mother and perhaps others from the rage would suggest a splitting of feelings. The original splitting of the breast into good and bad and finding all becomes bad with no good is repeated in the final theme of his drawing—boy is being encased, yet behaviourally he is sadistic. On the one hand, he tries to stop himself, yet on the other hand he tries to destroy. The splitting is suggested when John shows that he tries to get some support, even if it is from a jail. When he is not with others, John can be maintained, is certainly less destructive, and can even be co-operative.

If the jail had been able to provide John with a good-enough feeling of support and care, then perhaps he would have been able to integrate the split of the object and repair the phantasized damage he had done to the breast. But a jail is certainly a non-nurturing place; it is a lonely and isolated place, providing nothing except safety from destroying others and from being destroyed by them, and so it cannot help John. Splitting remains and forces John further and further away from reality. The phantasy of sadism and of being killed predominate, with little being able to be done to ameliorate these feelings and impulses. As Klein (1935) points out, jail becomes "a safeguard against one's own hate and against the hated and terrifying objects" (p. 288). There is no decrease in his frightening phantasies, and John cannot make any move to viewing reality as beneficial, as there is nothing that has not turned "bad" for him, both internally and externally. I think he demonstrates this very clearly in his drawings.

Perhaps the jail can also be reminiscent of the child who says, "I'm too bad, I belong in jail." Here the child seems to mean that he is so guilty for bad phantasies or bad acts that they deserve to go to jail. John could have meant this because at times he was described as "sad and even withdrawn". However, he had such difficulty coping with the anxieties aroused by sadness due to the feeling of having an insufficient supply of good internal objects that might allow him to control his sadism, that he quickly regressed to the paranoid persecutory phantasies of being attacked, hurt, and abandoned.

John could not really allow himself to experience the feelings of love, guilt, or anger. He was not able to establish an effective, loving relationship with his mother. He always perceived her as dangerous. His continual misbehaviour at home suggests that he was never able to make any kind of adequate reparation that would alleviate the feeling of discomfort that he was experiencing. In other words, whatever he did always created some kind of pain for him. It looks as if John has given up trying "to make reparations". He has become an, angry, sadistic child who sees himself in jail to protect himself from others. "Jail is where you belong" is John's feeling. His behaviour shows his workers that he cannot be helped by a therapeutic day-care centre alone—he requires individual play psychotherapy in order to help him recognize external reality as well as the interplay between phantasy and reality.

CHAPTER THIRTEEN

Tics and masturbation: symptoms associated with Oedipal and aggressive concerns

M atthew is 24 months old, and he has been described by his parents as a very pleasant, easy-going young boy who has not presented any unusual problems—or, at least, he has not presented any problems with which his parents could not or did not cope.

However, his father had a hernia operation, and Matthew, as expected by his parents, was quite upset. He did visit his father in the hospital, he talked about his father's return home, and he said that they would be "happy together" soon. Upon his father's return, an old back injury, along with the recent operation, prevented him from playing with Matthew as he had in the past. His father lay on the floor or on the bed and tried to involve his son in non-vigorous games that were primarily talking together, asking questions, and even using arms and hands, as long as this latter activity was not very active. While Matthew seemed to accept this phase of his father's recovery, he also asked to look at his father's "operation" and seemed very curious about it and its healing.

Unfortunately, before Matthew's father could once again become involved in their usual play, he had to leave for a conference. The night he left, Matthew said that he would "stand up to go to sleep", that he did not want to get into his bed; in fact, he demonstrated to his mother that he did not want to touch the bed at all. His mother said that this was all right, that she would lie on his bed, and they could talk together while he stood. Matthew said that he would not put his head on the pillow because there was a snake on it and it would hurt him. His mother responded to this by saying that she would throw the snake out, and she proceeded to shake the pillow outside the room, saying, "There, the snake is gone", and she replaced the pillow on the bed. Matthew then went into his bed, lay down on the pillow, and slept.

The next day his mother noticed that Matthew had a very definite eye-blink tic. He seemed all right upon first awakening, but shortly before breakfast his eye-blink tic developed and was present all day. His mother thought that he must be tired and distressed because of the day before when his father left and the bedtime difficulty. She expected that this tic would disappear the following day. However, it did not and was present just as full-blown as on the previous day. The tic was in only one eye, his right one, and appeared as a sudden, involuntary move-ment—present whether someone was with Matthew or was talk-ing to him or when he was alone playing.

I suggested that Matthew's mother try to make him "feel easier and safe", and by this I meant that she should try to do things with him that she had done when he was younger, say at 12 months of age. She accepted this recommendation and began to read a rhyme book that he had enjoyed at that age; this was a favourite book, and Matthew and his mother had often read it together. I suggested that she try to maintain the position of being his primary care-giver, that she take care of him, that she read this "younger" book to him whenever he seemed uncomfortable, that she not wait for him to finish the rhymes as he usually did, but that she read the whole rhyme to him—essentially, to take care of him totally, in order to reduce the feeling of pressure on him and to help him cope with these feelings that had now created the tic.

Matthew accepted this book very easily, enjoyed her "reads" to him, cuddled with her while she told him about "Mummy and Matthew when he was a little boy", smiled when she asked if she could feed him, and accepted some "feeds" from her—but moved to eat by himself, still smiling. Mother tried to create a setting in which Matthew did not have to demonstrate how capable he is ordinarily (Matthew is an exceptionally bright and verbally skilled child).

Matthew announced that he did not want "Mummy to sleep with Daddy", that "Mummy must sleep with Matthew". Mother replied to this by saying that when Daddy comes back Daddy has his bed and that Mummy has the same bed as Daddy, and that Matthew has his special bed which is now a safe bed. Matthew did not approve of this arrangement and asked if he could visit their bed at times. His mother agreed to this. Mother did add that Daddy would be back very soon, and that Mummy and Daddy would make things very safe for Matthew.

Matthew's eye-blink tic did not stop as dramatically as it had started, but it was not as prominent as it had been. When Matthew's father returned a few days later, the tic appeared whenever Matthew was anxious.

* * *

Helen, a bright, capable young ten-year-old, has been having difficulty at school right from the beginning. The particular problem that Helen has been having for about four years now was described to me as "seizures". Helen would suddenly be overtaken by a complete body shaking, during which time she did not respond to her name, nor to any calls made to her. This generalized body movement was followed by sweating, tiredness, and a desire to be quiet. Helen had many neurological examinations, and she had been involved in psychiatric care for over 15 months. While there was some disagreement as to the diagnosis, most diagnosticians felt that there was an "organic component involved"—implying that there was a possible central nervous system disease involved in Helen's problem. Over the four years that she exhibited this problem, there were no changes in the symptomatology. Her mother knew what kind of a day she had at school because sometimes she would come into her home sweating and bedraggled-looking, with her hair matted to her face.

Helen entered into play psychotherapy with me and talked about this problem very hesitantly. She usually said that "talk-

ing about it makes me feel worse". She also spoke in a remark-
ably high-pitched voice that was most often very difficult to
listen to. It seemed to pierce my ears and often "gave me a
headache"—or, at least, I often had a headache after Helen and
I had our sessions. I asked her about her voice, saying, "I
wondered why you speak in such a kind of whisper that sounds
like a whistle to me". Helen told me that she always speaks this
way, and that someone whom she had seen for treatment had
told her that she must always speak in a "deep-down voice",
but Helen noted that that hurt her throat, so she just did not
talk to that person. When she did, she said, "I usually start off
low and deep down, but I forget and talk this way". I told Helen
that she could talk however she wished, but I thought that she
talked in her squeaky voice because she wanted to make sure it
was never an "angry voice". Helen just went on playing a game
of "pick-up-sticks" as if she had not heard me.

After about seven months of play psychotherapy, Helen told
me that she did not "shake" in class any more, and, in fact, she
did not shake anywhere (she had never shaken with me). Her
schoolwork was coming along well and she enjoyed the classes,
but she added, "We're still going to see each other—we have
other things to do now". Helen was right. The relief from the
"seizure", or "shaking", as she called it, was only the beginning
of her treatment. While her voice was no longer squeaky, she
was able to talk about her feelings towards her father, who had
deserted the family, her mother, who had become engaged to
another man, and how she felt she was "nowhere" and "no one
wanted her". Helen talked about how her father seemed like
such a "strong man", and how he often teased her and her
mother. For example, in Helen's presence, he would telephone
her mother and tell her that Helen was missing, and that he did
not know where she was. When Helen tried to stop him from
doing this, he simply told her that if she wanted to visit him and
maintain his love, she would just have to put up with his
"jokes". Helen felt she had no choice but to "put up with him",
and while she really wanted to complain about him to her
mother, she felt helpless and powerless to do so. She saw herself as someone who could not take care of herself and, as she
told me, as a girl who "can't even talk properly, and who would
want to listen to such a funny voice like mine?" I think Helen

was able to project her anger with her funny squeaky voice and get others angry with her and trying to control her or threaten her by telling her she had to talk properly. In this way she did not "own" her angry feelings—she was just a "little girl" who could not take care of herself. She just made everyone angry with her and these others stopped her from becoming any more expressive of her anger.

I received an extraordinary telephone call from her mother after Helen and I had been working together for several months. Her mother stated, "Do you know why my daughter is shaking?" I answered that I thought I knew why, and before I was asked to explain, her mother said, "Helen is masturbating—she is not having seizures at all!" I told her that I knew this, that I did not think that she had been suffering from an "organic disease" but, rather, from several psychological problems. I asked her mother how she had found this out. She replied that she had pictures taken of Helen during one of her shaky episodes. She added that she had always suspected that there was nothing organically wrong, because, as she explained, "Helen never had a seizure when she wasn't at school. She never had a seizure at home and never when we were away together on a holiday." Her mother also tried to get Helen to stop this "shaking business" by offering her various rewards. At first Helen could stop, but very soon she resumed her shakes. Helen's anxiety seemed to be relieved at first because she stopped shaking, but she told me that she began to feel badly and very uncomfortable, and very soon the shaking business started again.

During our play psychotherapy sessions Helen did not have any "shakes". She mostly wanted to play "pick-up-sticks". She held the sticks up high and dropped them onto the floor with the exclamation usually of "then none of them will stop me". She often wanted to sit close to me, usually touching me, by having her arm against mine, or even her leg elevated upon my knees. At these times she would talk about her family, telling me the difficulties she was having with her father, how angry she was with her mother for not protecting her (although her mother in reality was trying to prevent her daughter's visits to her father, and the daughter was the one who insisted on the visits) and how she usually played alone at school. These aspects of her behaviour led me to conclude that the "shakes" was masturbation and that underlying the seizures were genital sadistic impulses directed towards the parents. Masturbation, which was the aim of the shaking, was directed at destroying the phantasized marital couple. Helen said that she did not think of anything when she did the shakes, but afterwards she thought of her parents and wondered how they were. I asked her if she thought that maybe when she did the shakes that they might get hurt. Helen responded: "Yes, but I don't know how that would happen. I just thought it might."

We tried to explore why she thought her parents might be hurt by her "shakes". Helen picked up the game of "pick-up sticks" and proceeded to jab each stick into the floor rug. She created a "deadly trap" of sticks pointing up, which would prevent anything from moving onto that part of the rug. I pointed this out to her, and she smiled and told me that that was what it was. We continued to talk about her trap, and at times Helen's voice became squeaky again. I pointed this out, telling her that she expected me to stop her from feeling angry now, that I was supposed to get angry with her voice and that would stop her from doing or feeling or thinking anything. Helen just kept adding to her "deadly trap". This play continued for several sessions.

Whenever we returned to the "deadly trap" game, Helen looked at me in a strange way. I responded to this by saying, "You're looking at me like a baby looks at its Mummy, and this Mummy won't stop you from feeling angry". Helen said, "That's foolish, you're not a Mummy, you're a Daddy". I agreed, but added, "Sometimes I can be either. You can imagine me to be a Mummy, or a Daddy, or even both together." Helen thought that was all right and said, "You can be both, but I won't hurt you—you're nice and kind". I answered "I try to be, but sometimes you might see me as not so kind, like when you want more sticks and I don't have any more. Or you want a white stick and I don't have one. Then you might be angry with me." The conversation continued.

HELEN: I don't think I would be angry with you ever.

ME: If I don't have what you want, you can feel angry with me, like I think you feel angry with your Mummy when she doesn't seem to know how to stop your father from teasing you.

HELEN: If I tell her and let her, she will help me.

ME: But you are afraid to let her because you think you might lose her. You think she's not strong enough to help you.

HELEN: Well, she wants to, and she does a lot, but she gets angry with me, just like my father.

ME: So you'd like to get rid of both of them sometimes.

HELEN: I guess so. Why don't we play the game?

ME: We can play the game if you wish, but all the sticks are making your deadly trap.

HELEN: So I'll just take them out.

ME: If you take them out, will you lose your protection? Do you think you might have to feel angry at times?

HELEN: I don't know. I'll try anyway. I don't think I'm afraid.

We continued with the game. I think that the externalization of "protection" by the "deadly trap" became Helen's way of explaining her shakes, her masturbation in class, which was essentially her aggressive motor discharge—both physical and sexual. The "deadly trap" would protect her, as her shakes had protected her. Protection was necessary for her phantasy of destroying the hated parents, with consequent fear of a revengeful attack from them. The masturbation was the equivalent expression of rage at them, and yet an experience of pleasure at the same time, as if she were hurting them and also robbing them of their pleasure, destroying them and then taking their pleasure for herself. She once again required some protection (the shakes and the trap) for these phantasized acts. Klein states an association between masturbation and tics: "the tic is not merely an equivalent of masturbation, but that masturbation phantasies are also bound up with it" (Klein, 1925, p. 124).

Gradually, as Helen was able to explore her phantasized masturbation attacks upon her parents, she was able to feel very angry in reality towards her father, she could refuse his visits and to visit him as well, and her relationship with her mother improved. She became interested in the things that her mother did. She liked the jewellery her mother wore, and she began to wear bracelets and a necklace as well as pins. She became interested in clothes and in having her mother design some clothes for her. Her play with the "pick-up sticks" gradually ended, and she wanted to talk rather than play other games.

* * *

Both Matthew and Helen seemed to be suffering from an inability to express and/or recognize the anger they felt towards their father and then towards their mother.

Matthew was very angry that his father was not at home—so angry that he could not look. He developed an eye-blink tic—an aggressive motor discharge, which acted to prevent him from seeing and looking at what he may have damaged. The eye tic became a depressive screen for his anger. He did want his father to be able to play with him as he used to, but an operation and back pain prevented him from doing so. Matthew no doubt phantasized that he had something to do with his father's pain, because, as his father said, he could not lift him and "rough-house" with him as he used to. He would have to lie on the floor and play that way with him. Then, when his father left the house, Matthew no doubt saw this as his fault. He had not only hurt his father but forced him to leave home. However, his father's separation was only partially mourned because now Matthew could sleep with his mother. Whatever pleasure he imagined they had together would now be his. To get rid of father and to sleep with his wife was both pleasurable and painful—painful because he had to get rid of father and suffer revenge, and pleasurable because he was the recipient of all mother's goodness. Retaliation anxiety took on the form of the Daddy/penis/snake set out to destroy Matthew. Since mother had protected him, she was his ally and, in phantasy, his lover. The following morning his full-blown eye tic represented Matthew's attempt "not to take in any more", not to recognize that he would have mother to himself, not to realize that he had sent father away, and not acknowledge that he was in any discomfort or anxiety. As long as the tic was present, Matthew could deny these feelings—he could make himself feel safe by blinking it all safe—by blinking to make it all go away.

It became very difficult for Matthew, because he was psychologically prepared to accept mother and father as a "couple"—that he saw them together became obvious. Not only did he not want Mummy to sleep with Daddy, but, perhaps more importantly, he had experienced no unusual problems in the past, either psychologically, intellectually or physically. He was developing as a very bright, capable young boy until father had his operation and left home. I am of the opinion that the child's normal development is an indication that he was working through aspects of the depressive position successfully. The blow to this success came when father was hospitalized. Matthew phantasized that his own ability to retain good objects—his internalized good father/penis—had been lost, and this constituted, as Klein notes, "a retreat from the object relations already achieved" (Klein, 1925, p. 123). His father's operation and departure precipitated a mistrust in his ability to recover this good object.

The resultant anxiety was not only experienced in relation to father but also towards mother. Matthew now needed to sleep with her to gain her love but, perhaps in addition, to make sure that she did not disappear as well and that his aggressive impulses had not been so powerful as to make them both sick and "gone". Sleeping with Matthew and not with her husband meant that the original separation from, and then loss of, the breast and its goodness, protection, and love was needed for Matthew's ego to maintain its functioning skills. Thus, when mother read to Matthew the books were those he knew and had loved as a baby and a toddler. The ego had reached a point where the assimilated object, the penis and breast, could not be maintained. Loss of the penis became a terrifying experience but was temporarily given up. Further cognition growth, and actually the continuing of his present cognitive skills, was in jeopardy—he had to give up further symbol formation. Matthew had to regress until his confidence in his ability to maintain good internal objects returned.

As his mother accepted her son's regression, helped him with his present anxieties, read "baby" stories to him, fed him, kept him home from his playschool, and stayed with him,

Matthew gradually experienced the good-enough breast and its love in reality—not its phantasized attacks. This, in turn, made him feel the capacity to love and to trust his love. The returned breast was not revengeful, and Matthew could resume his thinking and *see* that his father was not angry with him, he did not blame Matthew for his operation, and he had not left home (died) because of Matthew's anger. As this occurred, Matthew's tic improved, and he was again able to accept the combined parental couple—both externally as well as internally.

The eye-blink tic demonstrated anxiety related to his aggressive impulses to his father, his inability to continue to see and to think, and his great need to repair the "lost" good breast for himself. Matthew showed that his internal good objects were susceptible to damage. Through the fearful loss of part of the imago of the parental couple and the subsequent phantasized losses, his ego regressed to the point where it could recreate the original goodness. As his mother was willing to resume her original nurturing and care of Matthew, the child regained his good objects, along with the confidence that such a capacity brings with it—that is, Matthew felt much better now that he recognized that he had the ability to regain and maintain the love he had feared he had lost. I do not think that Matthew was angry with his mother for not protecting his father—rather, I think that Matthew's regression and eye blink were to prevent his thinking about, and knowing, how angry he was with his father, and that his loss could eventually mean mother's loss as well. Matthew could not bear the anxiety of losing her, of losing his loved internal object. As his anger subsided and trust in his capacity to be loved and to love returned, his sense of persecution became less, and his sense of feeling good and capable could be regained. Matthew resumed his pretend reading, his interest in books, and his talks with his parents. No longer was he afraid to look.

CHAPTER FOURTEEN

Group play psychotherapy: some concepts and research

A few years ago I had the opportunity of being involved with a small group of four-year-olds in group play psychotherapy. These children were attending a day-care centre for seriously emotionally disturbed children and had been attending the centre for several months by the time we met. I worked with their teacher–therapist, a young woman who had several years' practical experience in working with emotionally disturbed children along with professional training from an accredited academic setting. She noted that the children in her classroom were unable to interact, except to fight and throw things at each other, at the wall, or at pieces of furniture. In a more or less desperate manner she asked if I would consult with her regarding these children.

This situation presented me with an opportunity of following up on some work in group play psychotherapy that I had completed in one school setting with a group of mentally and physically handicapped children and in another day-care facility with a group of seriously emotionally disturbed children. Neither of these settings offered me the opportunity to do full-term work with the children or to have any kind of a control

198

group. I also could not use the children as their own control group by observing the children over a period of time to obtain a baseline for their behaviour in order to observe the effects of group play psychotherapy. The present day-care offered a full term (from October to May) as well as the possibility of setting up a control group within the same facility.

Before describing this research and the processes of the group play psychotherapy in this study, I would like to discuss some similarities and differences between group play psychotherapy, individual play psychotherapy, group day-care play, and sociodramatic play.

Group play psychotherapy with seriously emotionally disturbed children takes on a very different focus from individual play psychotherapy. I think that in individual play psychotherapy the psychotherapist is able to select the appropriate toys for the child, to interpret play within a unique transference–countertransference relationship, and to observe the readiness for termination (Weininger, 1989). However, in group play psychotherapy I found it impossible to choose appropriate toys for each child. I was aware of the transference–countertransference relationship, but this was a multiple relationship to several children, and then there was also each individual relationship of each child to the other. The number of ongoing interactive relationships was considerable, and, while some individual interpretations could be made, these did not seem as appropriate as interpretations that could be made at a "developmental level". By this I mean that an understanding of each child's development from a clinical Kleinian position would have enabled the psychotherapist to offer an interpretation of play that was appropriate to the group and not to one child in particular. I do not mean that the psychotherapist only spoke in "group terms" (certainly individual children were addressed and their play interpreted), but the interpretations that seemed to be most effective were those made related to the "group behaviour", and not necessarily through words, but through action as well.

Thus, for example, in one group I was able to offer small plastic "wild" animals—a bear, a lion, a tiger, a cougar, and a wolf—which the children used to express sadistic clawing and scratching. I offered a group interpretation of tearing at the breast, which seemed to be ungiving, and left the children very angry. I went on to suggest that their anger was felt at times to be dangerous because the breast could attack them, and that meant that they had to be even angrier and more destructive—essentially interpreting the retaliative phantasy. The children responded to my interpretations by becoming "fiercer" at first, and then making shelters out of Plasticine for each of the animals, saying that the animals will have to "learn to be good". Interestingly, this response to my interpretations appeared as a "group response" and seemed satisfying to the children, for their play continued, but this time a bit more co-operatively.

In another session, the sadism of these children again became disruptive. However, this time their behaviour appeared to me as "smashing" things, banging on the Plasticine and on the paper. I introduced an elephant, a hippopotamus, a horse, and a goat. This time the children used the animals to stomp on the Plasticine, and I suggested they were now able to stomp on the animals, which I saw then as murderous animals representing their phantasized sadistic attack on mother. The animals become dangerous because they can attack the children as well—that is, the rage of the animals becomes felt as the rage of the retaliative mother as well as their own rage towards mother. Interpretation of the retaliation is important in order for the play to continue. When I offered the children the interpretation that sometimes they even feel they might lose control over the animals and the animals could attack them, one child responded: "Well, we could put them in a zoo with a big lock and key." I replied that sometimes we can keep the good inside us, and we try to lock up the bad so it won't bother us. Another child replied: "I do that all the time. I don't want to see bad but I always am bad. My Mummy tells me I should be in a zoo behind gates." I said that it is hard always to be good, and one of the boys answered that he can be good by "playing very hard". I asked him what he meant by "very hard", and another child answered: "He means he just fights, like me."

The introduction of the stomping animals gave the children the opportunity to play out their anxieties regarding their own sadistic feelings and gave me an opportunity to offer group interpretation at the oral–sadistic paranoid–schizoid position. The children's play continued with the stomping of the animals on their paper constructions. While this play destroyed the constructions, their anxiety regarding retaliation seemed to be reduced. The play continued, but the hostility expressed did not disrupt their behaviour.

The same principles and "structure" that operate in individual therapy operate in group play psychotherapy. Sessions are regular, occurring perhaps up to four times a week at a fixed hour, in the same room, with its unchanging furniture, and with the same psychotherapist. Play materials along with words are introduced as interpretations. The children are told that they will be coming to this special room at a certain time each day and will be in the room with their special person, and that in the room they will be able to play and talk freely and privately. The group play psychotherapy room does not have "centres for various play activities". It is usually a smallish room with a table and a chair for each child and for the play psychotherapist. It is more like a small classroom than a free playroom.

Children are not encouraged to bring their own toys or materials into this room. If they say they want to bring toys into the room, they are asked to leave them in their "cubbies" (a shelf each child has for storing clothes, toys, and anything else they feel is important to them to store). In the room, the play psychotherapist does engage the child about his thoughts in bringing a particular toy into the room. My experience with this was to note that the child was very concerned that there would not be enough "stuff" for him in the room, or that someone else would have a "nicer" toy, or that he wanted to have the "best game in the room", or that someone would take all the toys for themselves and leave nothing for them. Interpretation of jealousy, greed, and envy helped to relieve their feelings and appeared sufficiently satisfying to permit the play to continue.

In one session a young girl of six decided that she was going to bring her four dolls, her dishes set, her cuddly bear, her set of crayons, and her snowsuit into the group room. I indicated that she could leave all these nice things in her "cubby". She told me that the "cubby" was not big enough, and she had all these things that she needed to take with her into the group room. I indicated that we had our toys in the room and that the room was ready for us to go and play. She said, "I just had to have all this with me", and she started to cry softly. I said that I thought I understood that she felt that she did not have as much as the other kids. She said, "I don't have very much. This is all I want to take into the room." I agreed that it was "our room", and that her things were very important to her and to me, and that she often felt "empty and maybe even that the kids seem to take your stuff from you". She agreed, still crying. I then indicated that we could leave her things just at the door of our room all piled up very neatly and "looking very nice", just waiting for her until we finished our group session. I was telling her that she felt that she had robbed mother and that she needed to make sure these things did not turn bad on her. If she left them outside, they could disappear, or they could turn bad and revengeful, and she would either have to rob again or feel very depleted and very angry. She agreed to leave her things just at the door, "all neat and nice", but the door had to be ajar "just a bit so I can peek out and see that my things are still all neat and no one has messed them".

While these interpretations were offered on our way into the group room with the other children close by, they did not seem to have a detrimental effect on the group as a whole. In fact, once in the room, we were able to talk about how we need so much, how we don't get what we want, and what we need to do to get the things that make us happy. As the talk went on, the children were sticking cut-out pictures of foods onto a large Bristol board onto which we had previously stuck pictures of babies, mothers, and fathers cut out from magazines and catalogues. The play activity was essentially an outgrowth of talk about babies never "getting enough", and that Mummies and Daddies were sometimes "mean and angry" and kept a lot for themselves. While the children did not specifically talk about their own parents, their words were about not gaining enough, that babies felt very hungry and didn't know how to get everything they needed. I brought in pictures of babies with parents, helped the children to make a collage with these cut-out pictures, then brought all these "baby foods" of milk, bread; cookies, and so on and helped the children to glue these to their baby-and-parents pictures.

By introducing these materials, I felt that I would be able to help the children symbolically to satisfy some of the psychological hunger and the resultant oral-sadism that was being expressed in their play and materials with each other. This gluing and collage-making lasted for two weeks, as I continued to supply pictures of babies, parents, and foods. The children glued and spoke about unsatisfied oral demands, but none of these sessions resulted in angry outbursts, crying, or withdrawal from the group room. All seven children were interested and participated in the activity. However, after two weeks it was obvious from their activity and talk that this episode was "over" for now. They became less energetic in selecting and gluing pictures onto the Bristol board. (The same Bristol board was used for the two weeks and was quite "full"!) They had begun to look around, as if looking for something else. At this point, I said that I thought that this gluing was finished for now and that we could come back to it later if we wished (all productions were saved).

I then introduced some new materials—popsicle sticks along with the glue—and began to make a room (as a room in a house). I reasoned that the oral-sadism and fear of retaliation made all situations feel very unsafe and dangerous for these children. There was always the fear of retaliation for their phantasized, if not at times real, aggressive outbursts. These, at least, had been reduced considerably as some of the oral-sadistic feelings had been worked through in the therapy. Therefore, the children should be more prepared to create for themselves a safe house, symbolically recreating mother's body. The children would then be able to fill mother's body with "good" things that they made. The children accepted this "materials and action interpretation" and began to work on the room to make the house.

I think that it is very important that the psychotherapist does not feel "rushed", nor should the group activity move on to another level before the children have had enough time to work through some particular group experience. Further, I have often observed that very seriously emotionally disturbed children initially cannot play. They need time within a safe room and in the presence of a consistent and understanding adult in order to "learn" how to play. Their play is often severely inhibited, if not prevented altogether. These inhibitions also prevent further ego functions from developing. Klein states that playing is an ego function that is inhibited because of libidinal fixation at a very early pre-playing stage (Klein, 1923). The capacity for the psychotherapist to be patient, to focus on the expressed and felt (countertransference) anxieties and the pains of the children, to contain them for the children and think about them, does have an effect on the children's problems. If psychotherapists are too concerned with action and making things, then it is important for them to try to understand why they find the children's destructive impulses and chaotic thoughts too painful to bear.

* * *

In another setting—a children's hospital—a group of four 7-year-olds and I were involved in group psychotherapy, trying to explore their physical diseases and the fact that they were going to die at a very early age. I had introduced Plasticine as a material to enable the children to create "whatever they wanted", and while I made a chair, the children made beds at first and rather quickly began to make "angels with wings". In this way they began to talk about what was going to happen to them—that they were soon going to be angels flying in the sky with "Jesus". One child said that he did not want to go away from his parents and that he could stay in the hospital, even though "they don't treat me very nicely". I repeated this last phrase, and another child said that he was being hurt because he was bad and that's "why I'm sick and going to die. I know that because I'm bad and maybe if I'm so bad I can fight Jesus and not fly away with him." The pain of separation seemed to be greater than the fear of death for this child and the others, who took up the theme of badness, sickness, and separation (Weininger, 1975).

After several such sessions, I was asked by a head nurse whether I thought it was wise for me to be talking about death to these young children. I replied that it was the children who wanted to explore their feelings about death and what might happen to them upon dying. The nurse became very angry with me, saying that it was not my business to be stirring up such feelings in children, and she added, "It is very hard for us to talk about death to the children. We want them to concentrate on living." I understood by these remarks that some nurses were unable to contain the children's pain and fears and that they needed to concentrate on looking after, on a day-to-day basis, their many physical needs, perhaps partly as a way of avoiding or maybe coping with their countertransference.

* * *

Group play psychotherapy is very different from the play that children demonstrate in a group day-care. In this latter situation, there are several day-care workers, the children have a variety of toys and materials to play with, and the structure of the day-care centre operates to control the behaviour of the child. There are rules and routines that must be followed, and "bad" behaviour is usually not tolerated. If a child is "bad", then he is sent for "time-out"—that is, sent to be alone in an empty room until he feels that he can return to the group and not show such behaviour. I think, rather, that at such a time a child needs a "time-in"—a time when the child is with an adult who can help to relieve the child's anxieties about his rage and destructive impulses. At such times, the strength and control that an understanding adult can offer enable the child to further his own ego development. If left alone, the child can either cry and kick to exhaustion and then seem to be under control because of lack of energy, or being alone can be so frightening that the momentary controls are brought into being, and the child returns to the group, only to lose these fragmentary controls under group stimulation and play.

Group play psychotherapy is somewhat like sociodramatic play among children in an educational setting, in that children are playing with materials and interacting with each other. In sociodramatic play the children develop a theme, either as a result of discussion or mutually co-operative play, which gradually evolves into a thematic play sequence (for example, going to the grocery store or playing at being a family or being in a school or work setting). The teacher may or may not be involved in sociodramatic play and may be invited to join in the play by the actors. The teacher may offer materials to encourage the development of a particular play theme—such as offering a baby bottle when the play of family and baby begins to falter, or offering two telephones so that children playing "garage" may now call into and out of the garage for car or truck problems (adding a pencil and paper alongside the telephone encourages pretend or actual writing, and it is a further aid to the elaboration of the play). The play is usually at the service of educational skill development, and this form of play is described as one of the most important tools available to the educator (Fein, 1981; Weininger, 1979). This pretend play and "role taking" helps participants to understand social situations more effectively by imaginatively acting out their understanding of the particular role they have adopted in the sociodramatic play.

In the classroom, this kind of play helps children to plan the dramatic undertaking, to relive and re-experience happy situations and/or painful memories, and to live through or work through the experiences and events that are important to him. While this play stimulates language receptivity and expression, co-operative behaviour, and sensitivity to others and their roles, it primarily allows children to understand experiences in their own way. Children try to work through their experiences and make sense of them by enacting these experiences, feelings, and events. By doing this, the experiences and feelings may become an integrated part of the child and not some mysterious split-off fragment of life. Apart from these important considerations, sociodramatic play has also been found to be an extremely valuable tool in the actual learning and mastery of academic subject material (Golomb & Cornelius, 1977; Johnson, 1976; Rosen, 1974; Smilansky, 1968; Weininger, 1988).

However, sociodramatic play is not group play psychotherapy, nor is it expected to be so. In the group play psychotherapy I was involved with, the emphasis was to help seriously emotionally disturbed children express their needs and receive both interpretations and materials to help them work through their frustrations. These sessions had a psychoanalytic object-relations perspective in that the interpretations and the presentation of materials were based primarily on the work of Melanie Klein. The children were not able to present dramatic themes to be enacted, nor did they show much capacity for social interactions. Rather, they were isolated, poorly integrated, angry young children. Their activities were chaotic and fragmented; often they flitted from one toy to another and often they hit one another or wandered off, only to run back, trying to smash whatever was present (furniture, games, walls, and so on).

I am aware that the seriously emotionally disturbed child does not "just start playing", but, rather, this child's play is rigid and stereotyped, with a general inability to make use of most materials. Often these children throw the materials about the room or at other children and at adults. These children may feel comfortable with only one kind of toy, and it is difficult to introduce other toys or materials to them. I think emotionally disturbed children do learn how to play with materials and toys, but a working-through of certain disturbing feelings is necessary before this can occur.

I did hope that some of the beneficial effects that have been noted in sociodramatic play may in fact also result from group play psychotherapy. Apart from academic stimulation, sociodramatic play has also had a social arousal-maintaining function—that is, it seems to help children maintain their motivation to play constructively, to be friendly, and to be responsive to peers and adults.

* * *

I will now describe the more extensive controlled research study I mentioned earlier. The children who participated in the group play psychotherapy were involved in a day-care facility for seriously disturbed young children. This group consisted of four boys aged four to five years.

One child had been diagnosed as "schizophrenic" two years prior to his involvement in this therapy. He showed no ability to play with the toys in the class playroom. Behaviourally he was jumpy and could not seem to sit still, and he usually shook his hands in front of his face as he talked. His talk was very difficult to understand, often sounding like "gibberish", but if one listened carefully one could make out words. He wandered about the room touching things, appearing to look at things, but not stopping to become engaged either with toys, materials, or people.

A second child was described and diagnosed as "paranoid" with hyperactive behaviour. He flitted from chair to chair, showing very little capacity to become engaged in any activity. He seemed unable to accept directions or instructions but wandered about repeating parts of the instruction. When he tried to do something, he usually could not carry out the task and would suddenly become very angry and then extremely disruptive of any classroom activity. At such times, which were frequent, he was both physically and verbally abusive, trying to hit others and/or swear and spit at them.

A third child was diagnosed as a "learning-disabled child with a perceptual handicap". His behaviour showed extremely poor frustration tolerance. He was unable to relate to other children or adults and showed temper outbursts, even when there appeared to be nothing in "reality" to frustrate him. As one teacher noted: "He is always angry and gets angry even when I think he is enjoying himself." This child's language was very difficult to understand, as he stuttered, was repetitive, and always seemed "very anxious".

A fourth child was extremely aggressive and was diagnosed as "schizophrenic with hostile reactions". This child had an exceptionally poor home life and had been physically abused by parents and several relatives. He was a child with an extremely poor frustration tolerance and appeared ready to hit out at any and every opportunity. His behaviour was "hyper", and his speech was very difficult to understand. He wandered about the room by himself, usually taking toys and materials and throwing them on the floor.

All four boys were reported in their psychological assessments to show "borderline intellectual functioning", but the examiner noted in each case that this cognitive functioning level may have resulted from uncooperative, antagonistic, and hostile behaviour. Thus, the children would refuse to answer the examiner's questions, or just stared at the examiner, or repeated parts of the questions over and over. The examiner felt that their observed intellectual functioning was more an indication of the children's serious emotional problems than an indication of their cognitive capacities, both currently and/or potentially.

Another group of four children, who were also observed at the same time, served as a "control group". These children were also diagnosed as seriously emotionally disturbed by the same psychologists, social workers, and psychiatrists. The children were suffering from such problems as schizophrenia, chronic hostility reactions, and learning disabilities, and they were functioning as well within a borderline intellectual range. The children were working with another person who also had several

years of training and experience with seriously emotionally disturbed children. While I was able to observe these children, I
was not involved in working closely with their teacher–therapist.
We would discuss problem children to some extent, but I did not
set up a group play psychotherapy experience for them. They
continued on with their regular program. Some of the children
were involved in individual play psychotherapy, and some of the
parents were also involved in family counselling and/or marital
therapy, as were some of the experimental group. These children remained together throughout the term, as did the children
involved in the group play psychotherapy. Very little change
occurred to the class composition. While occasionally another
child joined each class, that child did not remain as a stable
member of the class.

The children in group play psychotherapy and the children
in the control group were living with their natural parent or
parents. They had all experienced various amounts of separation from parent or parents over the previous four years. Some
of the children in both groups were involved in other day-care
programs as well as other activities—speech lessons, motor
exercises, and so on. It appeared that these two groups, each
of which was working with an experienced, sympathetic adult
and a classroom aide, were comparable. These women were
trained early-childhood care workers and were called teacher–
therapists.

The teacher–therapist who led the class of children involved
in group play psychotherapy became a group therapist, working under my supervision. We met once a week to discuss my
observations of the group and her impressions, and at such
times I presented her with the materials to bring into the classroom and/or the kinds of words to use as interpretations of
the children's behaviour and feelings. We had worked together
previously for over a year and had a comfortable relationship,
which, I think, allowed us to be helpful to each other and
honest about each other's contributions to the process in which
the children and we were involved. No problems arose that we
could not discuss and resolve.

In September, the teacher–therapist (a graduate student in
psychology) and I observed the children's functioning and
noted that as a group they demonstrated the following:

- very immature levels of thinking skills;
- expressive language at the two-year-old level;
- a great deal of hostile behaviour directed towards each other;
- very poor frustration tolerance, with aggression being shown every time the children were not able to accomplish what they were attempting—for example, kicking over the chair when the chair did not move with them as they tried to get at the table;
- anger and kicking when the teacher tried to help them;
- crying, screaming, and temper outbursts as typical behaviour;
- wandering about the classroom, "showing things" (carrying a toy, for example, and showing it to another child), sometimes screaming or swearing;
- uncommunicative behaviour, with rare attempts at co-operative play or even parallel play;
- little ability to orient themselves in relation to instructions—for example, it was very difficult to tell them that an event was going to happen in a few minutes, such as, "in a few minutes we will have snack"; the children wanted the snack immediately and became very aggressive and demanding of the snack;
- poor judgement—for example, they had a great deal of difficulty anticipating dangers or disapproval;
- unawareness of the presence of others; they behaved as though nothing else was happening in the room, and as if what each child was doing was the only event occurring;
- a poor sense of their own feelings with poor control over their impulses;
- poor interactions, and an inability to sustain any interaction, either with another child or with the adults in the room—while the interaction might seem appropriate at first, it gradually deteriorated and became characterized by anxiety and hostility;
- essentially a very poor capacity for attention and direction, along with a poor capacity for involvement in cognitive processes and an extreme difficulty in concentrating on a task or anticipating an event.

Personality organization appeared at the paranoid–schizoid position, with projection, splitting, and denial as primitive defence patterns. Dependency relationships were denied, and none was to be trusted, but, rather, the children seemed to have to fight others in an effort not to become attached to anyone. As a group, these children were impulsive and showed considerable dissociated behaviours and thought processes; their capacity to maintain some control over their feelings and impulses was very poor, and what controls they had were of a highly rigid and inflexible pattern. The children avoided inter-actions, they tried to do things the same way and discarded any introduction of new materials either by throwing them on the floor or spitting on them. Rational ego control indicated by sublimation of impulses was not observed. The children pre-sented as psychotic, and the adults in the classroom spent most of their time "catching" children, stopping fights, prevent-ing materials from being spilled or dumped, and trying to stop the children from running out of the room. There were no "real" observable differences in behavioural functioning between the two groups; rather, they both appeared to be composed of ex-tremely difficult children to change. The adults in both class-rooms did spend most of their time trying to "manage" one or another child, until yet another child began to "act up".

We began to work with one group of children in October while the other group continued with its "regular curriculum". The work and observations continued until mid-May. Since all the children in the group were attracted to toy cars and would push these cars in the classroom, I introduced the toy cars as the first material in the group play psychotherapy.

The room used for the group sessions was a small room, approximately 6' × 7' with a round, child-sized table and five child-sized chairs. The room did not contain any other furni-ture, and the walls were bare. The room had a one-way mirror for observation.

The children were told that they would be able to play with the toy cars in the small room with their teacher–therapist, four days a week, first thing every morning. We had observed that all the children pushed toy cars on the floor, on the furniture, on the walls, on any surface they could; in fact, they even pushed these cars in "air", always making a car-noise. I thought that it would be wisest to start with the toy that all the children were using and not introduce any new material until it was appropriate. These instructions were given to the children the Friday before the start of the play-group psychotherapy on Monday. The children seemed to "understand" but did not respond and continued with their random behaviour. We also determined that the length of time in the room would be only a few minutes at first, although we hoped that the sessions could eventually be extended to 60 minutes.

At the first session the toy cars were on the table, and each child went in and sat down. The teacher–therapist said, "We'll be in this room for a short while, and we can play with the cars". Since the children arrived by bus and they had travelled for up to an hour, we felt that it was appropriate also to provide them with a cereal snack. A box of cereal and five bowls were on the table, and each child was given as much cereal as he wanted.

The children sat on their chairs, pushed the cars along the table, bumped into each others' cars, made car-noises, kicked at each other, made guttural and swearing sounds, ate their cereal, and stayed in the room for about ten minutes. The teacher–therapist then said, "We will come into the room tomorrow morning first thing after you arrive, and we will have the cars and the cereal ready for you, just as it was this morning". (I felt that the consistency of routines was extremely important, as well as the "same room and same time" aspects of psychotherapy.)

The children continued to come to this room four times a week. They continued to push their cars on the table and to make all sorts of car-noises and other sounds (such as car crashes and cars back-firing, which one of the children called "farts"). They ate their cereal; this usually took about five minutes, after which they did not want any more cereal and the cereal and bowls were placed on the floor, but in view. The car activity continued throughout the eating and after the cereal had been taken off the table. The children and the teacher–therapist left the room when the children began to become violent. (I felt that it was important that the children view this room as "safe" and that tantrums and violence were not to occur there.) When hostile behaviour escalated to violence, the teacher–therapist suggested: "We will keep this room a safe place. We are ready to move back now to the classroom."

These destructive impulses were viewed as an attempt to destroy the room and, unconsciously, to destroy mother's insides, since the phantasy of the mother's retaliation was too severe for these children to endure. To protect them from suffering these phantasized attacks, the children were asked to return to their big classroom. This was not instituted as a punishment, nor were the children told that when they settled down they could return to the small room; rather, this move was viewed as an "interpretation" and a "containing" of the impulses by the teacher–therapist, because the children could not contain these impulses themselves. As an "action interpretation", moving out of the small room might be felt by the children as mother being able to maintain control rather than becoming angry and retaliative. The car noises and running the cars over the table seemed to represent the enormity of their hostility towards their phantasized mother and was expressive of their violent sadism. If this room (mother's body) could be kept safe, then the sadistic attacks by the use of the cars might not result in retaliation. Also, because of their personality dynamics, the children might unconsciously perceive that taking in the cereal was not robbing mother, because the food was always available, always in sight, and never exhausted. Therefore, unconsciously, they might expect an attack from the phantasy mother for robbing her, which would be observed as escalated hostile behaviour. However, since this was never allowed to happen, I thought that not only would the food remain good, but the room should also remain safe.

The anxiety that was seen in these children in their big classroom, with resultant deterioration of their behaviour, was, I think, the result of feared attacks by the mother for their sadism. The boys were attacking and expected a return attack, which forced them to view any further instruction or talk coming from an adult or any further internal feelings as the dreaded attack by a revengeful mother.

The children remained in the group room for about ten minutes each session and "zoomed" their cars and ate the cereal. This activity continued in the same way for the next four weeks, without much noticeable change in either the kind of play or in the children's behaviour. They remained an angry, difficult group to work with.

At the beginning of November, in order to begin to add more structure to the play, I suggested that the teacher–therapist introduce a large sheet of Bristol board, which she put on the table. The children ran their toy cars over the board and I asked the teacher–therapist to talk to the children at the same time about their bus ride to the day-care centre and to encourage them to talk about the bus ride and to demonstrate their feelings through the toy cars that they were using. At the end of the week, the teacher–therapist said that she would bring some crayons into the room.

When the crayons were introduced, the teacher–therapist made a long mark across the Bristol board using a black crayon and suggested that this might be a road on which they could drive their cars. When the line was added to the board, their activity became more "purposeful". Now they drove their cars along the line (the road), and they made some more roads along which to drive their cars. Since the Bristol board was not as large as the table and was rectangular, whereas the table was round, it provided the children with "angles" rather than "curves". Also, the line was angular rather than a smooth curve. I think that angularity is expressive of aggression and helped the children "feel" that their environment was receptive of their attacks and their expression of impulsive, hostile behaviour. However, perhaps more important, the line was symbolic of the penis. By being aggressive in a safe way to the penis, which I think the children phantasized as being within the mother's body, this object might not arouse as much "dread of an analogous attack from the external and the internal objects" (Klein, 1929, p. 212). Recall that Klein indicated that "the Oedipus conflict begins under the complete dominance of sadism" (Klein, 1929, p. 212). The children kept their cars on the "roads", they would crash their cars by going on the same roads, they would shout gleefully, "you're dead and you can't get me", and continue zooming their cars along the road.

In the second week of November I suggested that the teacher–therapist tell the children that their words were very important, and that she would write them in a special book that she would make and bring into the room every day with her. These words were the "stories" they wished to tell her. While the children were in the room for about ten minutes, there were more car noises, less screaming at each other, and more actual "organized play" in that the children were driving the cars on the roads.

In the third and fourth weeks of November the teacher–therapist introduced the idea that the roads they were crayoning could be a map, and she encouraged them to talk about where they were driving. The teacher–therapist said that some of the roads could lead to a house, and she asked where other roads could lead. She was presenting another helpful control to organize their constructive abilities. The children named places such as schools, homes, and churches on the map and pointed out where these buildings were located. The teacher–therapist made circles to represent these buildings.

At this time the teacher–therapist also introduced booklets which then belonged to each child and in which the child was given the time at the end of each session to write the story they had dictated to the teacher–therapist. Anticipating jealousy towards the teacher–therapist for having objects the children did not have, each child was given a booklet that was like the teacher–therapist's. Also, since they were able to tell a bit about their bus trip to the day-care centre and since the map was becoming organized and used, I felt that the children's emotional capacity to use their cognitive skills had proceeded sufficiently to allow them to "write" their own stories as well. Their inability to show their skills seemed to be the result of their sadism and concern about finding out that they could be attacked. I believe that the skills were not shown because to be able to do things and follow directions would mean that they could recognize others' feelings and impulses and that they might actually, in an omnipotent way, be able to then destroy their phantasized mother. In this way, then, the expression of a "successful hostility" (but without retaliation) and the sustained safety of the room allowed the children to "write" and think (Klein, 1923, pp. 59–76). They could recognize that their feelings were bad, that they could be successful in destroying the phantasized bad object, yet remain capable of continuing their activity. Gradually the hostility was being altered to aggressiveness, and some of the emotional energies used in hostility expression were now available for cognitive expression, which always requires aggression for completion—that is, to carry through a cognitive task takes some expression of aggression. Without aggression, the task just cannot be completed and peters out. However, if the aggression is so strong that it frightens the child into phantasizing retaliation, the aggression cannot be expressed creatively or in a sublimated form but must remain as a strong defence against the anticipated retaliation.

By now, two months after group psychotherapy had begun, the children were showing various aspects of co-operative behaviour: they were actually playing cars with each other; they showed sympathy towards each other (for example, when they bumped into each others' cars they looked surprised, moved their cars out of the way, and did not get "mad"); they were sharing ideas and said, for example, "Let's go on the road"; they talked to each other and described their actions, an obvious increase in language skills; they "listened" to each other and seemed to use the offered interpretation from each other; and they talked to the teacher–therapist, who continued to encourage the children to talk about their play by asking relevant questions. After the third week of November, the children remained in the room for about 20 minutes per session.

In the first week of December, materials such as Plasticine and popsicle sticks were discussed with the children and introduced that week. I thought that since the children were able to play and talk to each other and to the teacher–therapist, they would also be able to make use of "unstructured materials" such as Plasticine and popsicle sticks. The structure that the cars and map provided appeared sufficiently strengthened to allow for the introduction of this new material, which could be used for constructing things. Because the children were also showing the ego capacity to tolerate a degree of frustration, building and making things appeared as an appropriate activity. In our supervision meetings, it also appeared that the children were able to begin to examine and talk about the controls they were using. It was considered that if some form of talk about, and interpretation of, ego strengths could be made, then the children would also show further emotional gains.

To facilitate this, the teacher–therapist began to construct a "stop-sign", using a lump of Plasticine and sticking a popsicle stick into it and putting it at what seemed like an appropriate place on the road map. The children began to construct their own "stop-signs" and to place them on the map. This activity enabled discussion about having to stop, feeling angry that "you just can't go through the road when you want to", having to "take care about other cars on the road", and, in general, being able to talk in a symbolic way about ego controls and the way these controls made you feel.

The children also made bridges out of the Plasticine and popsicle sticks (simple bridges of two lumps of Plasticine with a stick over the lumps) and placed them on the map. The bridges became ways that "we can find out how to do things so that we won't make other people angry with us", also "how our angry feelings make us feel that we need to just drive our car right into somebody else's car because we are sure they will drive right into us". The bridge provided a beginning towards developing flexibility and an intellectual process for coping with strong hostile feelings. The ego defences of denial and projection were explored in this way, and the materials provided an avenue through which the therapist and children could explore these mechanisms. The others' cars as well as their own were not viewed as such dangerous objects and were becoming less and less hostile threats persecuting the children. Since the sadism was showing some signs of abatement (and this was confirmed by the sympathy the children had been showing), the very unfriendly, hostile setting was becoming altered to a much friendlier place, or at least to a less hostile setting. The ego defence mechanisms of projection and denial were operating less and less, and the opportunity to explore the change by use of the introduction of simple building materials seemed appropriate. The children were staying in the room for about 30 minutes now, and the extreme "hyper" behaviour had toned down considerably.

By the second week of December, sticky tape and circle-, square-, and triangle-shaped papers were introduced, having first been talked about as a way of representing buildings. Again, the introduction of this "symbolic representation" was considered a way of helping the children to talk about their imaginings. When the unconscious phantasy is expressed by primitive clinging, avoiding, or hostile behaviour, there is no way that the child is able to verbalize these unconscious phantasies. The child has the associated feelings but does not have the words to express them. As a more mature way of expression evolves, the child is able to talk about primitive feelings, but now in abstract or symbolic terms. Thus, for example, when a young child of four says, as he pulls a toy dog along the floor and the tail waves, "look at the puppy's tail", I think that the child is making reference to the penis. This child is not in psychotherapy with me, yet he engaged me in such a way as to indicate to me that he was worried about his penis. However, I do not say to him, "You are worried about your penis". Rather, my words are expressive of how strong the tail is, how it waves just right, how it stays on the puppy, and how the puppy will always have a tail. The point at issue is that I would use the same language-medium that the child used, and thus I could "talk to the unconscious phantasy" by making statements about the tail as penis.

Very seriously disturbed children do not have the opportunity to use abstract or symbolic ways such as the puppy tail to express their concerns and fears. Rather, there is an almost direct link between unconscious phantasy and expressed behaviour. It is as if the child thinks, "I am in danger, and I must destroy the danger". In order for the psychotic child to be gradually helped to work through his primitive defence systems and to reach a point where ego functioning is sufficient to talk about things, I think it is important to provide the "avenue" through which these "things" can be discussed. In the play psychotherapy group this was provided at first by lines on the Bristol board, and later on by Plasticine, popsicle sticks, pieces of paper, and sticky tape. These materials created an avenue for words to be used in a symbolic way that had not been available to them before. In this way, I think that there can be some communication between unconscious and conscious minds (Segal, 1973). The stop signs, the bridges, and the buildings also provided an opportunity for the child to begin to see himself put into another person's position—that is, if he used the bridge or if he stopped, then he would not harm the other child's car, and the other would not harm his. This beginning process of projective identification, which I think of as the beginnings of empathy, forms the basis for

the earliest form of symbol formation. By projecting parts of itself into the object and identifying parts of the object with parts of the self, the ego forms its first most primitive symbols. [Segal, 1973, p. 36]

This symbol development was encouraged by the introduction of these particular materials.

The group play psychotherapy continued until the Christmas break, with the eating of the cereal, the discussion about the children's bus ride, the use of the toy cars, the Bristol board with its elaborations, the children dictating to the teacher–therapist their stories about their work, and, prior to returning to their regular classroom, using their own writing booklets to "write" the stories they had just dictated. By the Christmas break the behaviour of the children was greatly changed. They looked at each other, they laughed at times, they were using words to say how they felt and what they wanted, they could now play in a "pretend" way, and they were co-operative in their play.

The teacher–therapist expected a considerable regression in behaviour when the children returned to the day-care centre in January after a Christmas break of about three weeks. It was both her experience and mine that children do not usually return to the day-care centre remembering the rules and routines, and that they once again experience the pangs of separation and express this feeling of loss by aggression and/or withdrawal. A bit surprisingly, to the teacher–therapist at least, the children seemed interested and anxious to return to their sessions, and they "fit" easily into the play and talk that they had left for three weeks. Her experience with children as emotionally disturbed as these children had been in October was that they would be upset, angry, and quite forgetful of the routines of the classroom.

By the end of January, the children were remaining in the room for 45 minutes, and there was only an occasional temper outburst or the beginning of a fight. When these emotions made their appearance, the teacher–therapist suggested that the child felt angry because he was not getting enough and felt others were getting much more than he, and she offered him more cereal, along with the opportunity to use the bridge as a way to get his car where he wanted it. Even if the child did not say that he wanted his car at a certain point on the map, the teacher–therapist indicated that he could use the bridge to get to his house and make sure his house was safe. In saying these words, she was attempting to put into words and use the available symbols to interpret to the unconscious demands that the internal objects were not going to be damaged, that his mother was not attacking him, and that she was safe and not destroyed. Usually this worked, and the child was able to follow up from this in an unexpectedly flexible way (for example, one boy said that he would go to the market and get some more bread).

Throughout February and March, the group play psychotherapy sessions continued with no change, except that, into the second week of March, the teacher–therapist suggested that if the children wanted to, they could read the story that they had dictated. At about this time it seemed that the emotional, libidinal energy, which at first was used in temper explosions and had altered to being used in constructing changes in ego strength and ego defence mechanisms, was now available for abstract purposes of learning.

> I have endeavoured to show that the fundamental activities exercised at schools are channels for the flow of libido and that by this means the component instincts achieve sublimation under the supremacy of the genitals. This libidinal cathexis, however, is carried over from the most elementary studies—reading, writing and arithmetic—to wider efforts and interests based upon these, so that the foundations of later inhibitions—of vocational inhibitions as well—are to be found, above all, in the frequently apparently evanescent ones concerned with the earliest studies. The inhibition of these earliest studies, however, are built upon play-inhibitions, so that in the end we can see all the later inhibitions, so significant for life and development, evolving from the earliest play-inhibitions. [Klein, 1923, p. 73]

In the same paper, Klein writes:

> The mechanism of inhibition . . . permits, owing to common sexual, symbolic meanings, the progress of the inhibitions from one ego-activity or trend to another. Since a removal of the earliest inhibitions also means an avoidance of further ones, very great importance must be attached to inhibitions in the child of pre-school age, even when they are not very strikingly apparent. [p. 73]

By the end of March the children's stories had progressed from words to sentences, and they were now attempting to put their stories in "pretend print". As the teacher–therapist read their dictations aloud, the children listened, asked questions, and elaborated their dictations. Interestingly, at this time, the children were "eager" to read their print—they remembered what they had dictated and written, and they "read" what they had said aloud. The children were "reading" words such as car, stop, and, too, the names of the other children, and the name E.T. (from the film "E.T."). They smiled a lot at being able to do this and appeared pleased with themselves. Their "pretend print" consisted of scribbles at first, but gradually the marks they made took on a letter character, and some of the children wrote in a pretend cursive style. Two of the children began to print their names (they noted that their teacher–therapist printed their names on their dictations and asked how to do it themselves). One boy printed his name vertically at first, and about one month later he printed it horizontally. The other child printed his name correctly. There was a great deal of interaction and copying, and the children seemed interested in what the others were doing. They did not appear "bored" and were not hostile to each other, nor to the teacher–therapist. They remained in the room for 60 minutes and had done so since the end of February. Even when they returned to their big classroom, they were no longer "hyper", hostile, destructive, or withdrawn. They played together constructively, usually using toy cars and trucks and blocks.

The group play psychotherapy sessions continued four times a week until mid-May, with no variations in themes or in materials. The routine continued as described in January. The children continued in the group room for 60 minutes. They would have stayed longer for many of the sessions, but I thought that the group sessions should have a definite time to them and not run the risk of the children experiencing the feeling they were taking more time from the teacher–therapist than was allotted. In this way the potential for fearing that they were robbing the teacher–therapist of her "time", her "internal objects", would in reality, but not necessarily in phantasy, be avoided.

Towards the end of the day-care term, the children's behaviour had changed considerably. The angry and/or withdrawn behaviour that was clearly seen in September and October was noticeably absent. While the children were "not always great" and at times refused to cooperate with each other, played alone, and swore when angry, there were considerably fewer temper outbursts. The children appeared to be in better control of their impulses, and their behaviour was more appropriate for the situation. They talked to each other, indicating that they were aware of the consequences of their actions. For example, one boy said, "If the truck dumps the dirt on the road, it'll bust up your road."

Specifically, the following was observed:

1. Children showed sustained purposeful play, with themes of driving the car to the store, having a pretend garage, "writing" notes to each other about car problems, family outings, and so on.

2. Children were able to pay attention, concentrate, and remember.

3. Children showed a desire to complete tasks successfully.

4. Children talked to each other and were able to play co-operatively.

5. Interpersonal relations had improved greatly, along with a great change in their expression of hostility.

6. Children still blamed each other for difficulties at play and were defensive about what they were doing—for example, the phrase "don't look" was often heard.

7. Children showed an improvement in their gross and fine motor skills—they did not seem to trip and fall as much, nor were they as clumsy.

8. When they left the small group room to go into their larger classroom, the children's play continued to be co-operative and sociodramatic with their own themes. They asked the teacher–therapist for help now and seemed to respond to her as a resource rather than a feared object.

9. Considerable change was observed in the children's language use, both in the session and when at play in their large classroom.

This language change may also be noted in their dictated stories, as, for example, in Marc's case:

Mid November: I want jeep.
I want dump-truck.

December: I brought a magazine to school. Santa Claus is in the magazine.
On the weekend I am going to the Dundas streetcar.

January: I like to ride on the St. Clair streetcar.
I want the shovel and the toboggan. I am going on a holiday and I will come back.
I want to sit on the chair. I will play bus with Steve.

February: I am a teacher. I tell Dave "get away from the door". Jimmy covered all the walls with silver paper.
I went to the library on Friday. The lady told a story. I saw some puppets. Bea took me because Sara is away.

March: I want to play with the toy car. I am upset today and Tim helped put the trucks away.
I made my day care and home on my map. I have a sore tummy today. I made Frosty in my book.

April: I made a road on my map. On the weekend I bought some chips. I went to Bloor Street and got some purple jogging pants.
I was late because there was too much snow. E.T. [of movie fame] was running for his spaceship but he didn't catch it in time. He was crying. Tim made a big aeroplane with blocks.

May: I was knocking at the door for a long time. Sara came to the door and opened it. Next time I will call the teacher.
I don't like it when Tim scratches his sweater. I will miss going swimming.

Another child, Vince, began his dictation with short sentences, quickly moving to longer and more descriptive statements.

November: I want the sports-car.
I want the school-bus, the boat and the sports-car.

December: I got mad because I want the black marker [crayon].
I want ten cars for Christmas.

January: I made two good ships. I made a calendar and a Christmas stocking.
I want to fall down in the snow and have a snow fight.

November

Figure 5.   Examples of Marc's "printing".

Bobby peed his pants. He got a spanking. Bobby cried so much. Bobby misses his Mum.

February: I taped the car box. I took three tapes off. I brought two cars to school.

I'm in a bad mood. I want to go to the big room.

March: I saw a film, "E.T.", and I saw my Mummy's boyfriend. [Vince was sick most of March and absent from day care.]

April: I made a fish and a road on my map. E.T. is at home playing with my army men.

I was crying and sad because Lorrie [teacher–therapist] was away but she came back.

December

I want Tim to come to my grandma's on the holiday.
I like to listen to "E.T." with Tim because I love "E.T."

May: The scary part comes when the man comes. E.T. phones home.

I like Tim to listen with me and Marc. I like the part where E.T. catches and misses the spaceship.

10. Changes in printing. Examples of Marc's "printing" are presented in Figure 5.

The observations of the children in the "control" group point out the very real achievement of the "experimental" group. At the conclusion of the work, the "control" group children were still acting in an isolated way, showing poor ego capacities,

January

inappropriate judgements, poor control over impulses, clumsiness, and poor cognitive skills—for example, poor language usage, poor attention span and involvement, and poor memory. They did not show the drive for mastery and competence demonstrated by the experimental group but, rather, flitted from one activity to another in a random way. Changes that one might expect as a result of maturation, or even general social experience with a trained worker, did not occur. The general emotional, cognitive, and physical capacities of these children were very different from those of the children who had been involved in group play psychotherapy.

In September these latter children had been at a similar developmental level as the "control" children and did not know

February

how to play. However, in group play psychotherapy the use of a limited number of toys and materials, along with the structure of psychoanalytic therapy, allowed the children to "learn" how to play without further damaging their fragile egos.

In an earlier group play psychotherapy project without controls, five children (three girls and two boys) aged three to four years showed similar developmental gains, and these gains were maintained. Their worker noted that the children were also functioning as well in September, after their two-month vacation. They continued and built on their gains, even though they were not involved in further group play psychotherapy but only in the regular day-care class curriculum. As Klein (1923) noted so many years ago:

April

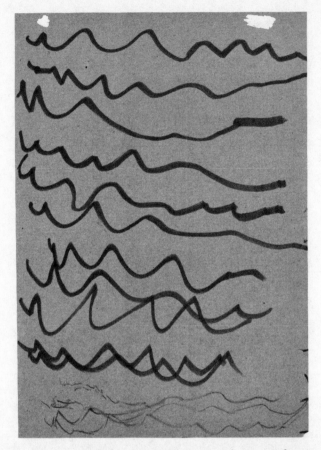

The teacher can achieve much by sympathetic understanding, for she is able thereby considerably to reduce that part
of the inhibition that attaches to the person of the teacher
as "avenger". [p. 76]

Segal (1973) notes:

When there is a predominance of good experiences over
bad experiences, the ego acquires a belief in the prevalence
of the ideal object over the persecuted objects, and also of
the predominance of its own life instinct over its own death
instinct. [p. 37]

I think this is what happened to these children in group play
psychotherapy.

REFERENCES

Bick, E. (1968). The experience of the skin in early object relations. *International Journal of Psycho-Analysis, 49:* 484–486. Also in M. H. Williams, *Collected Papers of Martha Harris and Ester Bick.* Strathclyde: Clunie Press.

Bion, W. (1962). *Learning from Experience.* London: Heinemann [reprinted London: Karnac Books, 1984].

Bion, W. (1967). *Second Thoughts.* London: Heinemann [reprinted London: Karnac Books, 1984].

Bion, W. (1988a). Attacks on linking. In E. B. Spillius (Ed.), *Melanie Klein Today, Vol. 1* (pp. 87–101). London: Routledge.

Bion, W. (1988b). Differentiation of the psychotic from the non-psychotic personalities. In E. B. Spillius (Ed.), *Melanie Klein Today, Vol. 1* (pp. 61–78). London: Routledge.

Bion, W. (1988c). A theory of thinking. In E. B. Spillius (Ed.), *Melanie Klein Today, Vol. 1* (pp. 178–186). London: Routledge.

Bowlby, J. (1979). On knowing what you are not supposed to know and feeling what you are not supposed to feel. *Canadian Journal of Psychiatry, 24:* 403–408.

Britton, R., Feldman, M., & O'Shaughnessy, E. (1989). *The Oedipus Complex Today: Clinical Implication,* J. Steiner (Ed.). London: Karnac Books.

Fein, C. G. (1981). Pretend play in childhood: an integrative review. *Child Development, 52:* 1095–1118.

Folch, G. C. de (1981). Communication and containing in child

229

analysis: Towards terminality. In E. B. Spillius (Ed.), *Melanie Klein Today, Vol. 2* (pp. 206–217). London: Routledge.

Golomb, C., & Cornelius, C. B. (1977). Symbolic play and its cognitive signification. *Developmental Psychology, 13*: 246–252.

Isaacs, S. (1930). *Intellectual Growth in Young Children*. London: Routledge.

Isaacs, S. (1933). *Social Development in Young Children*. London: Routledge.

Isaacs, S. (1948). The nature and function of phantasy. *International Journal of Psycho-Analysis, 29*: 73–97. Also in M. Klein, *Developments in Psychoanalysis*. London: Hogarth Press, 1952 [reprinted London: Karnac Books, 1989].

Johnson, J. E. (1976). Relations of divergent thinking and intelligence tests: social and nonsocial make-believe play of preschool children. *Child Development, 47*: 1200–1203.

Joseph, B. (1988). Projective identification: some clinical aspects. In E. B. Spillius (Ed.), *Melanie Klein Today, Vol. 1* (pp. 138–150). London: Routledge.

Klein, M. (1921). The development of a child. In *Love, Guilt and Reparation and Other Works 1921–1945*. London: Hogarth Press, 1975, pp. 1–53 [reprinted London: Karnac Books, 1992].

Klein, M. (1923). The role of the school in the libidinal development of the child. In *Love, Guilt and Reparation and Other Works 1921–1945* (pp. 59–76). London: Hogarth Press, 1975 [reprinted London: Karnac Books, 1992].

Klein, M. (1925). A contribution to the psychogenesis of tics. In *Love, Guilt and Reparation and Other Works 1921–1945* (pp. 106–127). London: Hogarth Press, 1975 [reprinted London: Karnac Books, 1992].

Klein, M. (1928). Early stages of the Oedipus conflict. In *Love, Guilt and Reparation and Other Works 1921–1945* (pp. 186–198). London: Hogarth Press, 1975 [reprinted London: Karnac Books, 1992].

Klein, M. (1929). Infantile anxiety situations reflected in a work of art and in the creative impulse. In *Love, Guilt and Reparation and Other Works 1921–1945* (pp. 210–218). London: Hogarth Press, 1975 [reprinted London: Karnac Books, 1992].

Klein, M. (1933). The early development of conscience in the child. In *Love, Guilt and Reparation and Other Works 1921–1945* (pp. 248–257). London: Hogarth Press, 1975 [reprinted London: Karnac Books, 1992].

Klein, M. (1934). On criminality. In *Love, Guilt and Reparation and Other Works 1921–1945* (pp. 258–261). London: Hogarth Press, 1975 [reprinted London: Karnac Books, 1992].

Klein, M. (1935). A contribution to the psychogenesis of manic-depressive states. In *Love, Guilt and Reparation and Other*

Works 1921–1945 (pp. 262–289). London: Hogarth Press, 1975 [reprinted London: Karnac Books, 1992].

Klein, M. (1936). Weaning. In *Love, Guilt and Reparation and Other Works 1921–1945* (pp. 290–305). London: Hogarth Press, 1975 [reprinted London: Karnac Books, 1992].

Klein, M. (1945). The Oedipus complex in the light of early anxieties. In *Love, Guilt and Reparation and Other Works 1921–1945* (pp. 370–419). London: Hogarth Press, 1975 [reprinted London: Karnac Books, 1992].

Klein, M. (1946). Notes on some schizoid mechanisms. In *Envy and Gratitude and Other Works 1946–1963* (pp. 1–24). London: Hogarth Press, 1975.

Klein, M. (1948). On the theory of anxiety and guilt. In *Envy and Gratitude and Other Works 1946–1963* (pp. 25–42). London: Hogarth Press, 1975.

Klein, M. (1952a). On observing the behavior of young infants. In *Envy and Gratitude and Other Works 1946–1963* (pp. 94–121). London: Hogarth Press, 1975.

Klein, M. (1952b). Some theoretical conclusions regarding the emotional life of the infant. In *Envy and Gratitude and Other Works 1946–1963* (pp. 61–93). London: Hogarth Press, 1975.

Klein, M. (1955). The psycho-analytic play technique: its history and significance. In *Envy and Gratitude and Other Works 1946–1963* (pp. 122–140). London: Hogarth Press, 1975.

Klein, M. (1957). Envy and gratitude. In *Envy and Gratitude and Other Works 1946–1963* (pp. 176–235). London: Hogarth Press, 1975.

Klein, M. (1958). On the development of mental functioning. In *Envy and Gratitude and Other Works 1946–1963* (pp. 236–246). London: Hogarth Press, 1975.

Klein, M. (1960). On mental health. In *Envy and Gratitude and Other Works 1946–1963* (pp. 268–274). London: Hogarth Press, 1975.

Klein, M. (1963a). Some reflections on *The Oresteia*. In *Envy and Gratitude and Other Works 1946–1963* (pp. 275–299). London: Hogarth Press, 1975.

Klein, M. (1963b). On the sense of loneliness. In *Envy and Gratitude and Other Works 1946–1963* (pp. 300–313). London: Hogarth Press, 1975.

Leach, P. (1984). *Babyhood: Infant Development from Birth to Two Years* (2nd edition). New Zealand: Penguin Books.

Meltzer, D. (1978). The Kleinian development (Part 1). *Freud's Clinical Development*. Strathclyde: Clunie Press.

Miller, L., Rustin, M., Rustin, M., & Shuttleworth, J. (1989). *Closely Observed Infants*. London: Duckworth.

O'Shaughnessy, E. (1988). W. R. Bion's theory of thinking and new techniques in child analysis. In E. G. Spillius (Ed.), *Melanie Klein Today, Vol. 2* (pp. 177–190). London: Routledge.

Piaget, J. (1962). *Play, Dreams and Imitation in Childhood*. New York: W. W. Norton.

Piaget, J. (1973). The affective unconscious and the cognitive unconscious. *Journal of American Psychoanalytic Association, 21* (1): 249–261.

Rosen, C.E. (1974). The effect of sociodramatic play on problem-solving behavior among culturally disadvantaged children. *Child Development, 45*: 920–927.

Rosenfeld, H. (1988). Contribution to the psychopathology of psychotic states: the importance of projective identification in the ego structure and the object relations of the psychotic patient. In E. B. Spillius (Ed.)., *Melanie Klein Today, Vol. 1* (pp. 117–137). London: Routledge.

Segal, H. (1973). *Introduction to Melanie Klein*. London: Karnac Books.

Segal, H. (1981). *The Work of Hanna Segal: A Kleinian Approach to Clinical Practice*. London: Karnac Books, and Free Association Books.

Sheleff, L. S. (1981). *Generations Apart: Adult Hostility to Youth*. New York: McGraw-Hill.

Smilansky, S. (1968). *The Effect of Sociodramatic Play on Disadvantaged Children*. New York: Wiley.

Spillius, E. B. (Ed.) (1988). *Melanie Klein Today, Vol. 1: Mainly Theory*. London: Routledge.

Tustin, F. (1958). Anorexia nervosa in an adolescent girl. *British Journal of Medical Psychology, 31* (3 and 4).

Weininger, O. (1975). The disabled and dying children: does it have to hurt so much. *Ontario Psychologist, 7* (3): 29–35.

Weininger, O. (1979). *Play and Education*. Springfield, IL: Charles C Thomas.

Weininger, O. (1979–80). The cognitive unconscious: figurative and operative processes in the learning of disturbed children. *Interchange, 10* (4): 1–11.

Weininger, O. (1984). *The Clinical Psychology of Melanie Klein*. Springfield, IL: Charles C Thomas.

Weininger, O. (1988). "What if" and "As if": imagination and pretend play in early childhood. In K. Egan & D. Nadaner (Eds.), *Imagination and Education* (pp. 141–149). New York: Teacher's College Press.

Weininger, O. (1989). *Children's Phantasies: The Shaping of Relationships*. London: Karnac Books.

Weininger, O. (1992). *Melanie Klein: From Theory to Reality*. London: Karnac Books.

INDEX

aggression, 46
  and anxiety, 74
  towards breast, 19
  and cognitive expression, 215
  dangerous, saving mother
    from, 33
  defence against, 31, 111, 112
  evacuation of, 47
  faeces as, 54
  and jealousy, 99
  and lack of containment, 7
  projected onto parent, 69
  towards mother, 34, 51, 79,
    83
  object destroyed by, 113
  towards parents, 124, 159,
    160
  to phantasized bad breast, 11
  projection of, 68
  and rivalry, 121–131
  and superego, 50, 64
aggressive inner world, 46
alpha-elements, 148
anorexia nervosa, 8, 98
anxiety
  anal and urethral, 44
  depressive, 59, 73, 88
  paranoid and depressive, and
    early eating problems,
    8–25
  persecutory, 44, 55

bad breast, 184
bad internal object, 137
  part-, 86
Bick, E., 100
Bion, W., 52, 86, 111, 119, 120,
    132, 136, 141, 143, 144,
    148, 149
Bowlby, J., 79, 80
breast
  bad, 184
  good, 17, 18, 31, 92, 197
    internal, 104
  as ideal object, 91
  /mother, 83, 84
  as part-object, 85
  persecuting, 12, 26, 176,
    200
  revengeful, 9, 10, 11, 12, 18
  split-off, 177
  as whole object, 32

233